Europe at the Edge of Pluralism

Editors:
Dorota A. Gozdecka
Magdalena Kmak

Europe at the Edge of Pluralism

intersentia

METRO

Ius Commune Europaeum

Dorota A. Gozdecka and Magdalena Kmak (eds.)

Europe at the Edge of Pluralism

Intersentia Publishing Ltd
Sheraton House | Castle Park
Cambridge | CB3 0AX | United Kingdom
Tel.: +44 1223 370 170 | Email: mail@intersentia.co.uk

ISBN 978-1-78068-306-5
D/2015/7849/63
NUR 823

Cambridge – Antwerp – Portland
www.intersentia.com | www.intersentia.co.uk

British Library Cataloguing in Publication Data. A catalogue record for this book is available from the British Library.

CONTENTS

Dorota A. Gozdecka*
Magdalena Kmak**

INTRODUCTION***

In May 2000 the European Parliament announced a new motto for Europe: Unity in Diversity. The motto was followed by the Commission's explanation that, via the European Union, Europeans are united in working together for peace and prosperity, and that the many different cultures, traditions and languages in Europe are a positive asset for the continent. Despite such bold declarations European countries and international organisations, including the European Union, have for years struggled to adopt laws and policies recognising and accommodating its growing cultural, ethnic, religious and linguistic diversity. Fourteen years after adoption of the motto European diversity more often than not appears to be a cause of discord rather than unity. This discord is more frequently visible in legal discussions at all levels. National constitutional systems struggle with adopting policies of recognition, while interpretation of the European Convention of Human Rights, instead of facilitating diversity, ever more often triggers irreconcilable conflicts. Similarly the European Union system is fraught with inconsistencies and systemic problems hindering the peaceful prosperity of many different cultures. Despite the existence of multiple debates.[1] Europe seems to be missing a clear vision of what diversity is supposed to entail. In 2015 Europe more than ever before appears to be standing at the edge of pluralism. This 'edge', just as the linguistic interpretation of the word 'edge', carries multiple meanings illustrating a multiplicity of problems related to cultural diversity. An edge may signify a line or border at which something terminates. It also means a brink or verge like the edge of a cliff or the edge of disaster. Alternatively it may also be used to describe a line at which two objects meet or the thin, sharp side of a cutting tool. To edge means to insert or work in or into something

* Australian National University and University of Helsinki.
** Erik Castrén Institute of International Law and Human Rights, University of Helsinki.
*** This book was funded by the University of Helsinki Project "Law and the Other in Post-Multicultural Europe".

1 *Intercultural Dialogue and Multi-level Governance in Europe: A Human Rights Based Approach.* PIE Peter Lang, 2012; Brems, Eva (ed.), *Diversity and European human rights: rewriting judgments of the ECHR.* Cambridge University Press, 2012; Kastoryano, Riva (ed.), *An identity for Europe: The relevance of multiculturalism in EU construction.* Palgrave Macmillan, 2009; Loenen, Maria Laetitia and Goldschmidt, Jenny (eds.), *Religious Pluralism and Human Rights in Europe: Where to Draw the Line?.* Intersentia, 2007; McGoldrick, Dominic, *Human Rights And Religion-The Islamic Headscarf Debate In Europe,* Hart, 2006: 320; Modood, Tariq and Werbner, Pnina (eds.), *The politics of multiculturalism in the new Europe: Racism, identity and community.* Palgrave Macmillan, 1997.

that is already shaped as in edging suggestions before the close of a discussion. To be on edge, on the other hand, describes a state of acute sensitivity, nervousness and tension. We encourage the readers of this volume to decide which of these meanings are the most relevant for Europe today. As the book attempts to illustrate, each of them has significance for current legal debates on diversity. We would like to pay particular attention to the sense of sensitivity and nervousness that permeates today's European debates on the problematic.

This nervousness might be exacerbated by multiple failures to examine, face and rethink many necessary premises and criticisms concerning cultural accommodation. The discourse on multiculturalism in particular reveals a deep cleavage between adopted premises and contemporary legal problems faced by culturally diverse European societies. Despite the difficulty of pointing out a single European country that would have officially adopted a policy of culturally diverse coexistence prominent European politicians have already announced the death of what they have called 'multiculturalism' and announced a politics of greater 'coherence' and 'security'. This abandonment of the project before its actual beginning signifies a state of suspension between the era of recognition and the era of critical reflection. As this book shows, many legal aspects of diversity in Europe exist in a state of suspension harbouring unsolvable legal conundrums in debates on pluralism, multiculturalism, human rights, constitutional aspects of European integration, regulation of migration and European citizenship, or accommodation of religious diversity and inclusion of minorities. This volume reveals, unpacks and examines multiple tensions related to diversity in contemporary interpretation of EU law, international human rights law, and domestic law.

In its first part, on LAW, DIVERSITY AND PLURALISM, the volume examines fundamental theoretical problems related to management of diversity, prominence of rights in accommodation of diversity and existing legal definitions dominating the area of recognition.

Beginning with a critique of traditional liberal democratic approaches Selen Ercan in her *"Democratizing Identity Politics: A Deliberative Approach to the Politics of Recognition"* unpacks dominant discourses in the language of recognition. She focuses on essentialism and constructivism that underpin dominant discussions on diversity. When culture is approached in an essentialising manner multiculturalism appears to exaggerate the unity and solidity of cultures and the intractability of value conflicts in culturally plural societies. Alternatively when constructivism is taken as a foundation its static nature encounters difficulties in institutionalising individual cultural affiliations that are subject to constant change. For that reason Ercan advocates deliberative strategies which avoid all or nothing approaches and prioritise inter-cultural dialogue securing conditions of social inclusion rather than purely legal inclusion. Pure extension of equal rights, argues Ercan, will never suffice to accommodate diversity. Legal recognition and a deliberative approach must be supported by recognition in a wider public sphere. In Ercan's words: *"It is this wide and rather informal understanding of recognition that first gives existing rights and opportunities their meaning. In other words, institutions or policies alone do not shape the politics of recognition. Similar institutional measures might have different effects in different contexts, depending on how citizens interact and the prevailing discourses of cultural diversity in a given society. The deliberative approach proposed here suggests that formal/legal forms of inclusion are necessary, but not sufficient, conditions for accommodating cultural diversity"*.

The lack a of wide and informal understanding of recognition is further examined in Ercan and Gozdecka's chapter entitled "*What is Post-Multiculturalism?: Recent Trends in Legal and Political Discourse*". The authors observe that the emergence of post-multiculturalism is partly a result of manufactured "crisis discourse". The article argues that the climate surrounding the topic of recognition has led to overemphasis on fragmented experiences of multiculturalism. The chapter examines three main tendencies in presenting multiculturalism that have led to the current shift toward post-multiculturalism. The first is an excessive focus on the maltreatment of women in minority cultures, frequently relying on stereotypical distinctions between liberal and illiberal, modern and traditional, enlightened and backward cultures. The authors observe that while non-minority women are presented as fully developed agents, the behaviour of women in minority cultural groups is regularly explained through their appeal to culture. The second observed tendency is religionisation of problems and issues that affect the shape of the public sphere and access to rights. As the authors observe, "*In recent years, religion has emerged as a major social signifier and was given a prominent role in understanding and resolving problems related to migrant integration in many European countries*". This phenomenon, as the authors argue, is also linked with the last tendency, overemphasising problems of social coherence. The climate of overemphasis on these selected issues rather than relieving the problematic features of multiculturalism exacerbates problems through "*racialising forms of essentialisation (...) underlining and exploiting difference. Culturalised subjects have become seen as unequally 'conditioned' and in need of being corrected for their religion, cultural difference, cultural origin and eventually political origin (citizenship)*".

The insufficiency of law to approach and categorise terms related to diversity of culture, origins, religions and citizenship also dominates Eliska Pirkova's chapter "*The Categorization of Minorities in the European Context: Unwrapping the box*". Pirkova argues that efforts to categorise minorities keep failing. Traditional definitions focus primarily on notions of national minority and fall short of recognising newly emerging cultural groups. Analysing contemporary European efforts to re-categorise and regroup minorities deserving protection, Pirkova argues that forced conceptualizations of different groups may become harmful to their individual members. The arbitrariness of definitions based on diverse cultural attributes can be abused for the purposes of racist propaganda. At the same time, she observes that recent developments in EU law prevent greater recognition of groups such as intra-EU migrants primarily due to the predominance of state and nationality centred definitions. In the new era, argues Pirkova, old categorisations cannot suffice and more flexible approaches are required in order to genuinely respond to the new era of European diversity. In her words: "*When discussing minority protection, we need to keep in mind both the complexity of personal identity as well as the structural complexity of the EU system of governance. Otherwise, we risk harming the interests of actual human beings within these groups, as too strict a categorization of minority protection, often based on just one, arbitrarily chosen feature, fails to pay due respect to all the diverse elements of their identity.*"

Further examining the necessity of more flexible approaches Marcin Kilanowski analyses the contemporary language of rights dominating the area of recognition in his "*From Universality to Responsibility in International Human Rights*". He challenges contemporary reliance on the language of rights primarily for its tendency to over-particularize. Following Kennedy's critique Kilanowski emphasises that the language and the strong moral stand of human rights is not innocent, neutral, universal or mirroring the objective reality or nature of humankind. Similarly to Giddens Kilanowski suggests a shift toward responsibility in the approach to rights. Against multiple European developments in the sphere of rights Kilanowski asserts that the language of rights cannot serve as the absolute truth and requires careful renegotiation. Even if such negotiation means compromises: "*We will never reach that final stage when we will understand all the relationships that are present or the potential basis for their appearance. However, that does not mean that we should not try to do our best to minimize the costs.*"

In similar vein, albeit relying on different philosophical premises, Ukri Soirila in "*Pluralisation through Legal Conflicts?: Rethinking Law and Cultural Pluralism*" deconstructs the language of rights, linking it even more strongly with the context of cultural pluralism. Following Rancière, Soirila insists that human rights "*are not the rights of a single subject that would be at once the source and the bearer of the rights and would only use the rights.*" Therefore in his analysis of contemporary pluralistic contexts Soirila emphasizes the process of subjectivization observing that the political subject can use human rights to create conflict over who is included and who is excluded. Following this analysis by encouragement of creating spaces of becoming but at the same time rejecting Deleuzian skepticism about law, Soirila convincingly argues that the project of radical pluralism should not simply discard everything we have assumed so far but instead play the different perspectives against each other in order to provide novel solutions: "*Where traditional theories of cultural pluralism treat pluralism mostly as a fact or a state of affairs and hence turn out to be fundamentally immunitary theories of order that concentrate on preventing de facto pluralism from culminating in catastrophe by facilitating a fair dialogue or competition between existing interest-groups, the project of progressive radical pluralism takes pluralization as its goal and vehicle for democratic contestation. The aim is to open possibilities for minoritarian becomings and drives of pluralization and hence to challenge existing power structures.*"

Part two focuses on migrant SUBJECTIVITIES AND BELONGING in contemporary Europe. It includes discussions on migration and citizenship, exploring them through the prism of different and frequently stratified forms of belonging – from full, through partial to marginalized and excluded. The three chapters by Magdalena Kmak, Sanne van de Pol and Sam Bennett show in particular how these stratified forms of belonging and, related to them, migrant subjectivities, are constructed by migration laws and policies and how stratification can be remedied or resisted by migrants themselves.

The underlying theme of this part of the book is the territorial order of citizenship deriving from hegemonic legal discourses which thought various technologies (such as border technology or technology of corrective citizenship) create the distinction between the citizen and the foreigner or the inside and the outside. Any attempt undertaken by a migrant to transform themselves from an outsider to an insider "does not come about without a struggle"[2] and is often resisted by the state. This transformation therefore creates different forms of belonging in the state based on a particular idea of who is considered a good (desirable) or bad (undesirable) foreigner. As a result, state migration policies often embed the conflict between state preferences and their obligations towards various categories of migrants, often forcing them not only to fulfil the necessary legal requirements but also to act as good and desirable foreigners.

First of all this conflict is visible in EU refugee policy which, according to Kmak, is based on the problematic categorisation of foreigners into three groups – the Good, the Bad and the Ugly. The latter term refers to asylum seekers towards whom the EU and Member States have international human rights obligations conflicting with their domestic policies and preferences. In her chapter, entitled "*The 'Ugly' of EU Migration Policy: The role of the Recast Reception Directive in Fragmentation of the Refugee Subject*", Kmak focuses on how the recently adopted Recast Reception Directive and in particular its provisions on detention of asylum seekers are guided by the philosophy of the Ugly. This approach results in fragmentation of refugee subjectivity into the genuine refugee and the bogus asylum seeker. This leads in consequence to the perception of all those arriving in the EU in an irregular manner as bogus asylum seekers. The Directive "*does so by allowing systematic detention of those asylum seekers entering EU territory irregularly or those whom states consider as abusing asylum systems in other ways, in a situation where EU law makes it very difficult to seek protection in a regular manner*".

Sanne van de Pol and Sam Bennet focus in turn on integration policies in the Belgian region of Flanders and in the UK. In the chapter entitled "*Welcome to the Margins of Society: An Analysis of (Civic) Integration Policy and the Fundamental Rights of Immigrants*" Van de Pol analyses the difficulties of transforming "outsiders" who often live on the margins of society into "insiders" in Flanders. This transformation happens through a policy of civic integration (*inburgering* – becoming a citizen) the aim of which is to help migrants to participate in and integrate with society. As van de Pol shows, however, the policy of civil integration, instead of turning migrants into "good" citizens contributes rather to their civic stratification and in consequence leads to diversified modes of belonging. In addition, even though civic integration is based on the core values of Belgian society (such as freedom, equality, solidarity and respect) which migrants are obliged to incorporate into their daily life, migrants themselves are often not treated in accordance with those values. As van de Pol claims, even though civic integration "*is supposed to encompass a recognition and appreciation of differences (...) in practice, tensions become apparent and civic integration courses are mostly designed top-down and one-way. They disregard the fact that integration is a multi-way and multilateral process*"

Bennett's chapter, entitled "*Performing Citizenship and Integration in the UK*", adds another layer to this problematic by outlining the symbolic importance of citizenship in processes of integration. Through the example of the UK Bennett explores the claim that migrants are increasingly being asked to 'perform' integration in symbolic and

2 van de Pol, Sanne, "Welcome to the Margins of Society: An Analysis of (Civic) Integration Policy and the Fundamental Rights of Immigrants", p. 95.

discursive ways and that only through such 'performances' can they acquire the perception of authenticity and similarity to existing members of society. Similarly to van de Pol, Bennett critically assesses the UK approach to integration which, instead of being a two-way process, is assimilatory and based on the neo-liberal concept of citizenship which migrants have to play out. In consequence migrants constantly oscillate between being considered as good migrants – those minimally different from the dominant group in society (usually a white middle class) and bad migrants – those considered to be radically different from them depending on how they perform various social roles. "*If migrants, especially asylum seekers, are discursively constructed culturally as radically different, and legally restricted from being economically self-sufficient, then in order to be accepted into society, that is, in order to integrate, they will be expected to alter this state. In effect they have to be, or at least act, like the dominant in-group by performing integration.*"

As the chapters point out, the subjectivities created by migration laws and policies, which lead to stratification of migrants, are however not static and various attempts are made to challenge them. On the one hand, Van de Pol underlines the emancipatory role of human rights in integration processes, emphasising that a general awareness of human rights is crucial for providing for a well-functioning society. "*Creating general awareness about this among migrants and wider society could have an important emancipatory effect, not only on migrants but also on society as a whole*". On the other hand, Kmak focuses on those who escape imposed categorisation and the territorial order of citizenship through new narratives of citizenship which dismantle the "*current hegemonic relationship between citizenship and territory and in consequence the binary distinction between citizen/foreigner and legal/illegal*". To be sure, such attempts deserve more academic attention.

This section is followed by RELIGION, AGENCY AND MINORS analysing the practice of pluralism in the educational environment. It goes to the heart of legal and cultural dilemmas in education and examines the agency of young people involved in the intersections of law and culture in diverse societies. It includes chapters by Sanna Mustasaari and Ryan Hill.

Mustasaari's chapter goes into the under-explored area of sexual rights of youth in increasingly diverse societies. It focuses on notions of agency in regulating sexual consent and education and examines how the question of agency has been framed as a conflict of private and public interest. Mustasaari shows that the significance of preserving and determining values that prescribe relationships in the family sphere frequently implies that young people might be perceived as a threat to the continuity of the social order and thus subjected to control through various discourses. Mustasaari examines the intersections of "*welfarist discourses defining the "normal" or the "healthy", religious or ideological discourses defining the "good" and the "sacred", cultural discourses defining belonging and identity, and legal discourses defining, for instance, the best interests of the child.*" She insists that the final say determining the shape of these "best interests" is based on a balance of interests between the minority and the majority.

Hill's chapter uncovers the tensions between different notions of proselytism and the friction at the heart of contemporary legal debates: who decides what offends, proselytises or can merely stand as a passive symbol in the education of children? Hill argues that regulation of dress code is propelled by concerns over social cohesion. The discourse of fragmentation or parallelism in Europe is linked with the desire of European states to maintain and construct the shape of the cultural community. In the case of children, however, Hill argues that considerations ought to be more complex: *"As they can be considered to be on a journey towards being full rights holders in their own right, children are not only current "incomplete" rights holders but also future "complete" rights holders. Thus states must not only consider the child's present interests and rights but also the future adult's interests and rights that relate to the "complete" rights holder the child will become* ". Hill insists that the key difficulty in contemporary societies lies in arriving at a satisfactory evaluation of what a child's current and future interests are within pluralist societies.

Finally part four concerning RESPECT AND MEMORY gets to the core of many contemporary discussions in Europe. Memory frequently reverberates in the majority of the previous discussions, whether touching upon migration, definition of a community or the role of certain symbolism. European discussions and legal developments in the area of diversity inherently link to the promises and threats of freedom of expression and legal protection of identity and memory. The difficult distinction between freedom of speech and unacceptable abuse of rights which is embedded in the balancing exercise and their relation to democracy, pluralism and protection of memory and diversity constitutes the main focus of the last three chapters by Jernej Letnar Černič, Aleksandra Gliszczyńska-Grabias and Mónica López Lerma.

Freedom of expression, as "a prerequisite for the functioning of democracy"[3] and its limitation in cases of hate speech, constitutes the main focus of Černič's chapter entitled "*Democracy as a Trump Card? Combating Hate Speech in Pluralistic Societies*". He analyses the recent case law of the European Court of Human Rights from the perspective of the relationship between prohibition of hate speech and democracy. In order to do so, he first discusses the two-tiered approach of the ECtHR towards prohibition of hate speech, which is based on the distinction between its most extreme and less extreme forms. The former concerns denial of crimes of genocide, crimes against humanity, war crimes and the Holocaust and in principle is absolutely prohibited by the ECtHR on the basis of article 17 of the European Convention. The latter category refers to cases where the ECtHR applies the principle of proportionality and assesses whether prohibition of hate speech constitutes interference with the rights and freedoms of individuals. This analysis leads Černič to pose an important question concerning the meaning of democracy and pluralism for freedom of expression: "*The question is whether an absolute prohibition of hate speech is necessary in a democratic society, or would it be better for the ECtHR to examine all complaints on the basis of the principle of proportionality*?" This problem constitutes one of the main themes underlying all chapters in this part of the book.

The question concerning the relationship between democracy and freedom of speech is in particular closely related to the role of law in protecting memory, which remains at the very heart of the analysis of the second author. In her chapter, entitled "*Coping with*

3 ECtHR *Özgür Gündem v. Turkey*, no. 23144/93, judgment of March 16, 2000.

the Past in a Multicultural Europe: The European Court of Human Rights on Memory and Law", Gliszczyńska-Grabias focuses on the difficult choice between on the one hand the need to legally protect the truth about certain historical events and the memory of victims of those events (in particular the truth about the Holocaust) and on the other hand the danger of imposing a state-sponsored orthodox version of history or even endorsing a lie. She focuses on the role of the ECtHR in negotiating between these two positions. "*Meeting halfway between these demands is not an easy task, but a necessary one, as law cannot stay indifferent to situations when under the cover of free academic debate some try to spread hatred, and at the same time are obliged to protect the rights and freedoms of the individual*". In addition, as Gliszczyńska-Grabias points out, these questions remain particularly relevant for multicultural communities where dominant views may easily overshadow minority narratives. However, no jurisprudence has so far focused on this particular dimension of memory legislation.

A concrete example of a dilemma relating to the role of amnesty and memory laws in a democratic state is analysed in López Lerma's article entitled "*What Judicial Memory for the Amnesty Law of 1977?*". The chapter's point of departure is the prosecution of Judge Baltasar Garzón for issuing a decision authorising a criminal investigation into crimes committed during the Franco regime in Spain. The decision was triggered by the Amnesty Law of 1997 which exempted those committing Franco-era crimes from prosecution. The situation has also not been remedied by the recently adopted Memory Law of 2007. The judicial initiative of Garzón was an attempt to align Spanish law with international legal obligations and provide remedies to victims of the Franco regime. However, the democratic origin of the Amnesty Laws combined with the legalistic approach of the court was used as a basis to protect the Amnesty and in consequence to prosecute Judge Garzón. This development yet again brings into the spotlight the question of the role of democracy in cases concerning respect and memory posed by Černič in the earlier chapter. As López Lerma concludes, "*In the Court's view, the Amnesty Law should be remembered as an essential milestone in the consolidation of Spanish democracy after Francoism and any critical assessment could be regarded "as a criticism of democracy itself." However, to open an investigation into the crimes of Francoism is not to question the legitimacy of the transition, let alone to threaten national reconciliation, but rather to comply with Spain's international obligations towards the victims in the present*"

Conclusions and input to contemporary discussion

The book illustrates that legal conundrums are often a result of the very terms of discussion that are dominant in contemporary discourses on diversity and pluralism in Europe. Neglect to re-examine these terms leads to a problematic oscillation between on the one hand struggles for greater recognition of diversity and on the other hand tendencies to preserve the current *status quo*. The chapters collected in this book illustrated the inefficiency of contemporary European legal tools and approaches to the question of recognition and their intended and unintended consequences. The collection urges law and diverse European legal systems to challenge their own presumptions before unconditionally withdrawing from rethinking multiculturalism. Instead of abandoning the discussion on cultural, ethnic and religious pluralism it encourages self-reflection and revision of contemporary approaches of law and its regimes to the problem of accommodating diversity. As the book illustrates, rights regimes and contemporary legal strategies often misdiagnose and misinterpret contemporary dilemmas of pluralistic societies. In consequence they frequently result in images of binary opposition between law and diversity which appear impossible to reconcile. These perceptions lead to multiple legal blind alleys and beg for new strategies to be involved in the complex balancing between law, society and politics. Without this revision Europe may permanently remain at the edge of pluralism – in a state of legal limbo where growing diversity lacks appropriate tools to resolve the problem of greater or lesser belonging.

PART I

LAW, DIVERSITY AND PLURALISM

Selen A. Ercan*

DEMOCRATIZING IDENTITY POLITICS: A DELIBERATIVE APPROACH TO THE POLITICS OF RECOGNITION**

Liberalism has often been regarded as the most suitable doctrine for accommodating and advancing individual differences in contemporary societies. However, when it comes to accommodation of ethnic or cultural differences, the liberal formula based on the separation of public and private spheres and the location of culture within the latter seems to reach its boundaries. Taking this deficit as their point of departure, critics of liberalism have suggested alternative strategies for accommodating cultural diversity under the rubric of the "politics of recognition."[1] The central claim of such politics has been to correct the subordinate position of disadvantaged ethnic groups by granting them special rights and entitlements. These policies, also known as multiculturalism, aim to facilitate greater inclusion and integration of marginalized groups in culturally diverse societies.

In this chapter, I aim to unpack the different forms the politics of recognition may take in multicultural societies depending on their underlying notions of culture. I argue that despite best intentions, if not crafted carefully, the politics of recognition may fail to provide productive ground for inclusive politics in culturally diverse societies. This is especially so when such politics is based on an essentialist account of culture. When culture is understood as a given and pre-politically extant entity, the subsequent politics of recognition and multiculturalism may easily lead to fixation and homogenization of the identities involved. I problematize these variants of multiculturalism, and offer an alternative way of conceptualizing the politics of recognition by drawing on insights suggested by deliberative democracy. To be clear, my criticism of multiculturalism is not that it has gone too far and led to the emergence of "parallel societies" – an argument that has gained momentum in recent years in nearly all migrant-receiving countries. Rather, I problematize some basic presumptions of this approach and try to offer remedies from a perspective of deliberative democracy. I argue that deliberative democracy opens up

* Institute for Governance and Policy Analysis, University of Canberra.

** An earlier version of this paper was presented at the Australian Political Science Association annual conference in 2007. I am particularly grateful to Ricardo Mendonca for his insightful comments and suggestions on the earlier version of this paper.

1 Charles Taylor, *Multiculturalism and "The Politics of Recognition"* (Princeton: Princeton University Press, 1992).

new ways of thinking about multiculturalism and politics of recognition which do not fall into the trap of essentialism.

Deliberative democracy is a growing branch of democracy theory that has important implications for the theory and practice of recognition in multicultural societies.[2] The deliberative approach draws our attention to the "constructed" nature of culture and identity, and suggests focusing on institutional and discursive conditions that facilitate an anti-essentialist, deliberative notion of recognition. As such, a deliberative approach offers a promising route to democratize identity politics in culturally plural societies.

The chapter is composed of four sections. In the first section, I outline existing critiques of the politics of recognition in the context of multiculturalism. I show that multiculturalism takes different forms depending on the underlying notions of culture and identity. In the second section, I highlight existing approaches to culture, and reveal their implications for the politics of recognition and multiculturalism. In the third section, I sketch the key characteristics of deliberative democracy, and finally in the fourth section, I discuss the institutional and non-institutional conditions required for a deliberative notion of recognition in culturally plural societies.

Critiques of the Politics of Recognition in the Context of Multiculturalism

Critique of multiculturalism is as old as the idea of multiculturalism itself. Since its first use in the 1950s, both the idea and the politics of "multiculturalism" have been subject to intense criticism. The reasons for its rejection vary considerably. The most common type of criticism that multiculturalism faces comes from its conservative critics. They argue that multiculturalism stands opposed to maintenance of a unified national identity, and it leads to segregation by undermining interpersonal trust and solidarity in culturally diverse societies. Conversely, liberal opponents of multiculturalism are less interested in problems associated with trust, solidarity or unity. For them, multicultural policies are dangerous as they undermine the liberal principles of equality and impartiality. Opponents are convinced that recognition of group-specific rights means denying equal treatment of the individual.[3] They argue that liberalism, by protecting individual freedom of association, already suggests the best possible strategy for accommodating cultural diversity.[4] Other liberals are concerned about the practicality of politics based on group identities. Claus Offe, for example, argues that:

2 Selen A. Ercan, "The Deliberative Politics of Cultural Diversity: Beyond Interest and Identity Politics?" in *Migration, Citizenship and Intercultural Relations. Looking through the Lens of Social Inclusion*, ed. Fethi Mansouri and Michele Lobo (Farnham: Ashgate, 2011), 75–91.

3 Brian Barry, *Culture and Equality* (Cambridge: Polity, 2001); Chandran Kukathas, "Liberalism and Multiculturalism. The Politics of Indifference," *Political Theory* 26, no. 5 (1998): 686–99.

4 Ibid.

> even the most demanding and utopian version of liberal universalism and individualism is a more promising and more realistic project of maintaining political unity than the alternative proposal of building a unity on the recognition of group identities.[5]

Some feminist scholars suggest that multiculturalism and feminism stand in tension to one another, notably Susan Moller Okin, who famously argues that multiculturalism is bad for women.[6] On her account, feminism requires liberal individualism, while cultural group rights allow for greater inequality between women and men. The most common concern is that multiculturalism leads to a fixation and homogenization of identities by "locking" individuals into certain features. Similarly, Patchen Markell points out the potential injustice that the politics of recognition might cause. He argues that although the politics of recognition aims to emancipate individuals, it binds them to certain identities and leads them to being "bound by recognition – honoured and constrained."[7]

It is possible to extend the list of critics of politics of recognition and group rights by focusing on internal differences within each stream of criticism. Instead, in what follows I focus on the commonalities between existing lines of criticism and argue that the existing literature on politics of recognition and multiculturalism suffers from two closely interrelated shortcomings. The first is related to critics' point of departure. Most critics of the politics of recognition tend to associate multiculturalism with an essentialised, fixed conception of culture. They are less interested in questions of where culture comes from, when it becomes a significant part of identity and under what circumstances it might be transformed. The second shortcoming of the existing literature relates to the way it conceptualizes multiculturalism. Multiculturalism is usually associated with the need for special group rights and criticized as such for standing in tension with individual rights. Scholars criticizing multiculturalism along these lines fail to take into account that multiculturalism can manifest itself in a variety of forms depending on the underlying conceptions of culture and identity. As I discuss in detail below, different approaches to culture and identity involve different implications for the consequent forms of multiculturalism as politics of recognition.

Two Approaches to Culture and Identity: Essentialism versus Constructivism

The question whether culture is relevant for the functioning of liberal societies has always been contested. In the existing literature, this issue has been debated in terms of the dichotomies between liberalism and communitarianism.[8] This debate is polarized around two strategies for accommodating cultural diversity that can be termed as privatization and protection strategies. The former is closely associated with liberalism. Liberals assert the need to protect the rights and freedoms of individuals against the

5 Claus Offe, "Political Liberalism, Group Rights, and the Politics of Fear and Trust," in *Herausforderungen der Demokratie. Zur Integrations- und Leistungsfaehigkeit politischer Institutionen*, ed. Claus Offe (Frankfurt: Campus Verlag, 2003), 334.

6 Susan Moller Okin, *Is Multiculturalism Bad for Women?* (Princeton: Princeton University Press, 1999).

7 Patchen Markell, *Bound by Recognition* (Princeton: Princeton University Press, 2003), 193.

8 Michael Sandel, *Liberalism and Limits of Justice* (Cambridge: Cambridge University Press, 1982).

claims of cultures. In the face of cultural heterogeneity, they tend towards solutions that distinguish the public from the private sphere and relegate issues concerning culture to the latter. Liberals maintain that privatization of culture is the best way to deal with the "problem" of cultural heterogeneity. This strategy aims to secure the neutrality of the state and the public sphere toward group identities which may potentially be divisive.[9]

Those advocating a strong protection strategy as an alternative to a privatization strategy see individuals as rooted in cultures and primarily as members of cultural communities. Emphasizing the meaning of culture for individuals, Taylor for example argues that without their membership in these communities, individuals would be "at sea"; they would no longer know who they were.[10] Given this, on Taylor's account when the state fails to protect and value culture, it undermines individual identity and sense of worth. As such, contrary to privatization strategy, scholars advocating the protection strategy, usually under the banner of communitarianism, emphasize the need to "protect" cultures in institutional terms. This requires adopting a wide range of public policies, legal rights and, in some cases, constitutional provisions for the accommodation of cultural differences.

The existing literature seems to oscillate between the privatization and protection strategies for accommodating cultural diversity. However, a close examination of this debate reveals that although these two strategies are framed as opposite alternatives, they depend on the same assumption. That is, they both assume that individuals' cultural attachments are given, fixed and pre-politically extant, and seek ways to accommodate culture understood as such. In so doing, both strategies presuppose an essentialist understanding of culture and identity. Before identifying the implications of such a starting point for the subsequent politics of recognition, let me briefly outline the core characteristics of the essentialist approach and explore its alternatives.

Essentialism can be defined "as a belief in true essence – that which is most irreducible, unchanging, and therefore constitutive of a given person or thing."[11] The essentialist approach claims that everything has a real essence that is unique, irreducible and unchanging. In the context of identity politics, to essentialise an identity means:

> to impute a fundamental, basic, absolutely necessary constitutive quality to a person, social category, ethnic group, religious community, or nation. It is to posit falsely a timeless continuity, discreteness or boundedness in space, and an organic unity. It is to imply an internal sameness and external difference or otherness.[12]

When based on an essentialist account of culture, multiculturalism tends to exaggerate "not only the unity and solidity of cultures but the intractability of value conflicts" in

9 Courtney Jung, "The Burden of Culture and the Limits of Liberal Responsibility," *Constellations* 8, no. 2 (2001): 221.

10 Charles Taylor, *Sources of the Self* (Cambridge: Cambridge University Press, 1989), 27.

11 Diana Fuss, *Essentially Speaking. Feminism, Nature and Difference* (Abingdon, Oxon: Routledge, 1989), 2.

12 Pnina Werbner, "Essentialising Essentialism, Essentialising Silence: Ambivalence and Multiplicity in the Constructions of Racism and Ethnicity," in *Debating Cultural Hybridity*, ed. Pnina Werbner and Tariq Modood (London: Zed Books, 1997), 228.

culturally plural societies.[13] Multiculturalism as such tends to suppress the heterogeneity and intra-cultural diversity that exist in each culture, and creates binary oppositions between cultures. Jon Stratton and Ien Ang argue that the cultural diversity embodied in the official multiculturalism of Australia presents an example of an essentialist notion of culture at work.[14] They note that here multiculturalism tends to construct a binary opposition between "ethnic communities" and Australian society, "as if the two were mutually exclusive, internally homogenous entities." This representation of ethnic communities not only constructs the latter as "'always devaluing, hierarchizing, othering' the former, but also pigeonholes 'the migrant' as permanently marginalized, forever ethicized."[15]

An alternative, anti-essentialist perspective on culture and identity is presented by constructivism. Constructivists claim that essence itself is a historical production; they reject the existence of true essence and argue that whatever appears as "natural" or "given" actually emerges "socially" and as a result of discursive practices.[16] In a similar vein, identity too is not fixed; it is continually renegotiated through interactive effort, via linguistic exchange and social performance.[17] Group members may emphasize different aspects of their identity in different contexts at different times.[18] As Taylor convincingly argues: "my discovering my own identity doesn't mean that I work it out in isolation, but that I negotiate it through dialogue, partly overt, partly internal, with others."[19] By emphasizing the relational feature of identity, a constructivist approach asserts that neither identity nor culture possesses an essence, and both are subject to constant change. The definition of culture and identity as such leads constructivists to focus on the mechanisms that produce and maintain the primacy of certain identities. These mechanisms may include not only formal institutional settings in a given society, but also prevailing social practices, systems of representation, cultural symbols and more broadly the role of ideology and discourses in shaping identities. The constructivist approach to culture recognizes that cultural identities do not exist prior to legal and political institutions, but are partly shaped, if not determined, by those institutions.

Given the differences between the essentialist and constructivist approaches to culture, the tendency in the existing literature is to regard ideas associated with "essential unity, integrity, discreteness and fixity" as reactionary, and constructivist ideas of "internal differentiation, interaction and fluidity" as progressive.[20] Although the

13 Anne Phillips, *Multiculturalism without Culture* (Princeton: Princeton University Press, 2007), 8.

14 Jon Stratton and Ien Ang, "Multicultural Imagined Communities. Cultural Difference and National Identity in the USA and Australia," in *Multicultural States. Rethinking Difference and Identity*, ed. David Bennett (Abingdon, Oxon: Routledge, 1999), 135–62.

15 *Ibid.*, 158.

16 Jung, "The Burden of Culture and the Limits of Liberal Responsibility."

17 Karen A. Cerulo, "Identity Construction: New Issues, New Directions," *Annual Review of Sociology* 23 (1997): 387.

18 Courtney Jung, "Race, Ethnicity and Culture," in *The Oxford Handbook of Contextual Policy Analysis*, ed. Robert E. Goodin and Charles Tilly (Oxford: Oxford University Press, 2006), 360–76.

19 Taylor, *Multiculturalism and "The Politics of Recognition,"* 34.

20 Tariq Modood, "Anti-Essentialism, Multiculturalism and the 'Recognition of Religious Groups'," *The Journal of Political Philosophy* 6, no. 4 (1998): 378.

essentialist and constructivist approaches seem analytically distinct, it is difficult to disentangle them in practice. In other words, the demarcation between essentialism and constructivism is not as solid as the advocates of both sides assume.[21] Ultimately, constructivism depends fundamentally on essentialism for the basis of its critique. What is important to acknowledge in the context of this chapter is that these two approaches to culture involve different implications for the subsequent politics of recognition and democracy.

Compared to the essentialist approach, the constructivist approach to culture seems to offer a more suitable point of departure for thinking about the politics of recognition in culturally plural societies. Yet one particular difficulty which this approach poses relates to the question how to institutionalize individual cultural affiliations if those affiliations are not static. To put it differently, if cultural identities are subject to constant change, as claimed by the constructivists, what kind of institutions do we need in order to capture this constant change? As noted by Judith Squires, it has become commonplace to criticize the essentialist notion of culture that underlies multiculturalism, yet an alternative version of multiculturalism that relies on the internal differentiation and fluidity of cultures remains undeveloped.[22] In what follows, I attempt to offer one such alternative version of multiculturalism from a perspective of deliberative democracy. A deliberative approach offers a promising starting point for articulating an expression of multiculturalism that avoids cultural essentialism, but nonetheless recognizes that culture matters. It helps us identify the normative conditions under which the value of culture can perpetually be re-formulated and re-negotiated according to the changing perceptions of members of a culture.[23]

Beyond Cultural Essentialism: Insights from Deliberative Democracy

I wish to argue that rather than categorically rejecting multiculturalism, we need to rethink the politics of recognition in ways that can help solve, or at least mitigate, the problems related to cultural essentialism. I start by arguing that if culture and identity are dialogically constructed, their recognition requires a particular model of democracy. The model of democracy sought must meet at least two tests: it should recognize cultural differences; and it should provide the conditions to facilitate interaction between and transformation of cultural differences. At the same time, it should recognize that cultural and ethnic identities and groups are not fixed but fluid and open to change. Before outlining the core characteristics of a deliberative politics of recognition which I think passes these tests, let me briefly define more broadly what deliberative democracy is, and what it offers in the face of cultural diversity.

21 Fuss, *Essentially Speaking. Feminism, Nature and Difference*; Judith Squires, "Culture, Equality and Diversity," in *Multiculturalism Reconsidered*, ed. Paul Kelly (Cambridge: Polity, 2002), 115–132.

22 Squires, "Culture, Equality and Diversity."

23 Mathew Festenstein, *Negotiating Diversity: Culture, Deliberation, Trust* (Cambridge: Cambridge University Press, 2005).

Deliberative democracy is a growing branch of democratic theory that has important implications for the theory and practice of recognition. Deliberative democrats suggest understanding democracy in terms of exchange of reasons rather than voting or aggregation or preferences. Deliberation involves a process of mutual justification where participants offer reasons for their positions, listen to the views of others, and reconsider their preferences in the light of new information and argument. Broadly speaking, deliberative democracy is a normative theory of democratic legitimacy based on the idea that those affected by a collective decision have the right, capacity and opportunity to participate and deliberate in the making of those decisions.[24] Here, collective decision-making is not understood in a limited sense as an aggregation of preferences; rather, it is conceptualized in broader terms as a series of interactions both in the formal and informal spheres. As such, deliberative democracy suggests more than a theory of decision-making. This approach is also concerned about the conditions facilitating *social learning*,[25] *mutual understanding*[26] and *cooperation* among deliberating individuals.[27] Given these attributes, a number of scholars regard deliberative democracy as the "key for securing just relations among ethnic or cultural groups"[28] and for providing "compelling answers to the challenges posed by multicultural demands."[29]

In this chapter, I am particularly interested in exploring the capacity of deliberative democracy to respond to the difficulties raised by the constructed account of culture. This concerns most notably the issue of how to take the constantly changing nature of culture into account and suggest a way of recognizing cultural differences without essentialising those differences. Three particular features of the deliberative democratic approach help facilitate a politics of recognition based on a constructed notion of culture: (i) the requirement of dialogical and intersubjective mutuality, (ii) a focus on the transformative potential of deliberation and (iii) emphasis on reaching collective decisions that are open to revision. Let me explain each of these features briefly.

The first key feature of the deliberative approach is the "dialogical and intersubjective mutuality" that it requires. The deliberative approach emphasizes "the intersubjective formation of individual identities through confrontation and interaction with other(s)."[30] This approach distances itself from liberal presuppositions of identity based on an *a priori* concept of human nature. The social contract tradition of liberalism assumes an historical account of human nature which leads "human beings [to] begin their history

24 Joshua Cohen, "Deliberation and Democratic Legitimacy," in *The Good Polity: Normative Analysis of the State*, ed. Alan Hamlin and Philip Pettit (Oxford: Basil Blackwell, 1989), 17–34.

25 Bora Kanra, *Islam, Democracy and Dialogue in Turkey: Deliberating in Divided Societies* (Farnham: Ashgate, 2009).

26 Amy Gutmann and Dennis Thompson, *Why Deliberative Democracy* (Princeton: Princeton University Press, 2004).

27 James Bohman, *Public Deliberation, Pluralism, Complexity and Democracy* (Cambridge, MA: The MIT Press, 1996).

28 Michael R. James, "Communicative Action, Strategic Action, and Inter-Group Dialogue," *European Journal of Political Theory* 2, no. 2 (2003): 157.

29 Seyla Benhabib, *The Claims of Culture: Equality and Diversity in the Global Era* (Princeton: Princeton University Press, 2002), 106.

30 *Ibid.*, 50.

endowed with a certain set of properties."[31] The deliberative theory puts emphasis on the intersubjective constitution of the self through dialogical practices. If cultural differences are not the reflection of pre-given ethnic identities but the results of interactive efforts, the dialogical feature of deliberative democracy gains particular significance. Rather than beginning with a notion of a pre-existing "subject" then trying to explain how that subject relates to others, a deliberative approach begins from a notion of interrelationship and its significance for identity building. The notion of recognition is embedded in the process of identity constitution. As such, it requires "mutuality" which goes far beyond the familiar plea for toleration. The dialogical notion of recognition requires reciprocal action in the process of identity constitution.

The second key feature of deliberation concerns its transformative potential. The deliberative approach is claimed to be "transformative," as it requires engagement in public dialogue, which subsequently leads to change in the judgments, preferences and attitudes of the deliberating individuals.[32] Deliberation can facilitate identity transformation through mutual, dialogical and intersubjective interaction. Some scholars argue that deliberation can even help transform the national identity so that it better reflects the cultural plurality in a given society.[33]

The third key feature of the deliberative approach is "revisability." Given the plurality and incommensurability of fundamental values in culturally diverse societies, no resolution can be definitive. From a deliberative perspective, every resolution must be open to further democratic dissent and renegotiation. Ideally, any proposed resolution should rest as much as possible on discussion and agreement between those affected by it. In other words, proposed resolutions should be seen as ongoing provisional agreements open to revision and correction. In the context of multiculturalism, the deliberative notion of recognition can be characterized as an ongoing struggle of identities that does not necessarily lead to a final state of resolution. In this context, recognition of cultural identities should not be seen as an end state, but rather as a provisional and continuous process of democratic activity.

James Tully's account of recognition captures the deliberative idea of revisability well, although Tully himself does not identify as a deliberative democrat. According to Tully:

> [r]ecognition in theory and practice should not be seen as a telos or end state, but as a partial, provisional, mutual, and human-all-too-human part of continuous processes of democratic activity in which citizens struggle to change their rules of mutual recognition as they change themselves.[34]

31 Bhikhu Parekh, *Rethinking Multiculturalism: Cultural Diversity and Political Theory* (New York: Macmillan, 2000), 118.

32 John S. Dryzek, *Deliberative Democracy and Beyond. Liberals, Critics, Contestations* (Oxford: Oxford University Press, 2000); Iris M. Young, *Inclusion and Democracy* (Oxford: Oxford University Press, 2000).

33 Monika Kirloskar-Steinbach, "National Identity: Belonging to a Cultural Group? Belonging to a Polity?" *JSRI* 8 (2004): 31–42.

34 James Tully, "Struggles over Recognition and Distribution," *Constellations* 7, no. 4 (2000): 477.

As Tully puts it, "in a free and open society existing norms of mutual recognition should be open to public questioning so these reasons can be heard and considered."[35] This approach is based on the idea that there can be no final resolution. As noted above, proposed resolutions should be seen as ongoing provisional agreements open to revision and correction. The aim of democratic politics is not to establish once and for all *the* just form of recognition. Rather:

> The primary aim will be to ensure that those subject to and affected by any system of governance are always free to call its prevailing norms of recognition and action coordination into question, to present reasons for and against modifying it, to enter into dialogue with those who govern and who have a duty to listen and respond, to be able to challenge the prevailing procedures of negotiation in the course of the discussions, to reach or fail to reach an imperfect agreement to amend (or overthrow) the norm in question, to implement the amendment; and then to ensure that the implementation is open to review and possible renegotiation in the future.[36]

In other words, on this account the aim of democratic politics is not to "discover and constitutionalize the just and definitive form of recognition" but to ensure the conditions enabling ongoing struggles of recognition.[37] In what follows, I will sketch some of the background conditions required to facilitate this form of recognition in practice.

Enacting Politics of Recognition within and beyond Formal Institutions

Deliberative democrats agree on the various benefits of deliberation in culturally diverse societies, yet they differ on the question of the institutional conditions this approach requires for its realization. One of the most contested issues among deliberative democrats concerns recognition of formal group rights and, more specifically, the institutionalization of formal group representation. For some, it is necessary to ensure a system of group representation to compensate the shortcomings of a system of individual representation.[38] According to Iris Young, for example, group representation serves as an "important enactment of political inclusion" in multicultural societies.[39] Yet at the same time she notes that institutionalizing group representation might have essentialist implications. Recognizing the dilemma that reserving seats for particular groups might "freeze both the identity of that group and its relations with other groups in the polity," Young argues that what multicultural societies need is "some more fluid procedure" of

35 James Tully, "Recognition and Dialogue: the Emergence of a New Field," *Critical Review of International Social and Political Philosophy* 7, no. 3 (2004): 98.

36 *Ibid.*, 99.

37 Tully, "Struggles over Recognition and Distribution."

38 Young, *Inclusion and Democracy*; Squires, "Culture, Equality and Diversity"; Melissa S. Williams, "The Uneasy Alliance of Group Representation and Deliberative Democracy," in *Citizenship in Diverse Societies*, ed. Will Kymlicka and Wayne Norman (Oxford: Oxford University Press, 2000), 124–54.

39 Young, *Inclusion and Democracy*, 123.

group representation.[40] Michael James expresses a similar concern, and suggests enacting the principle of group representation in the informal institutions of the public sphere.[41] He argues that institutionalizing group-specific policies within the formal decision-making sphere fails to capture the internal diversity of cultural groups as well as the changing nature of constructed identities. Similarly, several other scholars reject formal representation mechanisms and emphasize the role of the informal public sphere in facilitating inclusive deliberation across cultural difference. Most notably, Seyla Benhabib argues that "heterogeneity, otherness, and difference can find expression in multiple associations, networks, and citizens' forums" within the informal public sphere, rather than in formal institutions.[42]

Although I share the concerns of these scholars about the possible essentialist implications of formal group-specific rights in multicultural societies, I acknowledge that the question whether formal recognition of group-specific rights enables or hinders the inclusion of minority cultures in democratic politics is necessarily an empirical one, and thus difficult to answer in the context of this chapter. The deliberative approach I suggest does not categorically reject group-specific policies; rather, it emphasizes the necessity for a careful application of these policies. As long as these policies result from inclusive deliberative processes, and are seen as open to revision, they do not stand in tension with the deliberative democratic approach advocated in this chapter. In fact, the wholesale rejection of certain policies prior to any deliberative process runs against the logic of deliberative democracy. Furthermore, if we accept that culture and identity are dialogically constructed, we should also acknowledge that no single universal formula exists for the politics of recognition or multiculturalism that fits every society. As discussed above, multiculturalism manifests itself in different forms; a variety of institutional possibilities exists on the spectrum between individual rights and group-specific rights, each suggesting different forms of multiculturalism.[43]

The important point here is not to reduce the politics of recognition to the existence of formal group rights and entitlements.[44] The form that the politics of recognition takes in terms of institutions and formal rights should remain open to revision. What matters from a deliberative perspective is less the final, definitive form of recognition on institutional terms, but more the process of recognition understood in terms of open-ended and continuous struggle. This requires first of all the presence of institutional opportunities that facilitate both intercultural and intra-cultural deliberation.[45] In this context, it is particularly important to emphasize the need for intra-cultural deliberation.

40 *Ibid.*, 149.

41 James, "Communicative Action, Strategic Action, and Inter-Group Dialogue."

42 Seyla Benhabib, "Toward a Deliberative Model of Democratic Legitimacy," in *Democracy and Difference*, ed. Seyla Benhabib (Princeton: Princeton University Press, 1996), 84.

43 For example, compared to Australian multiculturalism, the Canadian experience presents a group-based form of multiculturalism by acknowledging corporate group rights such as the Quebec language laws.

44 On this point, see also Ricardo F. Mendonca, "Recognition and Social Esteem: A Case Study of the Struggles of People Affected by Leprosy," *Political Studies* 59, no. 4 (2011), 940–58.

45 Monique Deveaux, "A Deliberative Approach to Conflicts of Culture," *Political Theory* 31, no. 6 (2003):780–807.

As Monique Deveaux rightly argues, most of the time intercultural conflicts involve intra-cultural conflicts over the interpretation and meaning of certain cultural practices.[46] In this sense, intra-cultural deliberation can offer an important medium "through which the formation of identity and remapping of 'culture' occurs."[47]

Secondly, a deliberative politics of recognition is underpinned by the idea of what Jonathan Seglow calls "wide recognition."[48] Seglow differentiates between narrow and wide forms of recognition and argues that while the former is concerned solely about the vertical relationship between state and identity groups, the latter refers to a horizontal form of recognition that citizens should show one another. In practice, wide recognition means:

> for example that Islam is not disparaged as a religion and belief system; that non-European art is not considered primitive and savage; that speakers of Punjabi are not looked down upon; that gay relationships are not considered intrinsically inferior.[49]

The main point here is that "the majority need only affirm that the minority identity is different from their own, is valuable at least on its own terms."[50]

It is this wide and rather informal understanding of recognition that first gives existing rights and opportunities their meaning. In other words, institutions or policies alone do not shape the politics of recognition. Similar institutional measures might have different effects in different contexts, depending on how citizens interact and the prevailing discourses of cultural diversity in a given society. The deliberative approach proposed here suggests that formal/legal forms of inclusion are necessary, but not sufficient, conditions for accommodating cultural diversity. The liberal understanding of inclusion is solely about the extension of equal rights and opportunities to individuals who do not have them. A deliberative notion of inclusion goes beyond this form of inclusion by ensuring the conditions necessary for social inclusion. This is where the wide notion of recognition and existing discourses of cultural diversity in the wider public sphere gain importance. Ultimately, it is difficult to make sense of legal opportunities that are available to those who are publicly disregarded.

Conclusion

In this chapter, I sought to problematize the mainstream understanding of the politics of recognition underpinned by cultural essentialism and suggested an alternative notion of recognition from a perspective of deliberative democracy. I argued that the way culture and identity are conceptualized involves important implications both for the politics of

46 *Ibid.*, 784.

47 Ayelet Shachar, "Religion, State, and the Problem of Gender: New Modes of Citizenship and Governance in Diverse Societies," *McGill Law Journal* 50 (2005): 70.

48 Jonathan Seglow, "Theorizing Recognition," in *Multiculturalism and Identity Rights*, ed. (Abingdon, Oxon: Routledge, 2003), 78–93.

49 *Ibid.*, 88.

50 *Ibid.*, 84.

recognition and for democracy in contemporary multicultural societies. If identity is "dialogically created and constituted," as Amy Gutman argues, then its public recognition "requires a politics that leaves room for us to deliberate publically about those aspects of our identities that we share, or potentially share with other citizens."[51]

The deliberative perspective presented here contains three key lessons. First, it indicates that the politics of recognition is not an all-or-nothing affair, and that group-specific policies are just one form of implementing the politics of recognition. As argued above, recognition can manifest itself in a variety of ways depending on the contextual and institutional factors in a given society. Second, the deliberative perspective directs our attention to the importance of wide or informal types of recognition which first give institutional entitlements their meaning. In other words, formal rights are important, but not sufficient, conditions for a deliberative notion of recognition. Third, the deliberative approach suggested here requires the existence of rights and opportunities enabling legal and social inclusion of all affected parties, and ongoing, open-ended struggles for recognition. The most direct implication of a deliberative understanding of recognition is that no universal formula of politics of recognition exists. This approach helps us conceive recognition in broader terms, as a democratic activity and contestation, rather than as a narrowly defined relationship between cultural minorities and the state. As such, the deliberative democratic approach promises to go beyond the limitations inherent in essentialist responses to cultural diversity both on conceptual and institutional terms.

51 Amy Gutmann, "Introduction," in *Multiculturalism and the Politics of Recognition*, ed. Amy Gutmann (Princeton: Princeton University Press, 1992), 7.

Bibliography

Barry, Brian. *Culture and Equality.* Cambridge: Polity, 2001.
Benhabib, Seyla. *The Claims of Culture: Equality and Diversity in the Global Era.* Princeton: Princeton University Press, 2002.
— "Toward a Deliberative Model of Democratic Legitimacy." In *Democracy and Difference*, edited by Seyla Benhabib, 67–94. Princeton: Princeton University Press, 1996.
Bohman, James. *Public Deliberation, Pluralism, Complexity and Democracy.* Cambridge, MA: The MIT Press, 1996.
Cerulo, Karen A. "Identity Construction: New Issues, New Directions." *Annual Review of Sociology* 23 (1997): 385–410.
Cohen, Joshua. "Deliberation and Democratic Legitimacy." In *The Good Polity: Normative Analysis of the State*, edited by Alan Hamlin and Philip Pettit, 17–34. Oxford: Basil Blackwell, 1989.
Deveaux, Monique. "A Deliberative Approach to Conflicts of Culture." *Political Theory* 31, no. 6 (2003): 780–807.
Dryzek, John S. *Deliberative Democracy and Beyond. Liberals, Critics, Contestations.* Oxford: Oxford University Press, 2000.
Ercan, Selen A. "The Deliberative Politics of Cultural Diversity: Beyond Interest and Identity Politics?" In *Migration, Citizenship and Intercultural Relations. Looking through the Lens of Social Inclusion*, edited by Fethi Mansouri and Michele Lobo, 75–91. Farnham: Ashgate, 2011.
Festenstein, Mathew. *Negotiating Diversity: Culture, Deliberation, Trust.* Cambridge: Cambridge University Press, 2005.
Fuss, Diana. *Essentially Speaking. Feminism, Nature and Difference.* Abingdon, Oxon: Routledge, 1989.
Gutmann, Amy. "Introduction." In *Multiculturalism and the Politics of Recognition*, edited by Amy Gutmann, 3–24. Princeton: Princeton University Press, 1992.
Gutmann, Amy, and Dennis Thompson. *Why Deliberative Democracy.* Princeton: Princeton University Press, 2004.
James, Michael R. "Communicative Action, Strategic Action, and Inter-Group Dialogue." *European Journal of Political Theory* 2, no. 2 (2003): 157–82.
Jung, Courtney. "Race, Ethnicity and Culture." In *The Oxford Handbook of Contextual Policy Analysis*, edited by Robert E. Goodin and Charles Tilly, 360–76. Oxford: Oxford University Press, 2006.
— "The Burden of Culture and the Limits of Liberal Responsibility." *Constellations* 8, no. 2 (2001): 219–35.
Kanra, Bora. *Islam, Democracy and Dialogue in Turkey: Deliberating in Divided Societies.* Farnham: Ashgate, 2009.
Kirloskar-Steinbach, Monika. "National Identity: Belonging to a Cultural Group? Belonging to a Polity?" *JSRI* 8 (2004): 31–42.
Kukathas, Chandran. "Liberalism and Multiculturalism. The Politics of Indifference." *Political Theory* 26, no. 5 (1998): 686–99.
Markell, Patchen. *Bound by Recognition.* Princeton: Princeton University Press, 2003.

Mendonca, Ricardo F. "Recognition and Social Esteem: A Case Study of the Struggles of People Affected by Leprosy." *Political Studies* 59, no. 4 (2011): 940–58.
Modood, Tariq. "Anti-Essentialism, Multiculturalism and the 'Recognition of Religious Groups'." *The Journal of Political Philosophy* 6, no. 4 (1998): 378–99.
Offe, Claus. "Political Liberalism, Group Rights, and the Politics of Fear and Trust." In *Herausforderungen der Demokratie. Zur Integrations- und Leistungsfaehigkeit politischer Institutionen*, edited by Claus Offe, 321–48. Frankfurt: Campus Verlag, 2003.
Okin, Susan Moller. *Is Multiculturalism Bad for Women?* Princeton: Princeton University Press, 1999.
Parekh, Bhikhu. *Rethinking Multiculturalism: Cultural Diversity and Political Theory.* New York: Macmillian, 2000.
Phillips, Anne. *Multiculturalism without Culture.* Princeton: Princeton University Press, 2007.
Sandel, Michael. *Liberalism and Limits of Justice.* Cambridge: Cambridge University Press, 1982.
Seglow, Jonathan. "Theorizing Recognition." In *Multiculturalism and Identity Rights*, edited by Peter S. Haddock, 78–93. Abingdon, Oxon: Routledge, 2003.
Shachar, Ayelet. "Religion, State, and the Problem of Gender: New Modes of Citizenship and Governance in Diverse Societies." *McGill Law Journal* 50 (2005): 49–88.
Squires, Judith. "Culture, Equality and Diversity." In *Multiculturalism Reconsidered*, edited by Paul Kelly, 115–32. Cambridge: Polity, 2002.
Stratton, Jon, and Ien Ang. "Multicultural Imagined Communities. Cultural Difference and National Identity in the USA and Australia." In *Multicultural States. Rethinking Difference and Identity*, edited by David Bennett, 135–62. Abingdon, Oxon: Routledge, 1999.
Taylor, Charles. *Multiculturalism and "The Politics of Recognition."* Princeton: Princeton University Press, 1992.
— *Sources of the Self.* Cambridge: Cambridge University Press, 1989.
Tully, James. "Recognition and Dialogue: the Emergence of a New Field." *Critical Review of International Social and Political Philosophy* 7, no. 3 (2004): 84–106.
— "Struggles over Recognition and Distribution." *Constellations* 7, no. 4 (2000): 469–82.
Werbner, Pnina. "Essentialising Essentialism, Essentialising Silence: Ambivalence and Multiplicity in the Constructions of Racism and Ethnicity." In *Debating Cultural Hybridity*, edited by Pnina Werbner and Tariq Modood, 226–57. London: Zed Books, 1997.
Williams, Melissa S. "The Uneasy Alliance of Group Representation and Deliberative Democracy." In *Citizenship in Diverse Societies*, edited by Will Kymlicka and Wayne Norman, 124–54. Oxford: Oxford University Press, 2000.
Young, Iris M. *Inclusion and Democracy.* Oxford: Oxford University Press, 2000.

Dorota A. Gozdecka*
Selen A. Ercan**

WHAT IS POST-MULTICULTURALISM? RECENT TRENDS IN LEGAL AND POLITICAL DISCOURSE

Introduction

In recent years, culturally diverse societies have faced increasing difficulties in accommodating cultural and religious diversity. Multiculturalism, once celebrated as a long-sought solution to the issues cultural diversity may raise, seems to have lost popularity, at least at a discursive level.[1] The so-called retreat from multiculturalism has not only been confined to continental Europe, but it has been also evident in traditionally migrant-receiving societies such as Australia and Canada. Notwithstanding the absence of agreement about "what comes after multiculturalism," there seems to be a strong consensus in both scholarly circles and public discourse that we are now in a "post-multicultural" era.[2] In this chapter, we seek to unpack the meaning of post-multiculturalism and discuss its implications for culturally "conditioned" subjects. We define those subjects as individuals whose cultural, religious or ethnic identity is singled out from the rest of the population, and who are subject to legal and social discourses emphasising their differences. While unpacking the meaning of post-multiculturalism, we acknowledge that similar to the term multiculturalism, "post-multiculturalism" is a contested term. In fact, it seems to have different connotations in different countries, and is employed differently by various scholars and politicians. One important question the term post-multiculturalism raises is whether the prefix "post" implies the continuation of some sort of multiculturalism as a policy or a retreat from it. According to some scholars, such as Steven Vertovec, post-multiculturalism suggests a continuation with

* Australian National University and University of Helsinki (Law and the Other in Post-Multicultural Europe Project).
** Institute for Governance and Policy Analysis, University of Canberra.

1 Steven Vertovec and Susanne Wessendorf, *The Multiculturalism Backlash: European Discourses, Policies and Practices* (Abingdon, Oxon: Routledge, 2010).

2 Will Kymlicka, "The Rise and Fall of Multiculturalism? New Debates on Inclusion and Accommodation in Diverse Societies," *International Social Science Journal* 61, no. 199 (2010): 97–112; Steven Vertovec, "Towards Post-multiculturalism? Changing Communities, Conditions and Contexts of Diversity," *International Social Science Journal* 6, no. 199 (2010): 83–95; Dorota A. Gozdecka, Selen A. Ercan, and Magdalena Kmak, "From Multiculturalism to Post-multiculturalism: Trends and Paradoxes," *Journal of Sociology* 5, no. 1 2014): 51–64.

multiculturalism, yet it emphasises the need to foster maintenance of collective identity alongside recognition of cultural diversity.[3] In practice, this means that while existing policies for accommodating cultural diversity still have a place within a post-multicultural framework, they are complemented with new strategies designed to ensure some sort of collective identity in culturally diverse societies. According to Vertovec, these strategies may include interventions such as citizenship, language tests or citizenship ceremonies.[4]

When defined as such, and seen from a policy perspective, it is possible to argue that post-multiculturalism does not entail a radical departure from multiculturalism. Yet on a discursive level, the term post-multiculturalism seems to bring a new way of talking about and problematizing culturally different others. This is not to say that post-multiculturalism occurs only at a level of discourse; in fact, in some countries discursive changes have also led to institutional changes in immigration and integration laws and regulations.[5] Although such institutional changes are important, in this chapter we are primarily interested in capturing the discursive shift towards post-multiculturalism and its implications for accommodating cultural differences in contemporary societies. We focus on the way multiculturalism has been criticized in recent years, particularly in continental Europe, and identify new trends that are being developed under the banner of "post-multiculturalism" as a response to these criticisms. In doing so, we are particularly interested in exploring the implications of post-multiculturalism for those whose cultural or religious differences give grounds for diverse distinctions between them and the rest of the population.

The chapter is composed of three sections. In the first section, we explore the emerging literature on post-multiculturalism and focus on the meaning attached to this term by various scholars. In the second section, we seek to capture the distinguishing trends and changing discourses of cultural diversity in the post-multicultural area. Finally, in the third section, we discuss the possible implications of these changes on culturally conditioned subjects in contemporary plural societies.

What is Post-Multiculturalism?

Contemporary diagnoses around post-multiculturalism observe the emergence of a new trend but rarely underline the full range of its consequences. In his article on the rise and fall of multiculturalism, Will Kymlicka presents a rather optimistic view on the status of contemporary multicultural policies and acknowledges changes only in several areas, primarily those related to the management of migration. Similarly Vertovec and Wessendorf acknowledge a serious retreat of multiculturalism only in relation to immigrants, and argue that "without question, there has been a backlash against multiculturalism policies relating to post-war migrants in several western democracies."[6]

3 Vertovec, "Towards Post-multiculturalism?," 83.
4 Vertovec, "Towards Post-multiculturalism?".
5 See, e.g., Expanding language and citizenship tests requirements, examined in greater detail among others in Gozdecka, Ercan and Kmak, "From Multiculturalism to Post-multiculturalism," 51–64.
6 Vertovec and Wessendorf, *The Multiculturalism Backlash: European Discourses, Policies and Practices,* 41 (Abingdon, Oxon: Routledge, 2010).

Nonetheless they refrain from associating this tendency with a retreat from multiculturalism – a claim which they consider "overstated and misdiagnosed."[7] Kymlicka, Vertovec and Wessendorf, all emphasise that rather than multiculturalism coming to an end, we can talk about a shift in the application of multicultural policies, which in certain cases have encountered difficulties.[8] For Kymlicka, one of the examples which seemingly contradict alleged rejection of multicultural policies is the claim that retreat from immigrant multiculturalism is coupled with strengthening the institutional recognition of old minorities in the countries in question, such as the Frisian minority in The Netherlands or the Danish minority in Germany.[9] However, in our view such multicultural policies shifting the focus towards old and culturally assimilated minority groups constitute one of the examples of the post-multicultural era, namely reinforcement of the cultural *status quo*. To be sure, immigration has always been perceived as a challenge to integration, in both national and European Union discourses.[10] Recent developments, however, indicate a much stronger perception of immigration as a threat to national values and social cohesion. This, as we will discuss below, is due to a stronger and increasing emphasis on social cohesion and the need to emphasise the importance of citizenship as a form of collective identity in culturally plural societies.

Similar to Kymlikca's observations, Steven Vertovec rejects the diagnosis about the retreat from multiculturalism. In his article entitled "Towards post-multiculturalism" he considers post-multiculturalism as encompassing *inter alia* new measures designed to ensure integration of cultural minorities, such as citizenship tests, citizenship ceremonies or increased language requirements.[11] Vertovec acknowledges that such measures place the obligation "on immigrants to take up the values and cultural practices of the host country and to actively demonstrate their desire to belong."[12] Interestingly, though, in his view these developments do not imply renunciation of recognition of diversity. Rather, what they suggest is the emergence of an interesting mixture of a strong common national identity coupled with recognition of cultural diversity.[13]

Against these diagnoses, in their critical analysis presented in *The Crises of Multiculturalism* Alana Lentin and Gavan Titley point to several consequences of the current era, starting with a solidifying of the cultural *status quo*. They observe the role of so-called "recited truths" in regard to multiculturalism, and consider them as main reasons for the emergence of serious changes in the application of multicultural policies. These "truths" include primarily a widespread belief that multiculturalism has imploded,

7 *Ibid.*, 42.

8 Kymlicka, "The Rise and Fall of Multiculturalism?," 105.

9 *Ibid.*

10 Andrew Geddes, *The Politics of Migration and Immigration in Europe* (London: SAGE, 2003); Robert Miles and Dietrich Thränhardt, *Migration and European Integration: The Dynamics of Inclusion and Exclusion* (Madison, NJ: Fairleigh Dickinson University Press, 1995); Martin Kahanec and Klaus F. Zimmermann, "Migration in an Enlarged EU: A Challenging Solution?," in *Five Years of an Enlarged EU*, ed. Filip Keereman and Istvan Szekely (Springer Berlin Heidelberg, 2010), 63–94; Umut Korkut et al., *The Discourses and Politics of Migration in Europe* (Basingstoke: Palgrave Macmillan, 2013).

11 Vertovec, "Towards Post-multiculturalism?," 91.

12 *Ibid.*

13 *Ibid.*

a belief which emerged without due analysis of the concept itself. The manufactured "crisis" discourse, they argue, has led to changes and modifications based on fragmented experiences, which are read singularly and interpreted as evidence of crisis.[14] Similar to what we observe, these authors assert that the transition is problematic, as it entails serious implications for members of a community whose origins or culture are singled out. Before moving on to discussing these implications in greater detail, we will first outline the key manifestations of the post-multicultural era.

Manifestations of the Shift from Multiculturalism to Post-Multiculturalism

It is possible to identify the discursive shift from multiculturalism to post-multiculturalism in various areas. In what follows, we focus on three particular manifestations of this shift that we observe in the public and policy discourse of various culturally plural societies. These entail: i) overemphasis on gender inequality in minority cultures; ii) overemphasis on religious identities; and iii) emergence of the discourse of "parallel societies" and the need for "social cohesion."

i) Gender Inequality (Only) in Minority Cultures

The first and arguably the most common criticism of multiculturalism in recent years is its failure to ensure gender equality. This line of criticism is well-known in scholarly circles particularly since the publication of Susan Moller Okin's 1999 article entitled "Is Multiculturalism Bad for Women?" In her article, Okin forcefully argues that multiculturalism and feminism are not only in tension with each other, but that "multiculturalism is bad for women." In her view, liberal states should categorically avoid accommodating minority cultures as some cultures are harmful for female members of minority groups. The recognition of minority group traditions, she argues, exacerbates inequalities within minority groups. She maintains that even in the absence of special group rights and of multiculturalism as a state policy, it is important to remain cautious in response to cultures that are characterized by patriarchal beliefs and practices as such cultures tend to put women in a disadvantaged position. She substantiates this claim with her observation that many families in cultural groups in the United States, Canada and Europe place their daughters under significantly greater constraints than their sons.[15]

In recent years, this line of criticism has received renewed attention in nearly all migrant-receiving countries.[16] The dominant public discourse has depicted the issue of

14 Alana Lentin and Gavan Titley, *The Crises of Multiculturalism: Racism in a Neoliberal Age* (London: Zed Books, 2011), 40.

15 Susan Moller Okin, "'Mistresses of Their Own Destiny': Group Rights, Gender, and Realistic Rights of Exit," *Ethics* 112 (2002): 220f.

16 As Phillips and Saharso note: "Ten years ago, contestations around multicultural policy mostly proceeded without any mention of either gender or sexual violence. People debated the different bases for cultural claims, the relationship between individual and group rights, the balance between common citizenship and respect for diversity, or the nature and limits of toleration, but largely pursued these

gender inequality within traditional minority cultures as a strong indicator of multiculturalism's failure. This has been the case even in countries such as Germany, where multiculturalism has never been an official policy. Heated public and policy debate has occurred in both Europe and the Anglophone West over the treatment of girls and women in traditional cultures: women wearing the hijab; girls subjected to genital cutting; young people forced by their families into marriage with unknown and unwanted spouses; young women murdered by family members for behaviour said to offend the principles of community or family honour.[17] Such cases have usually been framed in the dominant public discourse as a culturally specific type of oppression that occurs only in minority cultures, and thus regarded as main obstacles on the way to integration.

One consequence of excessive focus on the maltreatment of women in minority cultures is that it reinforces the perception of such cultures as inherently oppressive and coercive; thus fundamentally different from mainstream society.[18] Gender inequality has been taken "as especially significant in exposing the gap between majority and minority cultures and degrees of integration are sometimes measured by degrees of assent to women's rights."[19] The way mainstream media and politicians frame these cases (as culturally harmful practices rather than gender-based violence) feed into stereotypical distinctions between liberal and illiberal, modern and traditional, enlightened and backward cultures. In this context, culture is taken to be something that applies only to minority groups whose "cultural practices" are blamed for resulting in a lack of cohesion in society more widely.[20] While non-minority women are presented as fully developed agents, the behaviour of women in minority cultural groups is explained through their appeal to culture.[21] Taken together, these tendencies have enabled sceptics of multiculturalism to represent it as "intrinsically separatist" and to frame "cultural difference as a major source of political instability."[22]

In this context, we do not wish to claim that gendered cultural practices, such as forced marriages or so-called "honour killings" are not problematic. Rather, we want to

without reference to gender concerns." Anne Phillips and Sawitri Saharso, "The Rights of Women and the Crisis of Multiculturalism," *Ethnicities* 8, no. 3 (2008): 293f.

17 See for example Anne Phillips and Moria Dustin, "UK Initiatives on Forced Marriage: Regulation, Dialogue and Exit," *Political Studies* 52 (2004): 531–51; Moira Dustin, *Gender Equality, Cultural Diversity: European Comparisons and Lessons* (London: The Nuffield Foundation, 2006); Sawitri Saharso and Doutje Lettinga, "Contentious Citizenship: Policies and Debates on the Veil in the Netherlands," *Social Politics* 15, no. 4 (2008): 455–80; Selen A. Ercan, "Same Problem, Different Solutions: The Case of 'Honour Killing' in Germany and Britain," in *'Honour' Killing and Violence. Theory, Policy and Practice*, ed. Aisha Gill, Carolyn Strange and Karl Roberts (London: Palgrave Macmillan, 2014), 199–217.

18 Anne Phillips, *Multiculturalism without Culture* (Princeton: Princeton University Press, 2007), 23–5.

19 Phillips and Saharso, "The Rights of Women," 293.

20 David Kahane, "Dispute Resolution and the Politics of Cultural Generalization," *Negotiation Journal* 19, no. 1 (2003): 11.

21 Conny Roggeband and Mieke Verloo, "Dutch Women Are Liberated, Migrant Women Are a Problem: The Evolution of Policy Frames on Gender and Migration in the Netherlands, 1995-2005," *Social Policy and Administration* 41, no. 3 (2007): 271–88.

22 Phillips, *Multiculturalism without Culture*, 24.

draw attention to the way such practices are framed in culturally plural societies. One recent example of this is offered by Selen Ercan in her analysis of "honour killing" debates in Britain and Germany. Ercan argues that although both countries have faced a similar challenge in addressing "honour killing," they have employed different "problem definitions" of these murders and debated them in substantially different ways. While the British debate has focused on the gender-related dimension of these murders and defined them ultimately as violence against women (VAW), in German public and policy discourse, "honour killing" has always been singled out as a culturally specific type of murder that occurs only in minority cultures. This is an important point, as the way such cases are framed affects not only the way migrants and cultural minorities are perceived in culturally plural societies, but also the relationship between them and the majority society.[23]

ii) Overemphasis on Religious Identities

Another tendency that characterises the post-multicultural era is the shift of focus from culture and/or ethnicity to religion. In recent years, religion has emerged as a major social signifier and was given a prominent role in understanding and resolving problems related to migrant integration in many European countries. Particularly in the post 9/11 era, we observe a strong tendency towards an "Islamisation" of identities and cultural issues.[24] A telling example of a tendency to underline religious difference is the statement by former French president Nicolas Sarkozy who noted that

> ... we must all respect differences, but we do not want a society where communities coexist side by side. Our Muslim compatriots must be able to practice their religion, as any citizen can, but we in France do not want people to pray in an ostentatious way in the street.[25]

The statement as such not only singles out Muslim citizens on the basis of their religion but also presents them as a coherent religious monolith rather than a culturally diverse mix of different identities.

One important consequence of the overemphasis on religion has been precisely such singling out of adherents of Islam and presenting them and their religious symbolism as religiously motivated fanaticism.[26] This representation of Islam triggered a widespread

23 Anna Korteweg and Gokce Yurdakul, "Islam, Gender, and Immigrant Integration: Boundary Drawing in Discourses on Honour Killing in the Netherlands and Germany," *Ethnic and Racial Studies* 32, no. 2 (2009): 218–38.

24 Ralph Grillo, "British and Others: From 'Race' to 'Faith'," in *The Multiculturalism Backlash. European Discourses, Policies and Practices*, ed. Steven Vertovec and Susanne Wessendorf (London: Routledge, 2010), 50–72; Ulrike Linder et al. ed., *Hybrid Cultures – Nervous States. Britain and Germany in a (Post) Colonial World* (Amsterdam: Rodopi, 2010); Christoph Ramm, "The Muslim Makers. How Germany 'Islamizes' Turkish Immigrants." *Interventions* 12, no. 2 (2010): 183–97.

25 "Nicolas Sarkozy joins David Cameron and Angela Merkel view that multiculturalism has failed," *Daily Mail*, January 11, 2011.

26 Michael Humphrey, "Conditional Multiculturalism: Islam in Liberal Democratic States," in *Ashgate Research Companion to Multiculturalism*, ed. Duncan Ivison (Surrey, Burlington, Ashgate, 2010), 199–

belief that its religious symbols cannot be reconciled with the values of democracy. This subsequently led to law's preoccupation with "fearful symbols" and initiated the expulsion of religious symbolism from an extremely broadly conceived public sphere.[27] The public sphere, originally understood as political,[28] became broadened to encompass not only the sphere of authority but also what Charles Taylor calls "the spheres of access and appearance."[29] Religionisation of identities brought legal changes primarily to the spheres of access and appearance, which both soon became protected from manifestations of religious symbolism. Examples of this trend are widespread throughout the world. Most notably, in 2009 following an Islamophobic campaign a Swiss referendum, "democratically" sanctioned a ban on the construction of minarets. The referendum changed the supreme legal source of the state; the very Constitution of Switzerland. Article 72 on Church and State under Section 3 currently reads: "The building of minarets is prohibited."[30] Despite the omnipresence of church towers in nearly every city, town and village of Switzerland, the existence of four minarets resulted in a ban on construction dictated by protection of "local culture."[31] The juxtaposition of local culture with the religionised subjects' symbolism relied on presenting claims by the traditional Christian population as legitimate and motivated by culture in contrast to claims by those wishing to build minarets, presented as motivated by alien and fanatical religious behaviour.

Similar to the minaret ban, the so-called "burqa bans" were also aimed at targeting the same group of believers by overemphasising the impact of a religious dress code on local culture and democracy. In 2011 France passed a law banning concealment of the face in public and penalising wearing a dress concealing the face with a fine of 150 EUR.[32] The broad scope of permitted forms of cover suggests that the ban is strictly aiming at women wearing full face veiling.[33] After entering into force, the law was executed by detaining a few women wearing full veiling. Soon after France, similar bans occurred in Belgium and Italy and have been debated in a few German states (*Länder*). All laws dealing with concealment of the face include similar provisions and have been passed with the support of democratically elected parliaments. The French ban has recently been challenged before the European Court of Human Rights (ECtHR). The case of

216; Rita Kaur Dhamoon, "Security Warning: Multiculturalism Alert!," in *Ashgate Research Companion to Multiculturalism*, ed. Duncan Ivison (Surrey, Burlington: Ashgate, 2010), 255–76; John L. Esposito and Ibrahim Kalin, *Islamophobia: The Challenge of Pluralism in the 21st Century* (Oxford and New York: Oxford University Press, 2011).

27 Jeremy T. Gunn, "Fearful Symbols: The Islamic Headscarf and the European Court of Human Rights" *Strasbourg Consortium: Freedom of Conscience and Religion at the European Court of Human Rights*, 2005.

28 Jürgen Habermas, *The Structural Transformation of the Public Sphere: An Inquiry Into a Category of Bourgois Society* (Cambridge, MA: MIT Press, 1991).

29 Charles Taylor, *Modern Social Imaginaries* (Durham, NC: Duke University Press, 2003).

30 Constitution of Switzerland, 18 April 1999, Amendment of 29 November 2009.

31 Nick Cumming-Bruce and Steven Erlanger, "Swiss Ban Building of Minarets on Mosques," *The New York Times*, November 30, 2009, www.nytimes.com/2009/11/30/world/europe/30swiss.html.

32 Loi 2010–1192 du 11 octobre 2010 interdisant la dissimulation du visage dans l'espace public (Law 2010–1192 of Oct. 11, 2010 Banning the Concealment of the Face in Public Space).

33 S. Nanwani, "The Burqa Ban: An Unreasonable Limitation on Religious Freedom or a Justifiable Restriction," *Emory International Law Review* 25, no. 3 (2011): 1431–76.

S.A.S. v. France[34] decided last year did not reverse the entitlement of the state to regulate religious dress code.[35] While approaching the claims of the applicant with greater respect, the objective of 'preservation of the conditions of "living together"' became the decisive factor upholding the ban on face covering.[36]

Meanwhile, analogical proposals have been considered in Quebec where the discussion on symbols allowed in the public sphere reaches deeply into the core values of the entire community.[37] A similar discussion briefly appeared even in the Australian context,[38] despite the comparatively low controversial nature of religious symbolism.

In some countries, an overemphasis on religious identity was a result of changes in migration and citizenship laws. Germany offers one such example. In 2000 a change occurred in the German Citizenship Law, in particular changing citizenship from the principle of *ius sanguinis*, that is, from a biological definition of citizenship, to one that includes facets of *ius solis*, the territorial principle that considers the place of birth in granting citizenship. This was followed in 2004 by the introduction of a new Immigration Act (*Zuwanderungsgesetz*). With this act, Germany recognized itself for the first time as a country of immigration (*Einwanderungsland*). Both developments contributed to Germany's move, however slowly, "in the direction of more formal acceptance of greater cultural pluralism and political inclusiveness."[39] Yet, paradoxically, both the new citizenship law and the new immigration act intensified rather than alleviated debates on identity and belonging and frequently revolved around religion.[40] In fact, lowering the citizenship threshold "has necessitated defining which values and competences characterize a truly democratic citizen, and screening out intruders who do not possess them."[41] In this socio-political context, ethnicity lost its major signifier status, and religious identity took over the differentiating function.[42]

34 *S.A.S. v. France*, no. 43835/11, pending.

35 See previous case law and commentaries, in particular: Dahlab v Switzerland, 42393/98 (European Court of Human Rights 2001); Karen Meerschaut and Serge Gutwirth, "*Legal Pluralism and Islam in the Scales of the European Court of Human Rights : the Limits of Categorical Balancing*", 2008, 431–65; Dorota A. Gozdecka and Amy R. Jackson, "Caught Between Different Legal Pluralisms: Women Who Wear Islamic Dress as the Religious 'Other' in European Rights Discourses," *Journal of Legal Pluralism and Unofficial Law* 64 (2011): 91–120.

36 *S.A.S. v. France*, para. 157.

37 Farzana Hassan, "Quebec needs to ban more than symbols," *Toronto Sun*, January 23, 2014, www.torontosun.com/2014/01/23/quebec-needs-to-ban-more-than-symbols.

38 Cory Bernardi, "For Australia's sake, we need to ban the burqa," *Sydney Morning Herald*, May 6, 2010.

39 Barbara Donovan, "Minority Representation in Germany," German Politics 16, no. 4 (2007): 476.

40 Frauke Miera, *Multiculturalism Debates in Germany*, Report for the EMILIE Project, A European Approach to Multicultural Citizenship: Legal, Political and Educational Challenges (Brussels: European Commission, 2007).

41 Per Mouritsen, "Political Responses to Cultural Conflict: Reflections on the Ambiguities of the Civic Turn," in *Constituting Communities. Political Solutions to Cultural Conflict*, ed. Per MOURITSEN and Knud Erik JORGENSEN (New York: Palgrave, 2008), 1–30.

42 Riem Spielhaus, "Religion und Identität: Vom Deutschen Versuch, 'Ausländer' Zu 'Muslimen' Zu Machen," *Internationale Politik* 3 (2006): 28–36.

iii) The Discourse of "Parallel Societies" and the Need for "Social Cohesion"

Finally, the third and related feature of post-multiculturalism discourse is the emphasis it places on the diagnosis of "parallel societies"[43] and "cultural disintegration."[44] The term "parallel societies" had been employed mainly by sceptics of multiculturalism to depict the threatening scenario of "non-integrated" immigrants retreating to "parallel worlds" and rejecting Western values. These worlds have been depicted as accommodating so-called "illiberal subjects" living in a strong patriarchal organisation with a high level of familial and social control over women. The dominant public discourse has presented such subjects and the "parallel societies" that inhabit them as serious threats to the liberal state and its "progressive" values. This has served to justify the need for stricter integration policies implying "love it or leave it"-type solutions particularly in continental Europe. In most cases, governments have responded to the threatening scenario of "parallel societies" by emphasizing the need for social cohesion which is manifested through various territorial security measures, and the revival of a "white nation" imaginary.[45]Not surprisingly, as part of their mission to secure social cohesion, most states in most immigrant-receiving countries, including those with multicultural policies in place have begun prioritizing citizenship as evidence of a strong link between population, territory and identity. With citizenship becoming a key tool for securing cohesion, acquiring citizenship has ceased being seen as a path to integration but instead as a "reward" for successful integration.[46] Introduction of citizenship classes as a compulsory part of the school curriculum (Britain, 2002) or strengthening language and local knowledge test policies (examples include the UK, Germany, Denmark, France, The Netherlands, Singapore, Australia, Finland) have created space for awarding citizenship only to those migrants who are capable of demonstrating knowledge of the language and values of the mainstream society. These corrective measures are seen as a remedy to counteract the "dangerously fragmenting" forces of multiculturalism and to replace them with a strongly integrated community. Even in traditionally migrant-receiving countries such as Australia, there has been a move away from multiculturalism to a social cohesion agenda, as a result of which the term "multiculturalism" was officially replaced by the word "citizenship."[47] In fact, as a manifestation of this move, in 2007, the Australian government changed the name of the *Department of Immigration and Multicultural Affairs* (DIMA) to the *Department of Immigration and Citizenship* (DIAC). More recently, in 2013 the name of this department changed again to the *Department of Immigration and Border Protection* (DIBP) heralding an era where strong border protection and

43 Gozdecka, Ercan and Kmak, "From Multiculturalism to Post-multiculturalism."

44 Lentin and Titley, *The Crises of Multiculturalism*, 42–48.

45 Kaur Dhamoon, "Security Warning," 258–273.

46 See Anne MacDuff, "Framing Migrants as Future Australian Citizens," Symposium Presentation, *Migrants Outside the Frames of Community*, ANU College of Law, Canberra, Presented on March 7, 2014.

47 Heba Batainah and Mary Walsh, "From Multiculturalism to Citizenship," in *Howard's Fourth Government*, ed. Aulich Chris and Roger Wettenhall (Sydney: University of New South Wales Press, 2008), 227–44.

security are viewed as part of the social cohesion agenda.As noted before, in recent years citizenship has also begun to be used a tool to ensure social cohesion and maintain territorial security. In this context, even the "best" migrants who have acquired citizenship continue being viewed through the lens of security needs.[48] In some countries, security measures include legal initiatives aimed at stripping those with double citizenship of their new nationality. The Netherlands has lately dealt with a government proposal to introduce a law that would put more restrictions on retaining double citizenship. Auke Zijlstra, a member representing the Freedom Party (PVV) in the European Union claimed that allowing immigrants from "Islamic countries" to retain dual citizenship had negatively impacted the integrity of Dutch society.[49]

Similarly, recent debate on the British law on citizenship illustrates a peculiar conjunction of security, cohesion and citizenship discourse. In the name of securing the territory from terrorism, an amendment to the Citizenship law first allows stripping those suspected of terrorism of their British citizenship if they hold the citizenship of another country. The amendment to section 40 of the British Nationality Act 1981 allows the British Home Office to deprive a person of citizenship if they are "satisfied that deprivation is conducive to the public good." The securitisation of migration as a form of controlling the migrant population has recently pushed proposed changes to the Nationality Act even further.[50] A legislative proposal by the Home Secretary suggested stripping citizenship from terror suspects even if it would leave them stateless.[51] While this proposal failed, the mere attempt to use such severe measures illustrates the extremity of steps taken in the name of cohesion and security. Statelessness, previously an unthinkable option, is currently considered a viable alternative to regular criminal proceedings. In sum, the need for social cohesion has escalated the use of extraordinary means to manage the lives of subjects seen as undermining the unity of territory, identity and the nation.

The New Imaginary of Cultural Minorities in the Post-Multiculturalist Era

The post-multicultural tendencies described above have cemented the position of traditional national communities. Legal and political discourses have shifted to target those selectively chosen segments of the population conditioned by their cultural origins. While most legal means appear neutral on the surface, the rationale and discourse behind them frequently is not.[52] Emphasis on the shortcomings of multiculturalism has become reflected in legal discourse and resulted in preoccupation with religious

48 Michael Humphrey, "Migration, Security and Insecurity," *Journal of Intercultural Studies* 34, no. 2 (2013): 179.

49 Krister Koskelo, "Dual Citizenship Worldwide," *Harvard Political Review*, 2012, http://harvardpolitics.com/covers/global-migration/dual-citizenship-worldwide/.

50 Humphrey, "Migration, Security and Insecurity."

51 Nicholas Watt, "Theresa May Plan Capable of Making Foreign-born Terror Suspects Stateless," *The Guardian*, January 30, 2014.

52 Humphrey, "Conditional Multiculturalism;" Milly Williamson and Gholam Khiabany, "UK: The Veil and the Politics of Racism," *Race & Class* 52, no. 2 (2010): 85–96; Nanwani, "The Burqa Ban."

symbolism, cultural practices and citizenship. Instead of focusing on possibilities for coexistence, these post-multicultural discourses reflect a constant perception of incommensurability and insecurity transforming the community into a stratified form based on a division between those belonging and those falling outside.[53]It can therefore be said that post-multiculturalism operates in "troublesome ways"[54] covering and disguising discriminatory policies and legal amendments under the spurious banner of being progressive. Bans targeting face covering well exemplify this tendency. While justified on the grounds of protecting freedom of expression, equality and freedom from coercion, in practice these legal means target specifically selected subjects. Those subjects, while nominally declared "equal," are in fact seen as inferior, without agency and in need of "saving."[55] Equality is thus not based on recognition of difference[56] and equal worth of those different from the majority population, but instead built on the assumption that equality must entail cultural sameness. The strong emphasis with which post-multicultural discourse and law targets "illiberal subjects" relies on the presumption of their "incapability" to adhere to Western norms of "equality" and constant exploitation of that alleged "incapability."[57]

Such targeting of those seen as "illiberal" reverses the logic of protection and recognition: protecting an individual from possible state injustice becomes replaced with protecting a state from "illiberal" others. This manufactured sense of insecurity, on the other hand, reinforces racial and cultural relations of power. The "illiberal" other is not racialised by reference to whiteness but is instead outlined by an uneven and asymmetrical set of power relations.[58] Post-multicultural discourses seem to reinforce rather than relieve racialising forms of essentialisation by underlining and exploiting difference. Culturalised subjects have become seen as unequally "conditioned" and in need of being corrected for their religion, cultural difference, cultural origin and eventually political origin (citizenship).[59]

Such inequality and racialisation "without race" has eventually led to social polarisation and stratification.[60] Culturally conditioned subjects are seen as excluded from the political community and thus by definition inferior and belonging at the

53 Etienne Balibar and Immanuel Maurice Wallerstein, *Race, Nation, Class: Ambiguous Identities* (Verso, 1991); Étienne Balibar, *We, the People of Europe?: Reflections on Transnational Citizenship* (Princeton: Princeton University Press, 2009).

54 Even though not branding them as post-multiculturalism, Barbara Arneil and Fiona MacDonald analyze contemporary multicultural policies and observe similar contradictory tendencies which they describe as "troublesome ways in which contemporary multicultural policy works," see: Barbara Arneil and Fiona MacDonald, "Multiculturalism and the Social Sphere," in *The Ashgate Research Companion to Multiculturalism*, ed. Duncan Ivison (Surrey, Burlington: Ashgate, 2010), 95–117.

55 Wendy Brown, *Regulating Aversion: Tolerance in the Age of Identity and Empire* (Princeton: Princeton University Press, 2008); Costas Douzinas, "The Paradoxes of Human Rights," *Constellations* 20, no. 1 (2013): 51–67.

56 Charles Taylor and Amy Gutmann, *Multiculturalism and "The Politics of Recognition": An Essay by Charles Taylor* (Fondo de Cultura Económica, 1992).

57 Kaur Dhamoon, "Security Warning."

58 Charles W. Mills, *The Racial Contract* (Ithaca, NY: Cornell University Press, 1999).

59 Balibar and Wallerstein, *Race, Nation, Class*, 21.

60 *Ibid.*

bottom of the social ladder.[61] Instead of parallel societies, post-multiculturalism recreates a different form of segregation – a quasi-class segregation.[62] Those perceived as culturally, religiously or politically "conditioned" became pushed to lower social strata and closed off in carefully selected, managed and controlled cultural "ghettos": ghettos the boundaries of which are as difficult to traverse as those of allegedly sealed cultures.

Conclusion

In this chapter we aimed to unpack the discourse of post-multiculturalism by identifying shifts in the politics of cultural diversity in contemporary migrant-receiving countries. We have argued that while post-multiculturalism does not at first glance appear to bring radical changes, it displays clear tendencies in particular areas pertaining to cultural difference. Due to the indistinctness of post-multicultural policies, the diagnosis concerning their impact may yield diverse results depending on the indicators one takes into account. It may be argued that, having taken into account a different set of indicators, the analysis of post-multiculturalism might prove its positive impact on recognition. As a problematic and fuzzy concept we argue that post-multiculturalism might mean at the same time more recognition in some areas and less recognition in others, particularly those targeting certain groups of the population. It appears that cultural, religious and place-of-origin conditioning is particularly strong and prone to being exploited. We believe that such exploitation might reinforce negative forces of multiculturalism rather than counteract them.

With the post-multicultural trend expanding around the world, it is likely that emerging changes will normalize and fix a more stringent immigration and citizenship policy. With a more controlled and selectively chosen population the cultural *status quo* risks becoming cemented and rigid. New cultural and social forces risk becoming simply controlled curiosities managed within the structures of existing hegemonic powers and pushed to lower social strata. With growing differences between the managed and the governing, post-multicultural societies seem to entail a high risk of cultural polarisation and cultural ghettoisation.

61 Etienne Balibar, "Europe, an 'Unimagined' Frontier of Democracy," *Diacritics* 33, no. 3 (2006): 37.
62 *Ibid.*

Bibliography

Arneil, Barbara, and Fiona MacDonald. "Multiculturalism and the Social Sphere." In *The Ashgate Research Companion to Multiculturalism*, 95–117. Surrey, Burlington: Ashgate, 2010.

Balibar, Etienne. "Europe, an 'Unimagined' Frontier of Democracy." *Diacritics* 33, no. 3 (2006): 36–44.

Balibar, Étienne. *We, the People of Europe?: Reflections on Transnational Citizenship.* Princeton University Press, 2009.

Balibar, Etienne, and Immanuel Maurice Wallerstein. *Race, Nation, Class: Ambiguous Identities.* Verso, 1991.

Batainah, Heba, and Mary Walsh. "From Multiculturalism to Citizenship. " In *Howard's Fourth Government*, edited by Aulich Chris and Roger Wettenhall, 227–44. Sydney: University of New South Wales Press, 2008.

Bernardi, Cory. "For Australia's Sake, We Need to Ban the Burqa." *Sydney Morning Herald*, May 6, 2010. www.smh.com.au/federal-politics/society-and-culture/for-australias-sake-we-need-to-ban-the-burqa-20100506-ubun.html.

Brown, Wendy. *Regulating Aversion: Tolerance in the Age of Identity and Empire.* Princeton: Princeton University Press, 2008.

Cumming-Bruce, Nick, and Steven Erlanger. "Swiss Ban Building of Minarets on Mosques." *The New York Times*, November 30, 2009. www.nytimes.com/2009/11/30/world/europe/30swiss.html.

Donovan, Barbara. "Minority Representation in Germany." German Politics 16, no. 4 (2007): 455–80.

Dustin, Moira. *Gender Equality, Cultural Diversity: European Comparisons and Lessons.* London: The Nuffield Foundation, 2006.

Douzinas, Costas. "The Paradoxes of Human Rights." *Constellations* 20, no. 1 (2013): 51–67. doi:10.1111/cons.12021.

Ercan, Selen A. "Same Problem, Different Solutions: The Case of 'Honour Killing' in Germany and Britain." In *'Honour' Killing and Violence. Theory, Policy and Practice*, edited by Aisha Gill, Carolyn Strange and Karl Roberts, 199–217. London: Palgrave Macmillan, 2014.

Esposito, John L., and Ibrahim Kalin. *Islamophobia: The Challenge of Pluralism in the 21st Century.* Oxford and New York: Oxford University Press, 2011.

Geddes, Andrew. *The Politics of Migration and Immigration in Europe.* London: Sage, 2003.

Gozdecka, Dorota A., Selen A. Ercan and Magdalena Kmak. "From Multiculturalism to Post-multiculturalism: Trends and Paradoxes." *Journal of Sociology* 50, no. 1 (2014): 51–64. doi:10.1177/1440783314522191.

Gozdecka, Dorota A., and Amy R. Jackson. "Caught Between Different Legal Pluralisms: Women Who Wear Islamic Dress as the Religious 'Other' in European Rights Discourses." *Journal of Legal Pluralism and Unofficial Law* 64 (2011): 91–120.

Grillo, Ralph. "British and Others: From 'Race' to 'Faith'." In *The Multiculturalism Backlash. European Discourses, Policies and Practices*, edited by Steven Vertovec and Susanne Wessendorf, 50–72. London: Routledge, 2010.

Gunn, Jeremy T. "Fearful Symbols: The Islamic Headscarf and the European Court of Human Rights." *Strasbourg Consortium: Freedom of Conscience and Religion at the European Court of Human Rights*, 2005. www.strasbourgconsortium.org/document.php?DocumentID=3846.

Hassan, Farzana. "Quebec needs to ban more than symbols," *Toronto Sun*, January 23, 2014. www.torontosun.com/2014/01/23/quebec-needs-to-ban-more-than-symbols.

Humphrey, Michael. "Conditional Multiculturalism: Islam in Liberal Democratic States." In *Ashgate Research Companion to Multiculturalism*, edited by Duncan Ivison, 199–216. Surrey, Burlington: Ashgate 2010.

— "Migration, Security and Insecurity." *Journal of Intercultural Studies* 34, no. 2 (2013): 178–95. doi:10.1080/07256868.2013.781982.

Kahane, David. "Dispute Resolution and the Politics of Cultural Generalization." Negotiation Journal 19, no. 1 (2003): 5–27.

Kahanec, Martin, and Klaus F. Zimmermann. "Migration in an Enlarged EU: A Challenging Solution?" In *Five Years of an Enlarged EU*, edited by Filip Keereman and Istvan Szekely, 63–94. Berlin and Heidelberg: Springer, 2010.Kaur Dhamoon, Rita. "Security Warnin: Multiculturalism Alert!" In *Ashgate Research Companion to Multiculturalism*, edited by Duncan Ivison, 255–76. Surrey, Burlington: Ashgate, 2010.

Korkut, Umut, Gregg Bucken-Knapp, Aidan McGarry, Jonas Hinnfors, and Helen Drake. *The Discourses and Politics of Migration in Europe*. Basingstoke: Palgrave Macmillan, 2013.

Korteweg, Anna, and Gokce Yurdakul. "Islam, Gender, and Immigrant Integration: Boundary Drawing in Discourses on Honour Killing in the Netherlands and Germany." *Ethnic and Racial Studies* 32, no. 2 (2009): 218–38.

Koskelo, Krister. "Dual Citizenship Worldwide." *Harvard Political Review*, 2012. http://harvardpolitics.com/covers/global-migration/dual-citizenship-worldwide/.

Kymlicka, Will. "The Rise and Fall of Multiculturalism? New Debates on Inclusion and Accommodation in Diverse Societies." *International Social Science Journal* 61, no. 199 (2010): 97–112. doi:10.1111/j.1468–2451.2010.01750.x.

Lentin, Alana, and Gavan Titley. *The Crises of Multiculturalism: Racism in a Neoliberal Age*. London: Zed Books, 2011.

Linder, Ulrike, Maren Mohring, Mark Stein and Silke Stroh, eds. *Hybrid Cultures – Nervous States. Britain and Germany in a (Post)Colonial World*. Amsterdam: Rodopi, 2010.

MacDuff, Anne. "Framing Migrants as Future Australian Citizens." Symposium Presentation, *Migrants Outside the Frames of Community*. ANU College of Law, Canberra, Presented on March 7, 2014.

Meerschaut, Karen, and Serge Gutwirth. "Legal Pluralism and Islam in the Scales of the European Court of Human Rights : the Limits of Categorical Balancing." In *Conflicts between Fundamental Rights*, edited by E. Brems, 431–65. Antwerp: Intersentia, 2008.

Miera, Frauke. "Multiculturalism Debates in Germany." *Report for the EMILIE Project, A European Approach to Multicultural Citizenship: Legal, Political and Educational Challenges*. Brussels: European Commission 2007.

Miles, Robert, and Dietrich Thränhardt. *Migration and European Integration: The Dynamics of Inclusion and Exclusion*. Madison, NJ: Fairleigh Dickinson University Press, 1995.

Mills, Charles W. *The Racial Contract*. Ithaca, NY: Cornell University Press, 1999.

Mouritsen, Per. "Political Responses to Cultural Conflict: Reflections on the Ambiguities of the Civic Turn." In *Constituting Communities. Political Solutions to Cultural Conflict*, edited by Per Mouritsen and Knud Erik Jorgensen, 1–30. New York: Palgrave, 2008.

Nanwani, Shaira. "The Burqa Ban: An Unreasonable Limitation on Religious Freedom or a Justifiable Restriction." *Emory International Law Review* 25, no. 3 (2011): 1431–76.

"Nicolas Sarkozy joins David Cameron and Angela Merkel view that multiculturalism has failed," *Daily Mail*, January 11, 2011. www.dailymail.co.uk/news/article-1355961/Nicolas-Sarkozy-joins-David-Cameron-Angela-Merkel-view-multiculturalism-failed.html.

Okin, Susan Moller. *Is Multiculturalism Bad for Women?* Princeton: Princeton University Press, 1999.

Okin, Susan Moller. "'Mistresses of Their Own Destiny': Group Rights, Gender, and Realistic Rights of Exit." *Ethics* 112 (2002): 205–30.

Phillips, Anne. *Multiculturalism without Culture*. Princeton: Princeton University Press, 2007.

Phillips, Anne, and Moria Dustin. "UK Initiatives on Forced Marriage: Regulation, Dialogue and Exit." *Political Studies* 52 (2004): 531–51.

Phillips, Anne, and Sawitri Saharso. "The Rights of Women and the Crisis of Multiculturalism." *Ethnicities* 8, no. 3 (2008): 291–301.

Ramm, Christoph. "The Muslim Makers. How Germany 'Islamizes' Turkish Immigrants." *Interventions* 12, no. 2 (2010): 183–97.

Roggeband, Conny, and Mieke Verloo. "Dutch Women Are Liberated, Migrant Women Are a Problem: The Evolution of Policy Frames on Gender and Migration in the Netherlands, 1995–2005. " *Social Policy and Administration* 41, no. 3 (2007): 271–88.

Saharso, Sawitri, and Doutje Lettinga. "Contentious Citizenship: Policies and Debates on the Veil in the Netherlands." *Social Politics* 15, no. 4 (2008): 455–80.

Spielhaus, Riem. "Religion und Identität: Vom Deutschen Versuch, 'Ausländer' Zu 'Muslimen' Zu Machen." *Internationale Politik* 3 (2006): 28–36.

Taylor, Charles. *Modern Social Imaginaries*. Durham, NC: Duke University Press, 2003.

Taylor, Charles, and Amy Gutmann. *Multiculturalism and "The Politics of Recognition": An Essay by Charles Taylor*. Fondo de Cultura Económica, 1992.

Vertovec, Steven, and Susanne Wessendorf. *The Multiculturalism Backlash: European Discourses, Policies and Practices*. Abingdon, Oxon: Routledge, 2010.

Watt, Nicholas. "Theresa May Plan Capable of Making Foreign-born Terror Suspects Stateless." *The Guardian*, January 30, 2014. www.theguardian.com/politics/2014/jan/29/theresa-may-terror-suspects-citizenship-clegg-approval.

Williamson, Milly, and Gholam Khiabany. "UK: The Veil and the Politics of Racism." *Race & Class* 52, no. 2 (2010): 85–96. doi:10.1177/0306396810377003.

Eliška Pírková*

THE CATEGORIZATION OF MINORITIES IN THE EUROPEAN CONTEXT: UNWRAPPING THE BOX

Introduction

For many decades, it has frequently been argued that only traditional or old minorities are entitled to minority rights under international law. The best example of such a practice is the Council of Europe's Recommendation 1201 (1993) of the Parliamentary Assembly of the Council of Europe (PACE), where the Assembly asked the Committee of Ministers to draft an additional protocol on rights of national minorities to the European Convention on Human Rights. The Committee has never done so and instead adopted the Framework Convention for the Protection of National Minorities (FCNM). However, the PACE Recommendation contained a definition of minorities, where one of the requirements was that the group maintains "long-standing, firm and lasting ties" with the state concerned. Although the FCNM does not include any definition, most state parties have limited its application to old or traditional minorities.[1] There is a view that the concept of minorities, and particularly national minorities, has a well-established meaning thanks to the famous definition by Francesco Capotorti and his study on the rights of minorities.[2] However, this concept excludes so called new minorities consisting of third country nationals and migrants, as it limits the range of minorities to groups of persons that hold the country's citizenship and have lived there traditionally.

The issue gets even more complicated if we take into consideration the remarkable diversity of the European Union (EU), consisting of numerous ethnic minorities. Notwithstanding the fact that after the Lisbon revision of the Treaties minority protection is one of the "values" of the Union, acting on this value remains highly challenging. Everyone in the EU belongs to a minority of some kind. The vulnerability of numerous groups can be seen as a result of EU integration as well. The EU treats issues of sexual orientation, ethnicity, race, religion, language, and nationality as discrete and unrelated phenomena, when in fact they interact. Moreover, they may interact in different ways at

* Doctoral researcher, University of Helsinki, Faculty of Law.

1 Asbjørn Eide, "The Rights of 'New' Minorities: Scope and Restrictions," in *Double Standards Pertaining to Minority Protection*, ed. Kristin Henrard. (Leiden: Martinus Nijhoff Publishers, 2010), 166.

2 Francesco Capotorti, *Study on the Rights of Persons Belonging to Ethnic, Religious and Linguistic Minorities* (New York: UN Publications, 1991).

the EU level than at the level of Member States.[3] As will be shown, the more the EU fosters freedom of movement, the fewer rights are given to members of minority groups. This concerns EU wide minorities, such as third country nationals residing in the EU, EU citizens who move to another Member State, as much as it does localized minorities, such as Baltic Russians in Latvia or Estonia.

This paper seeks to analyse the concept of a universal definition of minorities for international purposes in the European context. It explores the difficulties inherent in conceptualizing and legally defining the term "minorities." Further, the role of the EU in relation to its minorities will be discussed in the second part of this study. The main proposed argument is that too strict a conceptualisation of different ethnic groups as well as efforts to establish a common and unified definition of minorities may be rather counterproductive than useful. Moreover, it will be shown that the widely used dichotomy of old and new minorities is not plausible and that there is no ground to make such a general distinction between two supposedly main categories of minorities.

The following study begins by introducing and critically analysing the international discourse and positions on the definition of minorities. The next section deals with concrete definitional challenges of minorities at the EU level and addresses the main problems that occur in relation to the free movement provisions on the one hand and traditional definitions on the other. Finally, the main conclusions will be drawn.

Searching for an International Definition of Minorities

Despite many attempts there is still no officially accepted legal definition of the term "minority." Nevertheless, many have brought a significant effort to achieve an appropriate definition that would satisfy international as well as constitutional lawyers. Why is it such a difficult task? As Benoit-Rohmer points out, the majority of states and organizations "give no general definition of the concept of minority, on the basis of which to identify in abstract terms those groups (and their members) entitled to enjoy the rights attached to that concept."[4] She continues by claiming that it might be states' unwillingness to address and deal with their minority issues that has resulted in complete silence on a proper legal definition. Clearly, if there is no legal definition, there are no obligations for states to follow. Hence, the state can argue that nothing can or should be done for groups within its borders.[5] But one may still wonder who these supposed strangers or others are. The question that logically arises here is: "What and who qualifies to be treated as minorities?" And further, do we need to put these groups into different boxes and strictly conceptualise the term? In this chapter I will argue against categorization and a universally applicable definition of minorities. In order to do so, I will first examine widely used attributes of definitions of minorities suggested by prolific scholars and writers in the field. Further, I

3 Dimitry Kochenov, "European Union's Troublesome Minority Protection: A Bird's-Eye View," in *International Approaches to Governing Ethnic Diversity*, ed. Will Kymlicka and J. Boulden. (Oxford: Oxford University Press, 2014), 1.

4 Florence Benoit-Rohmer, *The minority question in Europe: towards a coherent system of protection of national minorities* (Strasbourg: Editions du Conseil de l'Europe, 1996), 12.

5 *Ibid.*

will discuss positions and general discourse on the definition of minorities. Many scholars and academics promoting a fixed definition of minorities rely on the generally accepted proposal designed by the UN special Rapporteur Francesco Capotorti in the context of Article 27 of the International Covenant on Civil and Political Rights (ICCPR). Although it has never received formal authorization by major international players, its features are commonly accepted and applied even today.[6] Besides, Kristin Henrard's definition draws from Cappotorti's proposition. According to Henrard, minorities are groups that have a distinctive ethnic, religious, or linguistic identity and are less numerous than the rest of the population of the state. These groups are not dominant and have a desire to retain their distinctive identities.[7] However, she also acknowledges the weaknesses of Capotorti's proposal and hence excludes from her own definition the original requirement of being a national of the state, as the requirement makes the concept too restrictive.[8] Roberta Meda-Windischer has gone even further and proposes a general definition of minorities that has potential to cover all kinds of minority groups. Nevertheless and for the purpose of this article, it should be seen rather as a working description. It consists of four conditions which states that minorities are: 1) residents within a sovereign state on a permanent or temporary basis, 2) smaller in number than the rest of the population of that state or of a region of that state, 3) whose members share common characteristics of an ethnic, cultural, religious or linguistic nature that distinguish them from the rest of population and 4) manifest, only if implicitly, a desire to be treated as a distinct group.[9] This definition is the best concept so far. Based on these well-known proposals, it can be suggested that at least a vast majority of attempts to define minorities share certain elements. These elements are the following:

a) Members of minority groups share ethnic, religious language, and cultural characteristics;
b) They are generally in a numerical minority in the entire state or in a region of the state;
c) They are in a non-dominant position;
d) The groups are recognized objectively to be a minority and by their own members subjectively that they constitute a minority.[10]

6 The definition states: A group numerically inferior to the rest of population of a State, in a non-dominant position, whose members – being nationals of the State – possess ethnic, religious or linguistic characteristics differing from those of the rest of the population and show, if only implicitly, a sense of solidarity, directed towards preserving their culture, traditions, religion or language.

7 Kristin Henrard, "An EU perspective on new versus traditional minorities: on semi-inclusive socioeconomic integration and expanding visions of 'Europe' culture and identity," *Columbian Journal on European Law* (2011): 30.

8 Henrard, "An EU perspective on new versus traditional minorities," 46.

9 Roberta Medda-Windischer, "Changing Paradigms in the Traditional Dichotomy of Old and New Minorities," in *Double Standards Pertaining to Minority Protection*, ed. Kristin Henrard (Leiden: Martinus Nijhoff Publishers, 2010), 206.

10 Bertus De Villiers, "Language, Culture and Religious Minorities: What and Who are They?," *University of Western Australia Law Review* 36, no. 1 (2012): 96.

The first of these criteria is logical and does not have to be discussed further. It describes common features shared by the members of minority groups, which are the core elements of their identity that distinguish them from the majority. It is mostly the second and third conditions that are troublesome. Firstly, as Fortman puts it, a group numerically inferior to the rest of the population of a state seems to be arithmetic nonsense.[11] Similarly, French philosophers Deleuze and Guattari emphasize that the opposition between the majority and minority is not simply quantitative.[12] Majority is rather a constant against which all evaluation is completed and by which all others can be evaluated and allotted to their "proper" social location. Minority is therefore that which differs from the majority regardless of number – a subsystem, as Deleuze and Guattari call it.[13] This creates the problem that, as Wendy Brown has demonstrated, marked "minoritarian" groups are seen as saturated by their group identity and hence less capable of participating in the universal.[14]

Furthermore, the whole formulation is rather unfortunate. The term minority refers not only to the numerical status of a group but also to a majority if that majority is in a non-dominant position.[15] Therefore the Whites during the apartheid regime in South Africa, who could have been numerically considered as a minority but were in a politically and economically dominant position, could not benefit from the international minority protection regime.[16] Another similar example could be Serbs living in Kosovo during the existence of the Yugoslavian Federation between the years 1989 and 1998. According to Fortman, there is also a dangerous aspect in using numerical inferiority as a characteristic feature of minorities. It undermines the dark side of minorities, meaning the potential of these groups to turn into exclusive collective identities that abuse their dominant position in the state.[17] Mohamed Salih rightly points out that the position of dominant minorities makes us realise that minorities are not necessarily passive recipients of majority oppression, or incapable of oppressing others. Nothing, not even minorities, is strictly black or purely white. He goes on to state that minorities are mostly social entities which reflect a social reality and their position within a nation state.[18]Secondly, self-identification as a subjective consideration of being a member of a minority group, together with objective external considerations expressed by others, is

11 Bas de Gaay Fortman, "Minority Rights: A Major Misconception?," *Human Rights Quarterly* 33, no. 2 (2011): 276.

12 Gilles Deleuze and Felix Guattari, *A Thousand Plateaus: Capitalism and Schizophrenia.* (London and New York: Continuum, 2004).

13 Deleuze and Guattari, *A Thousand Plateaus*, 116–17.

14 Wendy Brown, *Regulating Aversion: Tolerance in the Age of Identity and Empire* (Princeton: Princeton University Press, 2008).

15 A. Alen and Kristin Henrard, "The relevance for South Africa of minority protection in Belgium, against the background of the International and European framework, and some remarks on the federal structure of Germany and Spain," *Res Publica* 1998: 41–58, 108–109.

16 De Villiers, "Language, Culture and Religious Minorities," 97.

17 Fortman, "Minority Rights," 275–277.

18 Mohamed Salih, "Minorities and the Political in the Human Rights Deficit, in responding to the human Rights Deficit," In *Responding to the Human Rights Deficit: Essays in Honour of Bas de Gaay Fortman*, ed. Karin Arts and Paschal Mihyo. (The Hague: Kluwer Law International, 2003), 105.

another common condition contained within definitions of minorities. There are several examples that show positive results when a group had identified itself even without any external accountability. For instance in Ethiopia the Silte group desired to be recognised as a nation, nationality and people. In 2001 they achieved their own representation in the House of Federation and later on received their own administrative zone after separation from the Gurage group to whom they previously belonged. This was the result of long-term agitation to be recognised as a distinct group.[19] At the same time, if external recognition of a minority group is over-emphasized at the expense of internal identification, meaning that decisions on recognition are made on the basis of "objective" criteria as to who is entitled to qualify as a minority, the result can be an overly strict, perhaps even forced, group conceptualization, and hence a limitation of the individual's personal decision to stay or to exist within the group. Therefore a combination of objective and subjective criteria, and an acceptance that the individual may choose not to be a member of a group but to assert an individual or integrated identity, is the right path to take in crafting general minority policy.[20]

In order to better understand why all efforts to categorize minorities keep failing, the main discourse of the definition of minorities must be critically examined. Judging by the practice of international organisations and wide academic literature, there is a strong effort to classify, determine and box different ethnic groups. In general, national minorities are the first category separated from other groups. As Malloy indicates, the concept of national minority has become part of the lexicon of international law.[21] Although the Council of Europe's Framework Convention for the Protection of National Minorities (FCNM) contains no definition of national minorities, most Member States use the term in their legislation to refer to "traditional" or "old" groups that have existed in the country for a considerable length of time.[22] Historical, traditional or autochthonous minorities refer to communities whose members have a distinct language, culture or religion compared to the rest of the population. Usually these groups became minorities in a particular country because they have simply ended up on the wrong side of the border or they were not able to form a state on their own. In order for a group to be recognised as a national minority, two criteria must be met: each member must possess citizenship of the country of residence and secondly, the group has to have strong historical and long-established ties with the country.[23] Most European countries have limited the personal scope of the FCNM provisions by requiring fulfilment of these two conditions. However, some states do not impose the requirement of citizenship on an individual belonging to these groups. Newcomers can also be covered if they have the same language or share a religion and culture with the old traditional groups. Typical examples of such countries are Norway and Sweden.[24] On the other hand, Germany, together with Austria, defines their minorities in the most restrictive way. Members of

[19] De Villiers, "Language, Culture and Religious Minorities."

[20] Medda-Windischer, "Changing Paradigms," 205.

[21] Tove Malloy, *National Minority Rights in Europe* (Oxford: Oxford University Press, 2005), 16.

[22] Eide, "The Rights of 'New' Minorities," 174.

[23] Medda-Windisher, "Changing Paradigms," 201.

[24] Eide, The Rights of 'New' Minorities," 174.

national minority groups must be German citizens who have a distinctive identity they wish to maintain. Furthermore, not only do they have to have traditionally resided on German territory, but they must also live in their traditional settlement areas. The only exception from the rule is given to the Roma and Sinti, for whom, however, the criterion of holding German citizenship still applies. This means that other Roma and Sinti are not recognised as national minorities and thus do not belong under the FCNM scope of protection.

In 2006 the Council of Europe's Venice Commission published a report on non-citizens and minority rights. It argued that instead of constantly discussing the definition issue, the relevant stakeholders should be focused on non-restrictive exercise of minority rights in practice. Furthermore, it clearly stated that citizenship should not be considered as a decisive factor in defining the term "minority." The Advisory Committee on the FCNM has adopted a very similar approach. Although it can be concluded that citizenship is no longer seen as a general criterion for minority definition, it does not prevent individual states from limiting the use of minority rights only to their citizens. The citizenship requirement obviously excludes refugees, permanent residents, migrant workers and stateless persons. As Medda-Windischer points out, there are minorities in Europe whose members were illegitimately deprived of citizenship and their minority rights, as is the case of Roma in many European countries.[25]In the current discussion on minority issues, the dichotomy of new and old minorities is widely debated. The new minority groups stemmed from migration. These groups of people decided to leave their homeland and to emigrate to other countries for economic or political reasons.[26] Thus they consist of migrants, refugees and their descendants. Unlike old minorities, migrant groups very rarely oppose the requirement of states to learn the official language as a condition of citizenship or that their children must learn the official language in schools. New minorities have simply accepted the fact that their chances of a better life depend on their participation in the life of mainstream society in the host country.[27] Migrant groups tend to seek stronger recognition of their identities as well as accommodation of their practices but they do not require new forms of autonomy. In contrast traditional minorities resist assimilation more persistently and want to obtain autonomous use of their language and enjoyment of their culture from the state.[28] Evidently, old and new minorities are different. The question remains whether their distinctive features justify the dichotomy and several attempts to officially categorize these two on a different basis. It must be emphasised that while there are differences between these groups, their claims are essentially the same. In fact differences between their entitlements occur only in connection to certain specific minority rights, namely the right to use a minority language in public administration and on public signs and the right to education provided in a minority mother tongue.[29] All of these rights are usually conditioned by the criterion already described of traditional ties to the state. In that sense, the FCNM is

25 Medda-Windischer, "Changing Paradigms," 205.
26 Medda Windischer, "Changing Paradigms," 196.
27 Kymlicka 2001, 152.
28 Kymlicka 2001, 155.
29 Medda-Widischer, "Changing Paradigms," 212.

not exceptional either. Nevertheless, its explanatory report stipulates that the requirement of traditional ties does not refer only to historical minorities. The report goes on to claim that the term "inhabited traditionally" does not refer to historical minorities, but only to those still living in the same geographical areas."[30] All other rights of a more universal nature provided by the FCNM are dedicated to all individuals who are in the position of minorities, no matter if they belong to an old, new or a national category. To put it in different words, universal minority rights apply equally to all groups, while the more specific rights described above can be provided only to those who meet criteria imposed by the state. Such restrictions are allowed and should be considered as legitimate only in connection to those specific minority rights.

To conclude, a legal definition of minorities is neither necessary nor useful. Such a definition would amount to assuming that all minorities are entitled to all minority rights or that all groups falling outside the definition have no minority rights. The purpose of this section was to show that none of this is true. The needs of minority groups are so diverse that they cannot be addressed by one rigid definition. In other words, if the notion is applied to a set of more universal minority rights, there is no need to make a distinction between persons belonging to ethnic, religious or linguistic groups. In my opinion, this point is of significant importance especially in times of current economic turmoil and human rights crisis in Europe. A forced conceptualization of different groups may become harmful to the individual members with regard to their other, equally important, significant attributes.[31] As Kochenov correctly argues, Muslims in Germany or Russians living in Estonia are a religious, linguistic and ethnic minority at the same time.[32] Their arbitrarily chosen diverse cultural attributes can be abused for the purposes of racist propaganda. On the other hand, claims to use the minority language in relation to the official authorities or to have street names in the minority language are highly specific and should be differentiated. Minority groups, old or new, are not "indistinct monoliths."[33] In the words of Asbjørn Eide the scope of rights is contextual.[34] According to Deleuze and Guattari, a minority is always a subsystem. However, these thinkers emphasize that a minority can at the same time also be more than that. "It is important not to remain thinking about the relation between the majority and the minority in their fixed forms but instead to think about potentialities and becomings."[35] We think of minorities as objectively definable groups of ethnicity, language or sex but we should instead think of them as catalysts whose function is to

30 Explanatory Report of the Framework Convention for the Protection of National Minorities. Strasbourg, February 1995, H (95), para. 66. www.coe.int/t/dghl/monitoring/minorities/1_AtGlance/PDF_H%2895%2910_FCNM_ExplanReport_en.pdf.

31 Dimitry Kochenov, "EU Minority protection: a Modest Case for a Synergic Approach," *Amsterdam Law Forum* 3 (2011): 34.

32 Kochenov, "EU Minority protection," 34.

33 Medda-Windischer, "Changing Paradigms," 213.

34 UN Sub-Commission on the Promotion and Protection of Human Rights, *Possible ways and means of facilitating the peaceful and constructive solution of problems involving minorities*: report / submitted by Asbjørn Eide. 11 August 1993, para 27.

35 Deleuze and Guattari, *A Thousand Plateaus*, 118.

create novel, surprising movements that de-territorialize the majority.[36] The common feature of all minorities is that they manifest a desire to maintain their collective identity, which differs from the dominant culture. However, we live in a diverse world of overlapping identities.[37] The right to identity and diversity represents the essence of the case for minorities, no matter if they are considered by law to be old or new, religious or ethnic. Culture in this context is not synonymous with particular practices or customs. It is mostly a sense of "communal identity" that influences every aspect of life.[38] In the words of Steven Wheatley, it is the tradition of everyday life.[39] Or as Julie Cohen puts it, one's cultural identity is formed by the "play of every day practice."[40]

The European Union as a "Catalyst" for Different Identities: Unified in Diversity?

The need to respect rights of persons belonging to minorities is now, after the Lisbon revision of the Treaties, enshrined in primary law as a foundational value of the European Union (EU). As the EU has aimed primarily at economic integration from the beginning of its existence, minority issues have never been a priority for it. Therefore inclusion of minority protection as a criterion for membership of the EU imposes several challenges for the EU to handle. Although the Copenhagen criteria conditioned accession during the Eastern European enlargement, those criteria have never become decisive enough to be able to prevent candidate countries from joining the Union.[41] The Treaty of Lisbon lists protection of the rights of persons belonging to minorities as one of the fundamental values of the EU. Yet the enforcement mechanisms are not as well-defined as one would expect or perhaps hope for. In this chapter I will analyse the EU's approach towards conceptualisation of its minorities, as this contains many specificities and challenges worthy of discussion, especially compared to other international regimes active in the same field.

The EU has not taken an explicit position on what it considers to be a minority within particular Member States. Therefore the capacity to determine which groups should be recognized as minority groups is left within Member States' competence. Nevertheless the concept of minorities frequently appears not only in the EU's external documents but also its internal documents, which makes the overall logic less obvious.[42] The EU has never established its own standards nor does it provide any separate framework on

36 Soirila 2014, forthcoming.

37 Will Kymlicka, *Multicultural Citizenship: A Liberal Theory of Minority Rights* (Oxford: Oxford University Press, 1995).

38 Medda-Windischer, "Changing Paradigms," 362.

39 Steven Wheatley, "Deliberative Democracy and Minorities," *European Journal of International Law* 14, no. 3 (2003): 508.

40 Julie Cohen, *Configuring the Networked Self: Law, Code and the Play of Everyday Practice* (New Haven: Yale University Press, 2012), 224.

41 Kyriaki Topidi, *EU Law, Minorities and Enlargement* (Cambridge: Intersentia, 2010), 214.

42 Kristin Henrard, "An EU perspective on new versus traditional minorities: on semi-inclusive socioeconomic integration and expanding visions of 'Europe' culture and identity," *Columbian Journal on European Law* (2011): 57–99.

minority rights.[43] On the other hand by facilitating freedom of movement the EU is fostering its own cultural and religious diversity. Hence it seems to be logical to ask who minorities are within the EU context. If we consider traditional minorities and the requirement of citizenship, these would include long-standing minorities such as Hungarians in Slovakia or Turks in Germany. However, problems arise when EU citizens exercise their fundamental right to freedom of movement. As a consequence, a new type of hybrid group has come into existence, consisting of EU citizens residing outside their Member State of nationality. As Ahmed points out, the UN and Council of Europe definitions of traditional and long-standing minorities fail to protect the identity of many groups who, in the EU context, find themselves in a minority situation in their host Member State but do not hold that state's citizenship. These groups do not have to qualify as minorities in their country of origin but they find themselves outnumbered in their host state.[44] Hence intra-EU migrants are becoming a sort of minority in the state where they reside. However, not every individual that moves to another Member State immediately gains the status of a minority. The individual has to be the part of a group.[45] Nonetheless, in this context it is not so much about the existing attributes of minorities rather than about the minority position. As Makkonen argues, it is the minority position which serves as the rationale for minority rights.[46] It is not decisive whether the group fulfils a set of objective criteria in order to qualify as a minority or if the group is officially recognised by the state. Some persons can be minorities in some situations but not in others. Hence minorities may include migrants between EU Member States who are in a vulnerable position and wish to preserve their distinctive identities. A typical example of such a group is Muslims in Europe, who benefit from multicultural policies in the United Kingdom, yet at the same time struggle in France because of the constitutional principle of formal equality. Interestingly, the academic literature has been silent on this issue and has ignored the group of intra-EU migrants.[47] Although they could fall into different categories of minority, the challenges these groups are facing are not sufficiently discussed in the current minority rights discourse. Limitations of their rights can be experienced in different sectors. The joint cases of *Viking*[48] and *Laval*[49] represent efforts by Nordic countries to prevent workers from other Member States from entering their labour market and thus constitute a perfect example of limiting EU citizens' working rights in the EU. In other countries, the political rights of EU citizens may be restricted, based

43 Tawhida Ahmed, "A Critical Appraisal of EU Governance for the Protection of Minority Rights." *International Journal on Minority and Group Rights* 17 (2010): 267.

44 (Ahmed, A Critical Appraisal of EU Governance," 269.

45 Javaid Rehman, *International Human Rights Law, A Practical Approach* (Harlow, Essex: Longman Pearson, 2003), 299, citing Sub Commission on the prevention of Discrimination and the Protection of Minorities, UN Doc. E/CN.4/703.

46 Timo Makkonen, *Identity, Difference and Otherness, The Concepts of "People," "Indigenous people" and "Minority" in International Law* (Helsinki: University of Helsinki, Helsinki, 2000), 84.

47 Kochenov, "European Union's Troublesome Minority Protection," 4.

48 Case C-438/05, *International Transport Workers' Federation and Finnish Seamen's Union v. Viking Line ABP and OÜ Viking Line Eesti*, [2007] ECR I-10779.

49 Case C-341/05, *Laval un Partneri Ltd v. Svenska Byggnadsarbetareförbundet, Svenska Byggnadsarbetareförbundets avdelning 1, Byggettan and Svenska Elektrikerförbundet*, [2007] ECR I-11767.

directly on Article 22 of the Treaty on the Functioning of the EU (TFEU). While EU citizens residing in a Member State other than their own can vote and stand as a candidate in local and European Parliamentary elections "under the same conditions as nationals of that state,"[50] the national level of political representation in the Member State of residence is not covered. Article 22 TFEU does not grant voting rights to EU citizens but simply guarantees non-discrimination rights.[51] However, it allows for limitations of the right "where warranted by problems specific to a Member State." Therefore not only does the article fail to provide the right to elect and be elected at the national level, but is also enables limiting the extent of the non-discrimination right it contains.[52] To take Luxembourg as an example, if the percentage of EU citizens who do not hold the nationality of Luxembourg exceeds 20% of the population, the effect of the non-discrimination provision may be suspended for five years in the case of the voting right and for ten years in the case of the right to be elected. This limitation is obviously contrary to the objectives of the Treaty. Ironically, the more successful the functioning of free movement, the fewer the political rights granted to European citizens in their host Member State.[53]Third-country nationals (from non-EU countries) can also be singled out as a minority group suffering from discrimination. The attributions of EU citizenship are prescribed only for nationals of EU Member States. Those coming from third countries are excluded from its scope, even if they are long term EU citizens. This mainly applies to migrant workers, such as Turks in Germany or Algerians in France, who have lived on European soil for several generations. Thus and, as Étienne Balibar puts it, a new type of discrimination has been created within the EU context that did not exist in the national space - European racism. By radical separation of nationals from Member States from those of non-member countries, a new category of citizens is created.[54] Despite the fact that they enjoy permanent rights of residency, the members of this group are second-class citizens, at the service of Europeans.[55] Consequently a system of European apartheid is born.[56] The dichotomy of old and new minorities has been discussed in the previous section of this Chapter. Some commentators such as Kristin Henrard suggest that these third country nationals could be defined as new minorities.[57] However, this does not do them any justice because a large number of EU residents have lived in the Member States for generations. There are no old or new Turks in Germany: indeed, such a categorization is rather artificial. EU citizens cannot be treated as new minorities in their chosen Member States either. Within the EU citizenship context,

50 Article 22 TFEU.

51 Jo Shaw, *The Transformation of Citizenship in the European Union: Electoral Rights and the Restructuring of Political Space* (Cambridge: Cambridge University Press, 2007), 173.

52 Dimitry Kochenov, "Free Movement and Participants in the Parliamentary Elections in the Member State of Nationality: An Ignored Link?," *Maastricht Journal of European and Comparative Law* 16, no. 1 (2009): 213.

53 Kochenov, "Free Movement and Participants," 213.

54 Étienne Balibar, *We, the People of Europe? Reflections on Transnational Citizenship* (Princeton and Oxford: Princeton University Press, 2004).

55 *Ibid.*, 44.

56 *Ibid.*, 46.

57 Henrard, "An EU perspective on new versus traditional minorities," 59.

intra-EU migrants should no longer be seen as foreigners.[58] Member States are not allowed to use their nationalities as "legally relevant categories" because that would amount to a breach of the non-discrimination principle.[59]

The EU and its diversity impose highly specific challenges that require a special approach. As shown earlier, traditional definitions of minorities have proved to be insufficient in connection to the EU. Existing categories that are at the same time still used by EU agencies and Member States should no longer be applied as they can barely reflect who minorities actually are and who is a member of these groups. The Fundamental Rights Agency of the EU refers to Muslims as a religious minority,[60] rather than an ethnic one. But being religious is only one attribute out of many that describe this particular group and seems quite arbitrarily chosen. Minority characteristic features are "superimposed mutually diffused and intertwined."[61] Naturally, when identities overlap, so do possible grounds for discrimination. Therefore it is necessary to take into consideration different needs of different minority groups as well as minority experiences. When discussing minority protection, we need to keep in mind both the complexity of personal identity as well as the structural complexity of the EU's system of governance. Otherwise, we risk harming the interests of actual human beings within these groups, as too strict a categorization of minority protection, often based on just one, arbitrarily chosen feature, fails to pay due respect to all the diverse elements of their identity. Since the EU's commitment to facilitating freedom of movement can only lead to the growth of cultural, religious and other possible kinds of diversity in the Union in the future, there is a strong need for a new and more comprehensive approach to tackling minority-related issues. It remains to be seen how the EU will handle its minority issues and manage to preserve its high diversity.

Conclusion

Strict lines between categories or different labels of ethnic groups, such as national or new minorities, have become blurred and no longer correspond with current developments in the field. Rather than trying to label groups of people by using different terms, it is more productive to see them in a spectrum.[62] For many decades, international or national actors have used different definitions of minorities. We have now entered a new era, in which using the old rigid definitional concepts has become arbitrary. Old and new minorities are in many aspects alike. Therefore both groups should be entitled to broadly similar rights. If the EU Member States are serious about integrating immigrants and about freedom of movement, which they are obliged to respect, then they should not

58 Dimitry Kochenov, "Rounding up the Circle: EU Citizenship's Influence of the Nationalities of Member States," *EUI Working Paper* RSCAS 2010/23. (Florence: European University Press, 2010), 1.

59 Kochenov, "European Union's Troublesome Minority Protection," 5.

60 Henrard, "An EU perspective on new versus traditional minorities," 67.

61 Kochenov, "European Union's Troublesome Minority Protection," 5.

62 Michael Johns, "The European Union: Migrants, Minorities and the Changing Nature of Citizenship." *The Canadian Political Science Association Annual Meeting*, conference paper (2011), 11, www.cpsa-acsp.ca/papers-2011/Johns.pdf.

object to application of minority rights to new minorities as well. Moreover, in times when Europe is slowly recovering from dramatic economic, political and social struggles, it should be seen as an appropriate political gesture. This would underline the importance of the European integration project and send out a powerful message that all distinctive groups are integral parts of Europe.

It was demonstrated on the specificities of EU minority protection that traditional definitions of minorities fail to provide sufficient protection to different groups. Minorities are typically further subdivided into a number of categories, such as ethnic, linguistic, religious and so on. This restrictive way of defining and categorizing minorities leads to unnecessary specialization and compartmentalization in the EU minority protection literature and in legal practice. While discussing the current and future relationship between the EU and its numerous minorities, it should be emphasized that although the EU is not equivalent to a Member State it is nevertheless becoming strongly "minority oriented."[63] Hence it would be wrong for the EU to follow any state-centred definition. The Union is a polity in charge of half a billion citizens diverse enough not to boast any majority as well as creating new minorities through the operation of Union law. Keeping all this in mind allows us to readjust our expectations concerning what the Union can and should do with its minorities.[64] Therefore in the future the most appropriate path for the EU in the field of minority protection will be to become a promoter of minority rights rather than a legislator in the field.[65]

63 Dimitry Kochenov, "EU Minority protection: a Modest Case for a Synergic Approach," *Amsterdam Law Forum* 3 (2011): 36.

64 Kochenov, "European Union's Troublesome Minority Protection," 16.

65 Ahmed, "A Critical Appraisal of EU Governance," 284.

Bibliography

Ackers, Louise. "Citizenship, migration and the valuation of care in the European Union." *Journal of Ethnic and Migration Studies* 30, no. 2 (2004): 373–96.

Ahmed, Tawhida. "A Critical Appraisal of EU Governance for the Protection of Minority Rights." *International Journal on Minority and Group Rights* 17 (2010): 265–85.

Alen, A., and Kristin Henrard. "The relevance for South Africa of minority protection in Belgium, against the background of the International and European framework, and some remarks on the federal structure of Germany and Spain." *Res Publica* 1998: 41–58.

Balibar, Étienne. *We, the People of Europe? Reflections on Transnational Citizenship.* Princeton and Oxford: Princeton University Press, 2004.

Benoit-Rohmer, Florence. *The minority question in Europe: towards a coherent system of protection of national minorities.* Strasbourg: Editions du Conseil de l'Europe, 1996.

Brown, Wendy. *Regulating Aversion: Tolerance in the Age of Identity and Empire.* Princeton: Princeton University Press, 2008.

Capotorti, Francesco. *Study On The Rights Of Persons Belonging To Ethnic, Religious, And Linguistic Minorities.* E.91.Xiv.2 (Human Rights Study Series). New York: UN Publications, 1991.

Castellino, Joshua. "No Room at the International Table: The Importance of Designing Effective Litmus Tests for Minority Protection at Home." *Human Rights Quarterly* 35, no. 1 (2013): 201–28.

Cohen, Julie. *Configuring the Networked Self: Law, Code and the Play of Everyday Practice.* New Haven: Yale University Press, 2012.

de Gaay Fortman, Bas. "Minority Rights: A Major Misconception?" *Human Rights Quarterly* 33, no. 2 (2011): 265–303.

Deleuze, Gilles, and Felix Guattari. *A Thousand Plateaus: Capitalism and Schizophrenia.* London and New York: Continuum, 2004.

De Villiers, Bertus. "Language, Culture and Religious Minorities: What and Who are They?" *University of Western Australia Law Review* 36, no. 1 (2012): 92–114.

Eide, Asbjørn. "The Rights of 'New' Minorities: Scope and Restrictions." In *Double Standards Pertaining to Minority Protection*, edited by Kristin Henrard, 165–95. Leiden: Martinus Nijhoff Publishers, 2010.

Henrard, Kristin. *Devising an Adequate system of Minority Protection.* Hague: Kluwer Law International, 2000.

— "An EU perspective on new versus traditional minorities: on semi-inclusive socioeconomic integration and expanding visions of 'Europe' culture and identity." *Columbian Journal on European Law* (2011): 57–99.

— "International protection of minorities." In *Max Planck Encyclopaedia of Public International Law*, 2011. http://ilmc.univie.ac.at/uploads/media/minorities_empil.pdf.

Johns, Michael. "The European Union: Migrants, Minorities and the Changing Nature of Citizenship." *The Canadian Political Science Association Annual Meeting*, conference paper (2011): www.cpsa-acsp.ca/papers-2011/Johns.pdf.

Jones, Crispin. "State Education and Minority Rights." In *Education Rights and Minorities*, 7–9. London: Minority Right Group, 1995.

Kochenov, Dimitry. "Free Movement and Participants in the Parliamentary Elections in the Member State of Nationality: An Ignored Link?" *Maastricht Journal of European and Comparative Law* 16, no. 1 (2009): 197–225.

— "Rounding up the Circle: EU Citizenship's Influence of the Nationalities of Member States." *EUI Working Paper* RSCAS 2010/23. Florence: European University Press, 2010.

— "EU Minority protection: a Modest Case for a Synergic Approach." *Amsterdam Law Forum* 3 (2011): 33–53.

— "European Union's Troublesome Minority Protection: A Bird's-Eye View." In *International Approaches to Governing Ethnic Diversity*, edited by Will Kymlicka and J. Boulden, 1–20. Oxford: Oxford University Press, 2014.

Kymlicka, Will. *Multicultural Citizenship: A Liberal Theory of Minority Rights*. Oxford: Oxford University Press, 1995.Kymlicka, Will. 2001

Mahoney, Diana. "Expulsion Of The Roma: Is France Violating EU Freedom of Movement and Playing by French Rules or Can It Proceed with Collective Roma Expulsions Free of Charge?" *Brooklyn Journal of International Law* 37, no. 2 (2012): 649–82.

Makkonen, Timo. *Identity, Difference and Otherness, The Concepts of "People," "Indigenous people" and "Minority" in International Law*. Helsinki: University of Helsinki, 2000.

Malloy, Tove. *National Minority Rights in Europe*. Oxford: Oxford University Press, 2005.

Medda-Windischer, Roberta. "Changing Paradigms in the Traditional Dichotomy of Old and New Minorities," in *Double Standards Pertaining to Minority Protection*, ed. Kristin Henrard (Leiden: Martinus Nijhoff Publishers, 2010), 206.

Rehman, Javaid. *International Human Rights Law, A Practical Approach*. Harlow, Essex: Longman Pearson, 2003.

Robinson, Hana Li. "Preventing Sparks in Smouldering Ashes: Using Sweden's Internet Law To Combat Incendiary Speech in the Scandinavian Online Community." *Brooklyn Journal of International Law* 37, no. 3 (2012): 1215–41.

Salih, Mohamed. "Minorities and the Political in the Human Rights Deficit, in responding to the human Rights Deficit." In *Responding to the Human Rights Deficit: Essays in Honour of Bas de Gaay Fortman*, edited by Karin Arts and Paschal Mihyo, 105–29. The Hague: Kluwer Law International, 2003.

Shaw, Jo. *The Transformation of Citizenship in the European Union: Electoral Rights and the Restructuring of Political Space* (Cambridge University Press, Cambridge, 2007), 173.

Siddique, Haroon. "Roma expulsions by France overshadow EU summit opening." *The Guardian*, September 16, 2010.

Sobotka, Eva, and Peter Vermeersch. "Governing Human Rights and Roma Inclusion: Can the EU be the Catalyst for Local Social Change?" *Human Rights Quarterly* 34, no. 3 (2012): 800–22.

Soirila, Ukri. 2014

Topidi, Kyriaki. *EU Law, Minorities and Enlargement*. Cambridge: Intersentia, 2010.

UN Sub-Commission on the Promotion and Protection of Human Rights. *Possible ways and means of facilitating the peaceful and constructive solution of problems involving minorities*: report / submitted by Asbjørn Eide. 11 August 1993 E/CN.4/Sub.2/1993/34/Add.4. Accessed December 8, 2013. www.refworld.org/docid/3b00efc528.html.

Ward, Benjamin. "Europe's Own Human Rights Crisis." *Human Rights Watch*, January (2012): www.hrw.org/sites/default/files/related_material/eucrisis_2012.pdf.

Wheatley, Steven. "Deliberative Democracy and Minorities." *European Journal of International Law* 14, no. 3 (2003): 508–27.

Marcin Kilanowski*

FROM UNIVERSALITY TO RESPONSIBILITY IN INTERNATIONAL HUMAN RIGHTS. ANALYZING DAVID KENNEDY'S CRITICAL APPROACH**

Introduction: Universal Human Rights – Strengthening Existing Mechanisms?

Numerous international conferences, international regulations and institutions are designed to protect human rights. Rules and laws prohibit genocide, slavery, torture, racism, and are designed to protect women, children, and minorities. Surprisingly, we still witness ongoing violations. Slavery still exists, and the numbers go into the millions; sexual trafficking of children and women as well as the practice of torture remains. Ethnic cleansing is used by educated people as a means of solving cultural conflicts, and countless new sources of abuse exist in our changing, more global world. As in the past, self-interest guides people to the point where they treat others as mere means of reaching their own goals. In such a situation we often ask: are we doing something wrong?

That was the question that was also present after the Second World War when man were asking what could have been done to prevent its horrors. The post-war shock on finding out about the holocaust, gulags, and mass killing of civilians led to the establishment of an international system for the protection of human rights with a strong emphasis on the protection of universal "inherent human dignity." For many who had lived through those difficult times this seemed to be the only possible basis for securing recognition of the worth of every human being. Their answer was that "we" have to turn to the concept of inherent human dignity, to a recognition of our common humanity. This inherent human dignity was meant to be something that characterizes all people. But with the development of human rights, more confusion appeared about the status of human dignity and about what makes some human rights superior to others. The differing provisions of different international conventions drafted during the post-war period added to the puzzlement and did not allow the conclusion that "human rights are a set of claims and entitlements to human dignity, which the existing international regime assumes will be provided (or threatened) by the state."[1] Only a selective reading

* Ph.D., Nicolas Copernicus University.

** I would like to thank the John F. Kennedy Institute for North American Studies at the Free University in Berlin for the opportunity to use its resources while working on this paper as a recipient of a JFK Institute Library Grant in 2013.

1 Alison Brysk, *Globalization and Human Rights*, ed. (Berkeley, Los Angeles, London: University of California Press, 2002) 1.

of the conventions and court cases could have led the authors to make statements such as "claims found in paradigm cases of international law reflect some similar ideas about human dignity."[2] This is actually not the case, as Christopher McCrudden points out in his text *Human Dignity and Judicial Interpretation of Human Rights*. He asserts that analyzing the use of the term "inherent human dignity" or "human dignity" in conventions shows that there "is little common understanding of what dignity requires."[3] Additionally, as McCrudden notes, when we look at international adjudication, the term also "seems open to significant judicial manipulation, increasing rather than decreasing judicial discretion."[4] If this is the case, is it then still possible to improve our "common understanding" of human dignity when there are different substantive interpretations of this notion which are highly contextual – depending on politics, legal regimes, social and economic beliefs and circumstances? Instead of answering this detailed question, I would rather like to focus on a broader one: can we improve human rights by strengthening existing mechanisms to confront new challenges?[5]

It seems that the answer will depend on what one understands by "strengthening existing mechanisms". If this means strengthening our *understanding* of existing mechanisms, then I would agree – if this involves "improving awareness and analysis of the connections between different kinds of rights, different facets and implications of globalization, and the new forms of communication and governance to meet the new challenges."[6] But if, on the other hand, it means that "we must still continually improve on the eighteenth-century version of human rights, ensuring that the "Human" in the Universal Declaration of Human Rights leaves none of the ambiguities of "man" in the "hands of man"[7], then I would disagree. For this way of thinking omits something that may be far more constructive, "to review how we are part of the problem" and that we should "first identify it, and examine it carefully."[8] Ideas that we should leave "none of the ambiguities of man in the hands of man" are entrenched by thinking based on the sharp distinction that supposedly exists between universal and specific, values and rights, provisions and interpretations, law and politics. We should not be so naïve as to believe that it is possible to take rights from the hands of the people. People will always be involved, from prosecutors, judges, humanitarian workers to experts, parliamentary representatives, whose particular, subjective, ethnocentric views will impact their way of thinking and acting. This is especially so when human rights are at stake to the point at which the concept of universality of human rights and of human dignity as its basis is questioned.

The goal of this text is to highlight the difficulties that we face when analyzing the universality of human rights (in particular, when referring to their basis, which is the

2 Patrick Capps, *Human dignity and the Foundation of International Law* (Oxford and Portland, Oregon: Hart Publishing, 2009) 106.

3 Christopher McCrudden, "Human Dignity and Judicial Interpretation of Human Rights", 655.

4 Ibid.

5 As proposed by: Alison Brysk, *Globalization and Human Rights*, 19.

6 Ibid., 16.

7 Lynn Hunt, *Inventing Human Rights, A History* (New York London: W.W.Norton & Company, 2007) 212.

8 Walter W. Menninger, "Speech for the Conference on Human Dignity and American Democracy" in: *A Report on the Bicentennial Conference on Human Dignity and American Democracy*, ed. E.E. Grollmes (St. Louis: St. Louis University, 1976) 12.

universal value of "inherent human dignity"). Other difficulties include the reliance on the language of rights when protecting human rights, or reliance on the sharp distinction between law and politics. These are also some of the difficulties David Kennedy mentions when presenting the "downfalls" of human rights. However, one should not stop at this point and neither does this study. After presenting a critique, the the focus of the text moves towards a presentation of a way out of the trouble. The proposition is that human rights should rely more on language based on the value of responsibility, and rely more on critical assessment and dialog. This could be possible if we agree that our knowledge is fallible, that we make mistakes, and start to listen to other opinions and analyze other emancipatory projects instead of sticking to our own – of universal human rights with a set of fixed rights that should be protected. In other words, the second part of the text will try to answer the question of whether human rights could be improved by strengthening existing mechanisms to confront new challenges on a different basis to that used so far.

The Hegemony of the Language of Rights

Understanding that we are "part of the problem" means that we recognize our role in creating such problems. This is not a new discovery, as it was already described in some way by Judith Shklar, Mary Ann Glendon, or David Kennedy.[9] However, in the next part of this text, I would like to focus on David Kennedy's deeply insightful essay, *International Human Rights: Part of The Problem?*[10] It is particularly useful, as it helps us to understand how the legal language we create can be a problem. Part of the problem – as he describes – is our bias toward the universal, toward the abstract, but also toward a certain understanding of the rights of man. One might say that there is a problem with the philosophy embodied in human rights (its reference to universalism) as well as with the imagination of the world present in it (based on the concept of rights). The second point might be called a "structural" problem within human rights, which derives from the fact that the legal language of human rights determines the way we think – the way we understand this highly complex and problematic field – and how we perceive possible actions within it. This determined way of thinking stops different efforts, which are not articulated in existing human rights language. Such efforts are not considered valuable or worth taking into consideration. In other words, it is not the problem of a lack of resources or enough political engagement committed to narrowing the gap between the attention that civil/political rights receive and that given to social/economic rights. The problem lies in the reliance of human rights movement on the concept of rights that mirror – or are linked with – the concept of the right to property.[11] Because of this we

9 See: Judith Shklar, *Legalism, Law, Morals and Political Trials*, Cambridge 1964; Mary Ann Glendon, *Rights Talk. The Impoverishment of Political Discourse*, New York 1991; David Kennedy, *The Dark Sides of Virtue, Reassessing International Humanitarianism*, Princeton and Oxford 2004.

10 David Kennedy, *International Human Rights: Part of The Problem?*, in: David Kennedy, *The Dark Sides of Virtue, Reassessing International Humanitarianism* (Princeton and Oxford: Princeton University Press 2004) 3–37.

11 A careful reader of *The Dark Sides of Virtue, Reassessing International Humanitarianism* can see that David Kennedy sometimes says that human rights "limits human potential" (p.13), "generalizes" (p.15), "describes itself" (p.23), "promises a way of knowing" (p.21), "encourages people", or "reduces and

think that we "have" certain rights *vis-á-vis* those that also have them, or have some other rights. In other words, the human rights movement shapes our understanding of ourselves as "an instance of a preexisting general" – thus "general" covers the rights of the person, or sometimes the group – which are perceived as a "general good."[12] This promises "an available set of universal, extrapolitical legal rules and institutions."[13]

This reliance on the language of rights creates particular consequences, for example, in that way human rights over-particularize. Focusing on people as merely individual bearers of rights detaches them from the wider setting in which they exist. This "blunts articulation of a shared life"[14] and "reduces and distorts a more promising *real* experience."[15] Thinking of a person only as an individual, a bearer of rights, simplifies the complexity of their being part of the community and weakens the sense of solidarity. In consequence, such a move toward rights may create a loss – "a loss of the experience of belonging... of innovating collectively."[16] This loss is a loss of experience, of a variety of views and propositions, of creative possibilities that, even if expressed, are not taken seriously.

Institutional Hegemony

When discussing consequences Kennedy goes further. With human rights discourse presented as if universality, truth, justice, rationality, peace and harmony are on their side comes a certain positioning of the human rights movement – human rights institutions – as being at the center, while the rest is on the periphery – as being objective, right, neutral and natural when the rest is subjective, contextual, contingent. The human rights movement is presented as being on the side of internationalism, modernity and certainty and in opposition to the local and traditional. It represents modernization and progress. It "describes itself as a universal/eternal/human truth", but also "a pragmatic response to injustice"[17] that comes "from some place outside political choice, from the universal, the rational, the civilized."[18] On the opposite side, there are irrational, undeveloped social rules. With such positioning in mind, any discussion about possible solutions to a variety of problems can only lead to one conclusion: "the human rights way

distorts a more promising *real* experience" (p.16), and sometimes says that it is the human rights movement that "shares responsibility" (p.22), or "pays little attention" (p.12). A possible explanation for the change of narration is that when Kennedy says "human rights", he means either the "human rights idea", as he clearly says on page 8 of the essay, or "human rights vocabulary", as he says on page 19. In the second instance, one can say that when he says "human rights movement", he refers to a particular group of people acting in the name of the idea of human rights. Though we can agree that these are the people that "pay little attention" or "share responsibility", it is rather difficult to agree that a particular idea or vocabulary "generalizes" or "encourages people" to undertake given actions. Ideas or vocabularies do not encourage or reduce experience. We should be aware of such a rhetoric shortcut. It seems to be minor from the stylistic point of view, but may lead us to push the responsibility onto the realm of the abstract, onto concepts and constructs, rather than on those that use them – on the people themselves.

12 David Kennedy, *The Dark Sides of Virtue, Reassessing International Humanitarianism*, 13.

13 Ibid., 31.

14 Ibid., 15.

15 Ibid., 16.

16 Ibid., 20.

17 Ibid., 23.

18 Ibid., 21.

or no way". If we are the ones that understand what universal values are, what rights should be protected and in what way, then we cannot be wrong.

After the above observations, Kennedy goes on to say that we are witnessing the creation of institutional hegemony. This is the hegemony of one answer, of one solution without recognizing that there could be some other possible way of reaching the goal that will actually lead us to the point of achieving it, and not somewhere else. Because of this institutional hegemony other valuable emancipatory strategies are less available within the field to the point that it is not even possible to present them without being accused of criticizing human rights. Other ways of understanding harm and dealing with violations are pushed aside. For this reason, Kennedy says that human rights discourse often "occupies" the space of possible criticism of what is emancipatory or not. Moreover, it judges what is too political – thereby reducing other options of bringing "justice" through other means than just legal ones. This is why emancipatory movements representing, for example, women, the poor or minorities are increasingly looking for legal recognition in order to be able to rely on the state rather than focusing on economic, social or political conditions.[19] This also could be said about religion, which in human rights should ideally play no role. This is why Kennedy says:

> "Human rights encourages people to seek emancipation in the vocabulary of reason rather than faith, in public rather than private life, in law rather than in politics, in politics rather than in economics."[20]

This way of emancipating rests on "various false premises" and an "ultimately arrogant mode of thinking and speaking about what is good for people, abstract people, here and there, now and forever."[21] It is wrong and misleading as it encouraged "a global misconception of both the nature of evil and the possibilities for good."[22] In consequence, it demobilizes and constrains actors from thinking imaginatively and from going forward with other emancipatory projects.

Such words as "false premises", "arrogant mode", are examples of Kennedy's strong language and of a firm stand that comes from believing that what happens in the field of human rights is not innocent, neutral, universal nor mirrors the objective reality or nature of humankind. He believes that the human rights movement is too quick to make judgments about the good it produces, that it is the voice of reason, which reaches beyond emotions, passions and religion into the rational and secular.[23] Because of this, it hinders a discussion about different emancipatory steps. Why have a discussion when human rights vocabulary already promises "neutral and universalist mode of emancipatory intervention"?[24]

19 See: Hilary Charlesworth & Christine Chinkin, "The Gender of Jus Cogens", *Human Rights Quarterly* 15 (1993) 66–76.

20 David Kennedy, *The Dark Sides of Virtue, Reassessing International Humanitarianism*, 19.

21 Ibid., 15.

22 Ibid., 21.

23 Sometimes, however, Kennedy speaks with a "softer" voice, and that is perceptible when, for example, he says that the vocabulary that human rights is using "may have fully unintended negative consequences for other existing emancipatory projects, including those relying on more religious, national, or local energies." Here he chooses the word "may". Ibid., 9. I will refer to this issue in section IV.

24 Ibid., 23.

The Illusion of the Law and Politics Divide

Such a promotion of legal and political modernization, of which human rights is an example, is, according to Kennedy, a promotion of just an "illusion of cognitive control over the unthinkable" through "clinical antiseptic analysis."[25] "Modernization" in that case is not peace but conflict, because "rights conflict with one another, rights are vague, rights have exceptions, many situations fall between rights."[26] With such human rights comes a narrowing of "the range of socioeconomic choices available in developing societies in the name of 'rights'."[27] In consequence, as Kennedy points out, such an "attachment to rights as a measure of the authenticity, universality, and, above all, as the knowledge we have of social justice binds our professional feet."[28] In that way our possibilities as well as the possibilities of the human rights movement are narrowed down. Politics is pushed aside as not being a legitimate means of achieving the goals of the human rights movement. Thus, the human rights movement creates an additional illusion – "the illusion of affecting conditions both at home and abroad without being politically implicated in the distribution of stakes."[29] Human rights fosters the belief that emancipation can come only through "rights", through the recognition of rights, and not through politics. By fostering such a belief, it reduces the possibility of understanding that it is political conditions and the political context that determine the interpretation of rights and affect their meaning. In other words it misses recognition of the diversity of experience.

An acknowledgment of the existence of the political context of which rights are a part and the existence of various interpretations would lead to a recognition of the political process, of negotiations, and of dialog. These are, however, steps that the human rights movement does not want to take because they would lead to rearrangements and adjustments during which someone would have to become less privileged in order for another to "have" more. There is no need or will to take such a path. The development of law as a universal language of justice is perceived as emancipatory enough; it is a language that does not have to reduce itself to the politics of the streets. As a form of "knowledge", law functions in opposition to what politics is perceived to be affiliated with. Law is directed by the wisdom that rules should not engage in open-ended political fights and get their hands dirty. Unfortunately, even if there is some truth in such a perception of politics, the outcome is that the baby is thrown out with the bath water. Kennedy observes:

> "A 'universal' idea of what counts as a problem and what works as a solution snuffs out all sorts of promising local political and social initiatives to contest local conditions in other terms."[30]

Such a human rights approach does real damage, as Kennedy says. It is harmful because "it discourages political engagement or encourages reliance on human rights for results

25 Ibid., 34.
26 Ibid., 22.
27 Ibid., 20.
28 Ibid., 31.
29 Ibid.
30 Ibid., 11.

it cannot achieve."[31] Not much changes in the public sphere, only the field of human rights itself, by producing more literature, and not action that would bring relief. Propositions for policies that are not expressed in the language of "rights" are not considered. Moreover, such abandonment of the possibility of engagement – of politics – among right holders and reliance on the absoluteness of the rules "makes compromise and peaceful adjustment of outcomes more difficult"[32], which is, for example, the case when economic arrangements are the issue. In that way economic arrangements are not challenged due to the strong practice of reaching for rights claims against the state rather than on focusing on distribution. The main issue for those dealing with human rights is the development of law, and not distribution. In that light Kennedy asserts:

> "Encouraging people to imagine themselves as right holders, and rights as absolute, makes the negotiation of distributive arrangements among individuals and groups less likely and less tenable."[33]

From the Dark Sides to Responsibility and Pragmatism

Kennedy's arguments are part of his list of the "dark sides" of human rights and comprise a significant proportion of his critique of these rights. Is there any solution to the problems he mentions? Is there any answer to the question posed previously as to how to improve human rights and strengthen the mechanisms of protection?

Keeping in mind the above-mentioned problems, we can suggest changing our perception of the discourse of rights, which we even do not perceive as a discourse, but as the only existing reality. Our first step could be to increase our consciousness to be able to say, like John Quataert, that closer analysis shows that "rights are not self-evident, self-policing, or ethically monolithic; they are historical constructs rooted in struggle and are even at odds with one another."[34] Because of this situation, the cause of rights "continuously contested by calculations of power and self interest… alone cannot ensure a fair and equitable outcome."[35] It would be good to understand, like Clifford Bob, that "human rights are political, and their precise scope will always remain disputed."[36] The fact that we will have to argue about their scope is not the end of the world, as critics predict. Communication can be liberating and not enslaving as long as we are prepared for it by having the right means to conduct it and we understand the individual role that we play in it.

Unfortunately, we are having a hard time seeing our own role and understanding the consequences created by the language that we use as well as the consequences of a lack of communication. This is so because we do not think and perceive ourselves not only as those with an impact on the current situation, but also as those who often create it. What we need instead, as Kennedy claims, is to "develop professional habits… for taking

31 Ibid., 24.
32 Ibid., 22.
33 Ibid., 17. See also: Ibid.,11 and 32.
34 John H. Quataert, *Advocating Dignity, Human Rights Mobilizations in Global Politics*, 4.
35 Ibid., 4.
36 Clifford Bob, ed., *The International Struggle for New Human Rights* (Philadelphia: University of Pennsylvania Press, 2009) 13.

responsible action as a ruler."[37] We need more responsibility that we share instead of thinking that it is others that govern and should be held responsible.

As we can see, previous criticism of Kennedy is not for criticism's sake. Kennedy points to a direction where we could find a solution and even tries to show a path towards it. He asks that we should be more conscious of what we do, look at the consequences of our actions and feel responsible for them, instead of looking for universal foundations. We can see how this argument plays out in his thinking, when he refers to humanitarianism being part of the human rights movement:

> "My hope is that bringing the costs of humanitarianism [and the language that it uses – MK.] to the surface will encourage an attitude of responsibility for the difficulties our endeavors inevitably bring."[38]

In other words, what is crucial is the sense of responsibility; not responsibility that appears afterwards, when actions are judged in the name of the law and one is "held responsible", but the attitude of responsibility when one chooses an action, the attitude that comes with the desire to reach the best outcome by analyzing the pros and cons, by listening to different voices and imagining the consequences of particular decisions. One could add that the appearance of such an attitude would require a push toward a pragmatic evolution of human rights – towards development of a habit of making assessments. This assessment would require the human rights movement to understand its position better than it does – to understand the "human side of the story", which "takes us to the difficult terrain of desire, power, knowledge, and responsibility" as Kennedy says.[39]

It is also Kennedy's proposition, that the human rights movement should start thinking about itself more in pragmatic terms "rather than theological terms."[40] He suggests that we should move toward pragmatic human rights. This is why he is in favor of pragmatization of the field of human rights and criticizes its underdeveloped pragmatic potential, which would allow it to respond better to political and social conflicts.

Language of Responsibility?

Even though Kennedy makes some suggestions about how to overcome the difficulties he mentions, he is not presenting an integrated program of how to deal with the dark sides of human rights. He hopes "that those who wish to keep the humanitarian impulse vigorous in the world will add to our toolkit of diagnostic and remedial vocabularies."[41] This remedial vocabulary is necessary and we can actually look for it where Kennedy is pointing, to a pragmatic approach. I believe such an approach can be studied when one refers to pragmatic philosophy.

It is the philosophy of Dewey, Rorty, Habermas and Putnamthat shapes the vocabulary that can help to deal with the issue of vanishing universality, the decentralization of

[37] David Kennedy, *The Dark Sides of Virtue, Reassessing International Humanitarianism*, xxv.
[38] Ibid., xix.
[39] Ibid., xxv.
[40] Ibid., 31.
[41] Ibid., xx.

knowledge, recognition of ambivalence, while still defending the attitude of responsibility. This vocabulary can be the basis for a new way of thinking and can help to shape the practice which "embraces the freedom and responsibility that come with an ongoing awareness of the dark sides"[42] (to put it in Kennedy's words) of the human rights movement. This vocabulary would emphasize the need for dialog, recognition of the fallibility of our knowledge and the need to understand freedom as responsibility, and in that way it would create a new discourse.[43]

Such a discourse based on the understanding of the notion of freedom as responsibility has the potential to be useful in the field of international human rights. This would be a discourse that does not center on the necessity to discover an absolute and universal truth or universal values.[44] It would not focus on defining issues in universal terms, according to which we should act, but would direct us toward the unsettled process of critical cooperation with a sense of responsibility for the outcome. It would recognize our need for dialog, need for mutual understanding and search for consensus. It would rely on the fact that we are developing our knowledge, constantly pushing ourselves to critically rethink our position with the ultimate goal being better understanding and knowledge. This would emphasize the fact that we make mistakes.

It is important to add that responsibility in such a discourse would not and should not be understood as a duty, as Giddens rightly points out when he asserts that "responsibility is not duty" because it lacks the "imperative power which the call to duty draws."[45] He adds:

> "Responsibility implies the spelling out of reason, not blind allegiance. It runs counter to fanaticism, but has its own compelling power, for commitments freely undertaken often have greater binding force than those which are simply traditionally given."[46]

Giddens is right, but again, as in the case of others, only to a certain extent. He is right when he says that an attitude of responsibility, which is necessary, does not come from obligation and duty. But he is not correct when he says that the "values of the sanctity of human life, universal human rights" imply "ethics of individual and collective responsibility", values that are "able to override divisions of interest."[47] Responsibility is not an implication from universality and it is not only characterized by "spelling out reason". Moreover, the issue is also not to overcome "divisions of interests."[48]

42 Ibid.

43 See: Marcin Kilanowski, *Ku wolności jako odpowiedzialności. Dewey, Rorty, Habermas o nowej jakości w demokracji.*, Wydawnictwo UMK, Toruń 2013.

44 By saying that the new language does not have to "rely on the necessity to discover an absolute and universal truth or universal values" I am not saying that the universal truth or universal values do not exist, but that discovering them is not necessary if our goal is to protect human beings and recognize their needs. For further argumentation please see: Marcin Kilanowski, *Truth, Universality or Dialog?* in: *Beyond Rorty*, ed. Randy Auxier, Chris Skowronski, Lexington Press 2015.

45 Anthony Giddens, *Beyond Left and Right, The Future of Radical Politics*, 21.

46 Ibid.

47 Ibid.

48 Interests do not have to be something that will stop us from engaging in dialog. See: Jane Mansbridge, with James Bohman, Simone Chambers, David Estlund, Andreas Føllesdal, Archon Fung, Christina

Responsibility comes from redescribing our position in society and understanding our freedom in a new way. It also comes not only from a definitive reliance on reason, which sometimes cannot even be "spelled out", but also on, and probably sometimes primarily sentiment and compassion, as Rorty and Habermas have pointed out.[49] We should then say that "issues of dignity and self-worth depend far more on the attitude of people towards one another, parents toward children, teachers toward students, than on the country's governmental structure"[50] and rights alone. We could support that claim by referring to the history of human rights, which "shows that rights are best defended in the end by the feelings, convictions, and actions of a multitude of individuals, who demand responses that accord with their inner sense of outrage."[51] Of course, we should not forget that this "inner sense of outrage" should rely on a critical and responsible assessment of the situation and the means deployed to deal with it. We should not rely uncritically on rights or on any absolute truth during this process. We can by analogy say that rights as a philosophy should be treated as tools, and that they should be constantly questioned and evaluated. That way we have a better chance of not becoming dependent on any kind of "regime", be it totalitarian, "democratic" or international.

Summing Up

It can be said that nowadays the "language of rights has largely replaced the language of responsibilities" and it has separated individuals from one another.[52] Moreover, as Arthur Dyck says, "many of our contemporary views of what constitute knowledge have also separated individuals, groups, cultures, and notions from one another."[53] It is hard not to agree with such a view even though it is not that certain that we previously had a better language, which was later replaced. Rather, such a language has to be developed today to replace the language of fundamental rights being treated as the property of individuals strengthening their position with reference to universal values. The need for such a change can be supported with criticism of the kind David Kennedy expresses when he points to the unanticipated consequences of human rights language and the human rights movement.

Kennedy's criticism makes us aware that we should be careful if by chance we are not violating someone's "rights" or constraining someone's needs, by believing that we are only doing "good", that we are only protecting their and others' human rights, by defining their situation in the language of rights. This is the case when we perceive law as going

Lafont, Bernard Manin, and José Luis Martí. "The Place of Self-Interest and the Role of Power in Deliberative Democracy." *Journal of Political Philosophy* 18 no 1 (2010) 64–100.

49 See: Richard Rorty, *Human Rights, Rationality, and Sentimentality*, in: *On Human Rights*, ed. S. Shute, S. Hurley, The Oxford Amnesty Lectures, Oxford 1993.

50 Walter W. Menninger, "Speech for the Conference on Human Dignity and American Democracy," 9.

51 Lynn Hunt says: "Courts and governmental organizations… will always be slowed down by considerations of geopolitics", see: Lynn Hunt *Inventing Human Rights, A History*, 213.

52 Arthur J. Dyck, *Rethinking Rights and Responsibilities, The Moral Bonds of Community*, (Washington, D.C.: Georgetown University Press, 2005) 1. Dyck also mentions "obligations".

53 Ibid., 328. To put it in different words: "If duties without rights make slaves, rights without duties make strangers." See: David Selbourne, *The Principle of Duty*, (London: Abacus, 1997) 123.

together with good. In this way, everything that is an outcome of legal regulation must be good and everything that is outside legal discourse is bad. Kennedy also makes us aware that the human rights movement strengthens "the habit of understanding international governance in legal rather than political terms", which "weakens its ability to perform what we understand domestically to be these political functions."[54] Such a transformation of "political questions into legal questions, and then into questions of legal "rights"" can make other forms of "collective emancipatory politics less available"[55], as it did in the past.

Kennedy's list of downsides, as presented here, seems to be of great value. It can motivate our undertaking what I call a linguistic turn in human rights, as took place in social science or philosophy thanks to Wittgenstein or Rorty. Kennedy makes some of the points function as expressions of certain intuitions that should be explained further to become real guidance for those willing to transform the field of human rights and to achieve the necessary change in the lives of ordinary people. It is hard to say how far Kennedy would go because he sometimes seems to be saying that the problem with human rights is not structural but rather situational.[56] However, it is certain that his criticism does not lead to deconstruction of the field in order to tear it apart and leave only scraps of no use to anybody. The point is to make us aware that our actions have consequences and these can be dangerous, which applies in the field of human rights as much as anywhere else.

We can add that it is good to have a list of possible risks and costs, of what can go wrong, and to think about the field in pragmatic terms. However, thinking that we will eliminate these risks would be a mistake. We will never reach that final stage at which we will understand all the relationships that are present or the potential basis for their appearance.[57] However, that does not mean that we should not try to do our best to minimize the costs. We will not avoid problems and difficulties by not engaging in conversations about them. What's more, we have the pragmatic philosophical tradition on our side at this point with its strong support for the concept of critical pragmatic assessment. It teaches us that we have to soften the attitude toward our fundamental rights, universal values, the legal structure we rely on and enrich it, strengthen it, with recognition of the ambivalent as well as the attitude of doubt and critical assessment. We have to understand that to a great extent we have always been a construct of the ideas that became central to our thinking. We have lived by past philosophical arrangements and we still do when we live by the private-public dichotomy and think about ourselves as individuals with our private sphere *vis-á-vis* the public, and when we think about ourselves as separate individuals in contrast to the community in which we live.[58]

54 David Kennedy, *The Dark Sides of Virtue, Reassessing International Humanitarianism*, 31.

55 Ibid., 33.

56 He says for example: "A checklist of possible downsides is not a general critique of human rights. Benefits and harms must be analyzed in particular cases, under specific conditions, at particular times." Ibid., 5.

57 Kennedy is also aware of this when he says: "For all our good intentions and careful attention to costs and benefits, dark sides, blind spots, biases all will remain with us." Ibid., xix.

58 A significant number of philosophical and legal authors are already emphasising this point, from John Dewey and Hannah Arendt to Horatia Muir Watt and Mary Ann Glendon.

I mentioned in the introduction that relying on dialog and the value of responsibility seems to be more appropriate for human rights. I hope that through the above analysis the reader will see where such an intuition comes from – from employing language which places greater emphasis on dialog and responsibilities in place of language centered on one universally correct answer. A more anti-foundationalist language, based on a redefined notion of individuality and freedom seems to be more appropriate in order to accommodate different points of view in a changing world, as well as during the processes of the formation of law, its interpretation and adjudication. That would be the language of engagement and of criticism, encouraging participation and not allowing others to decide for us. This is not only crucial for a well-functioning democracy but also for better protection of human "rights" and strengthening current mechanisms. We have to learn how to question and we have to question what we learn.

Bibliography

Bob, Clifford, ed. *The International Struggle for New Human Rights*. Philadelphia: University of Pennsylvania Press, 2009.

Brysk, Alison, ed. *Globalization and Human Rights*. Berkeley, Los Angeles, London: University of California Press, 2002.

Capps, Patrick. *Human dignity and the Foundation of International Law*. Oxford and Portland, Oregon: Hart Publishing, 2009.

Charlesworth, Hilary, and Christine Chinkin. "The Gender of Jus Cogens." *Human Rights Quarterly* 15 (1993): 66–76.

Dyck Arthur J. *Rethinking Rights and Responsibilities. The Moral Bonds of Community*. Washington, D.C.: Georgetown University Press, 2005.

Giddens, Anthony. *Beyond Left and Right, The Future of Radical Politics*. Redwood City, CA: Stanford University Press, 1994.

Glendon, Mary Ann, *Rights Talk. The Impoverishment of Political Discourse*, New York: 1991;

Hunt, Lynn. *Inventing Human Rights, A History*. New York, London: W.W. Norton & Company, 2007.

Kennedy, David. *The Dark Sides of Virtue, Reassessing International Humanitarianism*. Princeton: Princeton University Press, 2005.

Kilanowski, Marcin. *Ku wolności jako odpowiedzialności. Dewey, Rorty, Habermas o nowej jakości w demokracji*. Toruń: Wydawnictwo UMK, 2013.

Kilanowski, Marcin. "Truth, Universality or Dialog?" In *Beyond Rorty*, edited by Randy Auxier and Chris Skowronski. Lexington Press, 2015.

Mansbridge, Jane, with James Bohman, Simone Chambers, David Estlund, Andreas Føllesdal, Archon Fung, Christina Lafont, Bernard Manin, and José Luis Martí. "The Place of Self-Interest and the Role of Power in Deliberative Democracy." *Journal of Political Philosophy* 18, no. 1 (2010): 64–100.

McCrudden, Christopher. "Human Dignity and Judicial Interpretation of Human Rights." *The European Journal of International Law* 19, no. 4 (2008):655–724.

Menninger, Walter W. "Speech for the Conference on Human Dignity and American Democracy." In *A Report on the Bicentennial Conference on Human Dignity and American Democracy*, edited by E. E. Grollmes. St. Louis: St. Louis University, 1976.

Quataert, John H. *Advocating Dignity, Human Rights Mobilizations in Global Politics*. Philadelphia: University of Pennsylvania Press, 2010.

Shklar, Judith, *Legalism, Law, Morals and Political Trials*, Cambridge: Harvard University Press, 1964.

Rorty, Richard. "Human Rights, Rationality, and Sentimentality." In *On Human Rights*, edited by S. Shute and S. Hurley. Oxford: The Oxford Amnesty Lectures, 1993.

Selbourne David, *The Principle of Duty*. London: Abacus, 1997.

Ukri Soirila*

PLURALISATION THROUGH LEGAL CONFLICTS? RETHINKING LAW AND CULTURAL PLURALISM

Introduction

It is not easy to combine law and cultural pluralism.[1] Indeed, it would seem at first sight that the two concepts are fundamentally at odds with each other. Law is supposed to be predictable and permanent and is hence typically conceived of as something categorical, rigid and fixed. The term "pluralism," on the contrary, tends to evoke visions of contingency and freedom. If law is seen to bring stability at its best and totalitarianism at its worst, then a similar dichotomy of cultural pluralism is usually conceived to be one between flexibility and chaos. It would therefore be easy to argue either that law and cultural pluralism are incompatible, and pluralist accommodation through legal measures impossible, or that the two can be used as reciprocal checks and balances against each other, law bringing rationality and stability to the chaos of pluralism, with pluralism preventing law from slipping into an overly rigid totalitarian system. Unsurprisingly, in this Chapter, I reject both the overly optimistic and the equally pessimist options. Instead, I argue that a solution should be sought somewhere between these two extreme poles. The argument I put forward is not, however, a banal realist one, according to which law and cultural pluralism do indeed manage to balance each other to some extent, but not entirely, as reality is more complex than theory – even though I admit that such a conclusion is indeed true for the most part. Rather, my aim is to challenge the picture on a conceptual level. What is the relation between law and cultural pluralism if law is not as rigid and pluralism as flexible and contingent as commonly thought? How to combine the concepts if law is actually contingent and pluralism threatens to become fixed? I do not therefore want to discard either law or cultural pluralism but to look at the two from a fresh perspective in the hope of discovering new avenues for a more dynamic, progressive and radical pluralist project.

The Chapter is structured as follows. First, I discuss the standard approach to cultural pluralism in order to argue that it tends to paint too fixed a picture of the different

* Faculty of Law, University of Helsinki.

1 I employ the term "cultural pluralism" here to distinguish my subject of research from that of legal pluralism, which is usually taken to mean the existence of several legal systems within one State, region, or the world.

cultures and communities forming a single society, with the result that the standard approach may turn out to be a tool for biopolitical management of society, rather than a way to increase freedom. Second, I suggest that focus should be shifted from this notion of pluralism to flows of pluralization. To be more precise, I argue that social movements, as well as pluralist laws and policies, should aim to release these flows that lead to always ongoing processes of becoming. Change is never easy, however, especially when it can be seen to threaten the hard-won privileges of existing interest groups, and flows of pluralization may therefore be blocked not only on a macro level, but also on a micro level. Thirdly, then, I point out that law may sometimes be a tool for change and contingency, helping flows of pluralization push through all kinds of micro level barriers. I conclude the Chapter by arguing that both law and pluralism are necessary but that it is important to expose both of them to scrutiny from various perspectives in order to cultivate a truly pluralist and multicultural ethos.

Conservative Cultural Pluralism?

Cultural pluralism aims to achieve a fair balance of power between different religious, ethnic and geographical groups within one area and to give each group adequate voice in making socially binding decisions. As William E. Connolly puts it, "the system is celebrated not because it performs any single function perfectly, but because it is said to promote, more effectively than any other known alternative, a plurality of laudable private and public ends."[2] As the traditional cultural pluralist vision goes, society is divided into several clearly distinguishable groups that enable the individual to develop powers and a sense of purpose that lead to a fully developed personality. Participation in politics through group assimilation leads to a more stable regime and to a mode of rationality that transcends the specific interests of the participants, leading to overall best consensual solutions.[3]

Such a view is not, however, satisfactory from a more progressive political perspective – such as that of Connolly, for example. It is all too easy to sediment groups that have merged in the past through political struggles as the only possible interest holders in society and to divide the population under these interest groups.[4] And it is equally easy to start treating the rules used to negotiate interests between interest groups as the only possible way to solve conflicts within society. The result is the kind of post-political system that the French thinker Jacques Rancière describes with the term "policing" or "politics of *consensus*." Policing means all the administration – all the balancing of

2 William E. Connolly, *William E. Connolly: Democracy, pluralism and political theory*, ed. Samuel A. Chambers and Terrell Carver (London and New York: Routledge, 2008), 15.

3 Jürgen Habermas, "Three normative models of democracy," in *Democracy and Difference: Contesting the Boundaries of the Political*, ed. Seyla Benhabib (Princeton: Princeton University Press, 1996), 24; Jürgen Habermas, *Between Facts and Norms* (Cambridge: Polity Press, 1997), 296; Seyla Benhabib, "Toward a deliberative model of democratic legitimacy," in *Democracy and Difference: Contesting the Boundaries of the Political*, ed. Seyla Benhabib (Princeton: Princeton University Press, 1996), 68; John Rawls, *Political Liberalism*. (New York: Columbia University Press, 1996).

4 Connolly, *William E. Connolly: Democracy, pluralism and political theory*, 39.

interests of existing, pre-destined classes, groups and stakeholders – that we read about daily in newspapers under the term "politics." Yet policing has nothing to do with politics proper which, according to Rancière, consists of contesting the very definition of the community by multiplying litigious objects and disputing subjects and hence challenging the supposed tranquility of consensus. The aim of policing is to manage the basic dispute about the constitution of the community by setting limits to the terrain where political discourse can be had and by creating rules on who can participate in this discourse (who can act as a representative), what matters can be disputed, and what one can do and what not. Struggles are transformed into managed conflicts with strict rules and all truth and reality is absorbed into the only thing(s) possible, according to the guidelines of realism, with the result that it seems that no one has been prevented from taking part in the determination of common life.[5] Society is ready, unified and whole, and all there is to do is to negotiate interests between existing interest groups.

This vision of the world plays by the rules of biopower, the term referring to detailed management of human life, in order to make the population as healthy, efficient and productive as possible.[6] When the population is divided into clearly distinguishable parts, it becomes easier to manage. This management is achieved through governmentality, the directing of crystallized power relations, or forces, in order to achieve different biopolitical aims. While biopower does tolerate differences, even uses them, they must be certain types of differences that are manageable. Individuals that do not fit the scheme are either normalized or excluded and rendered invisible so that in the public eye the mosaic of society appears seamless and complete. This is also one of the main points of Wendy Brown's well-known critique of the tolerance discourse.[7] Represented as the only possible response to and a positive moral attitude towards difference, tolerance reifies and naturalizes all difference and its interpretation. A potential, public justice project is therefore replaced with a private therapeutic or behavioural one. There is no political struggle, just tweaking of individuals. The tolerance discourse is therefore a way of depoliticizing and controlling the social that shapes conflict and difference and hides political struggle.

My point so far has been that traditional approaches to pluralism tend to paint a ready-made and fixed picture of society, and hence risks depoliticizing political struggles and hiding those individuals that do not belong to any of the existing interest-groups – in other words, those that Rancière calls "the part of no part." My second point, then, is that traditional approaches to pluralism also risk essentialising those interest-groups, communities and cultures, what is going on inside them, and their members. Roberto Esposito shows in his *Communitas: The Origin and Destiny of Community* that Western

5 Jacques Rancière, *Disagreement: Politics and Philosophy*, trans. Heikki Kujansivu (Helsinki: Tutkijaliitto, 2008). See also Joseph J. Tanke, *Jacques Rancière: An Introduction* (London and New York: Continuum, 2011), 43–48.

6 Michel Foucault, *The History of Sexuality, vol. 1: An Introduction* (Penguin Books, 1978); Michel Foucault, *Society Must Be Defended: Lectures at the Collège de France, 1975–1976* (New York: Picador, 2003).

7 Wendy Brown, *Regulating Aversion: Tolerance in the Age of Identity and Empire* (Princeton and Oxford: Princeton University Press, 2008).

thought on community has always been haunted by the assumption that a community is some fixed totality: a common attribute or property that joins together the members of the community and qualifies them as belonging to the same whole. It is presupposed that a community gives a quality that is added to the subject so that they are also subjects of a community; that "what is common for the members of the community is what is most properly their own."[8] This is clearly visible in contemporary legal approaches to issues of pluralism and multiculturalism. For example, while it seems impossible to decide on an internationally accepted definition of minorities, it is generally accepted that the definition should more or less follow the suggestion by Francesco Capotorti, the Special Rapporteur of the United Nations Sub-Commission on Prevention of Discrimination and Protection of Minorities, which includes for example the requirements that members of a minority possess ethnic, religious or linguistic characteristics differing from those of the rest of the population and show a sense of solidarity towards maintaining their culture.[9] There must therefore be some kind of essential property or attribute that is to be maintained for the group to be recognized.

Yet, as Esposito emphasizes, there is in reality no such essential positive property within the community, nor is any community as full and total as the mainstream notion assumes. Deriving the Latin word *communitas* from the word *munus*, meaning both office and gift, Esposito shows that community is based on an absent gift that does not belong to any member of the community but that they are obliged to give to each other. The members of the community do not therefore have in common something positive; the community is not a totality of persons united by a common property.[10] What the members of the community have in common is an obligation or a debt. Community is not a matter of addition but subtraction: it is minus, not plus.[11] This means that we do not possess any attributes that would naturally make us part of one group or another. Hence forcing such an attribute is necessarily a violent act, forcing the "I" to submerge into the "We."[12] Traditional approaches to pluralism thus also risk hiding the violence that goes on inside interest-groups, towards minorities inside minorities. Further, the compulsive search for the essence of a community which is never found – for there is only void to be discovered – is potentially a destructive process that may often culminate in violence towards the Other, whether other groups or the Others within the community that are not really part of "us" and hence make achievement of the pure community impossible (to take an extreme example, this is the role that the Jews played for the Nazis, acting as a concrete scapegoat to explain how the German community could have ended in the miserable situation it was in after the first World War). Finally, such a fixed notion of individuals and communities would make emphatic relations between groups and individuals impossible for, as Giorgio Agamben points out, if we were already this or

8 Roberto Esposito, *Communitas: The Origin and Destiny of Community* (Stanford: Stanford University Press, 2010), 3.

9 Francesco Capotorti, *Study on the Rights of Persons Belonging to Ethnic, Religious and Linguistic Minorities*, UN Working Group on Minorities, doc E/CN.4/Sub.2/384/Rev.1, para. 568.

10 Esposito, *Communitas*, 3–6.

11 *Ibid.*, 6–7.

12 Costas Douzinas,"The Paradoxes of Human Rights," *Constellations* 20, no. 1 (2013), 59.

that, instead of remaining in a state of potential, if we already had this or that (fixed) identity, we could never have any communal relations, only factual connections and breaks.[13] In other words, it would be impossible for us to be flexible enough to adopt the Other's perspective and adapt to new situations with new people. These dangers involving the community have been perceived by modern thinkers who with the lead of Thomas Hobbes[14] have replaced relations within the community with a vertical rule of the Leviathan for the preservation of all.[15] Having discovered the risk included in the tradition of community, these thinkers have deduced that the only way to save us from this risk is to eradicate all communal relations altogether. But all that is left after such a move is nihilistic individualism. According to Esposito, in their extreme reaction to the *munus* these thinkers repeat the mistake of the communitarians. As nihilistic reasoning goes, the options are the dangerous debt of the community or no community at all. The concept of community is therefore just as totalitarian as it is in the communitarian vision, with the crucial exception that the nihilists emphasize the perils of this bond, whereas the communitarians emphasize its bright side. Hence a seemingly unsolvable tension and a never-ending oscillation are born between the communitarian and nihilistic visions. I will return to this communitarian-nihilist dichotomy, and the solution that Esposito provides to it, in the next Section of this Chapter. However, I first want to conclude my main argument of the present Section. What is suggested by my points about the traditional cultural pluralist way of perceiving, first, society and, secondly, the groups or communities that build that society, is that cultural pluralism may not be as contingent and flexible as commonly thought. Cultural pluralist theory can be conservative, too, and often freezes current dominant identities that are the results of past political struggles. As William E. Connolly points out, "while demands for close ethnic or religious unity are resisted, many pluralists bound diversity by the territorial state, the normal individual, and monotheistic or monosecular conceptions of morality."[16]

The true obscene underside of pluralism is therefore "fascism," as Deleuze and Guattari employ the term, not referring so much to the historical fascism associated with Hitler and Mussolini as the fascism that, operating inside all of us and at the molecular level of family, friendships and communities, makes us love power and "desire the very thing that dominates and exploit us."[17] Pluralism may indeed work as a counterforce against top-down totalitarianism but as Deleuze and Guattari remind us, it is easy to fight against the state and corporations but more difficult to detect that we tend to reiterate the same state power in our personal relationships, communities and everyday practices.[18] It is not easy to remain open to destabilizing change after having received

13 Giorgio Agamben, *Means Without an End*, trans. Juhani Vähämäki (Tutkijaliitto, 2001), 16.

14 Thomas Hobbes, *Leviathan* (Oxford: Oxford University Press, 1996).

15 Esposito, *Communitas*, 12–14.

16 Connolly, *William E. Connolly: Democracy, pluralism and political theory*, 39.

17 Michel Foucault, "Preface," in *Anti-Oedipus: Capitalism and Schizophrenia*, Gilles Deleuze and Felix Guattari (London and New York: Continuum, 2004), xiv–xv.

18 Gilles Deleuze and Felix Guattari, *A Thousand Plateaus: Capitalism and Schizophrenia* (London and New York: Continuum, 2004), 236–37.

certain benefits or recognition as a consequence of hard-won past struggles. And what makes things even more difficult is that such micro-level fascism operates not only through explicit exclusions and repressions but also through such open-minded practices as the tolerance discourse, as Wendy Brown has demonstrated.[19] Tolerance implies a certain hierarchy and distance in which some are marked as potential objects of tolerance whereas others, who have the capacity to tolerate, form the norm – the universal against particular Others. This is what Slavoj Žižek calls "racism with a distance," a self-referential, empty form of racism which conceives the other as belonging to a self-enclosed "authentic" community, against which the "pluralistically" minded autonomous individual maintains a distance enabled by their universal position. Multiculturalists do not try to force their "superior" values on the Other but nevertheless maintain their superiority.[20]

Towards Pluralization!

It is against this threat of micro-fascism, included in any sedimented theory, system or norm, that Deleuze and Guattari set their rhizomatic thought, based on becomings and lines of flight. If the danger of traditional approaches to pluralism is that they may lead to a fixed, frozen situation, dominated by the Majority as a constant against which all evaluation is completed and by which all others can be evaluated and allotted their "proper" social location –the standard measure – then it is possible to escape this deadlock only by endless processes of becoming-minoritarian. In other words what are needed are flows of pluralization that prevent cultural pluralism from freezing into a fixed system.[21] Such flows and the constant becoming-minoritarian should not be confused with the individualism of nihilist answers to the dangers of the communitarian *munus*, however. As William E. Connolly explains, "individual*ism* presupposes a model of the normal or rational individual against which the conduct and interior of each actual self are to be appraised."[22] The individual is pictured as stiff and steadfast and the logic of individualism is easily turned into a doctrine of normalization through individualization – not by excluding or normalizing explicitly but through leaving unchallenged "dualities already inscribed into the culture" that is idealized.[23] On the contrary, Connolly's pluralization relies on the theory of individual*ity*, which "gives primacy to the individual while qualifying or problematizing the hegemony of the normal individual [and] stretches the boundaries of identity officially given the normal self and brings new issues into public life through resistances."[24] The theory can thus take into consideration Étienne Balibar's complex notion of the self, according to which the individual and their identity is constructed by a myriad of ongoing processes that are singular but nonetheless trans-individual, always in transit between several symbolic

19 Brown, *Regulating Aversion*.
20 Slavoj Žižek, *Living in the End Times* (London and New York: Verso 2011).
21 Connolly, *William E. Connolly: Democracy, pluralism and political theory*, 39.
22 *Ibid.*, 155.
23 *Ibid.*
24 *Ibid.*, 156.

references.[25] Hence the theory escapes the nihilism of individualism as well as the totalizing effects of the communitarian vision of community. So how then to vision the community if it is necessary to leave room for flows of pluralization and individuality, while still avoiding the pitfall of nihilism? The answer is provided by Esposito. Community is, according to Esposito, defined by a *no-thing*. The community is not an entity, a totality or a collective of subjects. It is rather a relation that makes its members something more than individual subjects, not because it adds some common feature to them but because it necessarily alters them.[26] As Esposito explains, as soon as we can understand how that *no-thing* keeps the community together, we can grasp that "the subject of the community is no longer the 'same'," that is added to every subject, but an other – "not another subject but a chain of alterations that cannot ever be fixed in a new, whole, identity."[27] It is "with" or "between" and always in the process of change.[28]

But even if we manage to conceive individuality as a singular yet trans-individual process and the community as a relation that is in a process of change at the same time as it alters its members, releasing drives of pluralization from their shackles is still no easy task. Connolly writes that social pluralism "is often presented as an achievement to be protected, while the eruptions of new drives to pluralism are often represented as perils to this achievement."[29] Further, claims for recognition of new possibilities of being create panic and insecurity in the self-confidence of established identities and create counter-reactions that tend to aim at maintaining the status quo.[30] Those who have struggled hard to gain recognition are not always willing to let go of their established identities and may resist new processes of change. There is therefore a correlation between pluralization and fundamentalisation: "each drive to pluralization is countered by a fundamentalism that claims to be authored by a god or by nature [and] any drive to pluralization can itself become fundamentalised."[31]

To conclude, I argue that we need a more progressive pluralist project to replace traditional notions of cultural pluralism. This is important because these traditional notions are too easily turned into a fixed system of order that presents society as ready. As such, they risk hiding possible oppression both of those who do not belong to any of the recognized interest groups in society, and of those that are in a minority position within recognized groups. Where traditional theories of cultural pluralism treat pluralism mostly as a fact or a state of affairs and hence turn out to be fundamentally immunitary theories of order that concentrate on preventing *de facto* pluralism from culminating in catastrophe by facilitating a fair dialogue or competition between existing interest-groups, the project of progressive radical pluralism takes plurali*zation* as its *goal* and vehicle for democratic contestation. The aim is to open possibilities for minoritarian becomings and drives of pluralization and hence to challenge existing power structures.

25 Étienne Balibar, *Politics and the Other Scene* (London and New York: Verso, 2002), 27–28.
26 Esposito, *Communitas*, 138–40.
27 *Ibid.*, 138.
28 *Ibid.*, 139.
29 Connolly, *William E. Connolly: Democracy, pluralism and political theory*, 39.
30 *Ibid.*, 40.
31 *Ibid.*, 37–38.

But this is easier said than done. As I explained above, those who have won their privileges through hard struggles may be reluctant to accept new forms of being, while every flow of pluralization creates counter-flows of fundamentalisation. Hence, sometimes force (in immaterial, not physical form) is needed to push through the barriers of conservatism. It is here that law can become useful.

Law as Progressive Force?

If drives to pluralization tend to be blocked at the molecular level through all kinds of attitudes, discourses and practices of micro-fascism, perhaps law can give these drives a push that helps them thrust through these barriers? I argued earlier that the bright side of cultural pluralism is the freedom and flexibility that it can produce, but that its dark side may not be chaos and disorder, as commonly claimed, but rather fascism, in the meaning Deleuze and Guattari give to the term. Perhaps the inverse is true when it comes to law. The obscene underside of law is indeed totalitarianism. Abstract law can never grasp life in all its complexity. Law always needs to categorize and classify and sometimes this rigidity can get out of hand. Yet the bright side of law is not necessarily the stability it brings, although it does sometimes bring that too. Perhaps the truly positive effect that law brings could potentially be flexibility, conflict and contingency?

Rancière suggests just such a capacity of law and rights in his insightful essay *Who Is the Subject of the Rights of Man?* According to Rancière, legal rights are not useful merely because they manage to capture some essential part of humanity or because they would be some kind of higher form of (divine) law, but because they can, as written and formally equal, indeterminate, and written rules, open a space for contesting the borders of the political and turn their acclaimed subjects (potentially everyone) into political subjects, capable of forming political claims. Rights are useful as catalysts of conflicts. Commenting especially on human rights, Rancière argues that they can evade the trap set by Arendt, according to which human rights are either the rights of the human as such or the rights of the citizen – meaning that they are either the rights of those without rights, amounting to nothing, or the rights of the citizen who has rights, amounting to tautology. As Rancière explains, there is a third option: human rights are "the rights of those who have not the rights that they have and have the rights that they have not." Human rights "are not the rights of a single subject that would be at once the source and the bearer of the rights and would only use the rights." Instead of talking about the subject of rights, we should talk about the process of subjectivisation that closes the gap between rights as written rules, as something given, and use of those rights to "build such and such a case." The human of human rights is a political subject and not necessarily part of a definite collective. This political subject can use human rights to create conflict over "who is included in their count [...] what they exactly entail and whom they concern in which cases."[32] In Deleuzean terms the political subject deterritorialises and reterritorialises rights and thus creates a line of flight that may lead to larger processes of change.

32 Jacques Rancière, "Who Is the Subject of the Rights of Man?," *The South Atlantic Quarterly* 103, no.2 (2004), 302–3.

In this way, law can actually work as a vehicle for change and pluralization. New forms of being can use the rights won by previous movements against those movements themselves if they have stabilized into dominant, fixed groups, preventing new becomings. Changes can occur at the molecular, subject level through slow changes in the consciousness of dominant groups and individuals, but they could potentially also happen through Court decisions. Taking into consideration the indeterminacy of law, much hinges on the way we perceive the act of judgment. Here we need to turn to Deleuze's thought, an important part of which is critique of dogmatism. According to Deleuze, dogmatism is based on common sense and opinions and reduces thinking to the act of recognition, meaning that encounters new things assimilated with the concepts and categories used in recognition. As Alexandre Lefebvre writes, "[a]ccording to Deleuze, the essence of dogmatism is the assumption, implicit or explicit, that everything encountered can be recognized."[33] Dogmatic judgment is therefore about subsuming cases under rules. A teleological judgment is an upgrade from a dogmatic judgment but is ultimately based on the same logic. The problem, as Lefebvre explains, is that a true encounter, which according to Deleuze is a condition of thinking (in a strict sense that does not include recognition) and creation of the new, is bypassed as the complexity of the case is flattened and forced under existing categories. It is this dogmatism that Deleuze wants to replace with a more creative act of judgment. For example, an important difference between dogmatic law and Deleuzean jurisprudence has to do with repetition. Law in the traditional sense is based on the notion of calculative and bare repetition. Such repetition makes its subjects mutually interchangeable and the future predictable. Deleuzean repetition, however, has nothing to do with an identically repeating series. Instead it is differential repetition, meaning that it produces change and is hence creative.[34]

Deleuze is therefore not against law as such, as is commonly claimed, but simply against reflective judgment which assigns a function to the organisms of law and their organs, flattens cases and prevents the emergence of new modes of existence. He is also not against rules, tradition, customs and the past of law. According to the concept of time that Deleuze borrows from Bergson, the entire virtual past is always contemporary with the present. It is not simply assumed, as in teleological judgment, but it ontologically *is*. As Lefebvre demonstrates, a Deleuzean judgment is therefore cumulative and experimental. Attempts are made to apply different "memories" and parts of the virtual past to the case one after another and every experiment opens new possibilities, creating something new, with the result that the case becomes singular, constructive and creative but not in any way arbitrary.[35] The aim of such judgment could perhaps be to maximize life – not empty life reduced to survival but creative affirmative life. As John Protevi writes, "it is not a matter of applying a transcendent standard to the facts of the case but judgment felt as intensity at a singular point, allowing lines of a virtual multiplicity to be

33 Alexandre Lefebvre, *The Image of Law: Deleuze, Bergson, Spinoza* (Stanford: Stanford University Press, 2008), 59.

34 Gilles Deleuze, *Difference and Repetition* (London and New York: Continuum, 2004); Lefebvre, *The Image of Law*, 59–62, 65–68.

35 Lefebvre, *The Image of Law*, *passim*.

actualized as the solution of a problem."[36] It is a way of allowing concrete individuals to use rights immanently in concrete situations; a matter of rights of life that allow life in all its multiplicity to fight all the dominant norms that try to capture it. In Edward Mussawri's words:

> [w]hen Deleuze and Guattari counter the major ontology based on 'man' with various minor becomings, such as becoming-minority, part of the point is to show that rights are not borne from attaining for oneself a certain status, but from pushing status itself toward the side of its minority and minorization.[37]

It is therefore important not to completely discard law as a tool for cultural pluralism. Sometimes law can provide the solid ground on which to base claims for further pluralization in order to break conformist barriers. These kinds of breakthroughs are rare, however, and the legal project should not therefore replace more grass-roots projects that slowly create change through alterations in subject-level attitudes. But legal projects can supplement these other projects and even when a Court decision is negative, the publicity of the case may have planted the seed of change in the minds of individuals. Ultimately all depends on the prevailing *ethos*, as Connolly employs the term, meaning our sensibilities or the "customs, priorities, habits, and norms" that guide our institutions and practices.[38] It is unlikely that much can be accomplished through courts either, if the *ethos* is highly conservative, affecting the judges as well, and smothering any incentive for more creative judgments. But in a more blurry situation a court decision may well be what finally breaks the conservative walls. Hence, it is strategically extremely important to remember that law can act as a vehicle for change, just as well as it can act as a barrier against it.

Conclusion

This chapter has engaged with the assumption that law and pluralism can act in harmony, that both are in fact needed as checks and balances against each other. As that assumption goes, law, through its stability, can balance the chaotic contingency of pluralism whereas pluralism can prevent law from becoming totalitarian. What the analysis provided in the article suggests is that law and pluralism are indeed both needed, but that the concepts and the relation between the two are more complex than sometimes supposed. Pluralism can indeed bring flexibility and contingency but it may also freeze into a fixed system that maintains existing identities, interest groups and communities and blocks further flows of pluralization. On the other hand, law can act as a tool for opening these blockages and returning the conflicts, deterritorialisations and lines of flight necessary for further

36 John Protevi, "The Terri Sciavo Case: Biopolitics, Biopower and Privacy as Singularity," in *Deleuze and Law: Forensic Futures*, ed. Braidotti, Colebrook and Hanafin (Hampshire and New York: Palgrave Macmillan, 2009), 69–71.

37 Edward Mussawri, *Jurisdiction in Deleuze: The Expression and Representation of Law* (Oxon and New York: Routledge, 2011), 57.

38 William E. Connolly, *Pluralism* (Durham: Duke University Press, 2005), 6, 135.

pluralist becomings. But as law, because of its indeterminacy, can also lapse into totalitarianism, it is often actually pluralism that is needed as a stable basis that guides legal decisions into rights directions. It is important not to focus too exclusively either on micro-level or macro-level processes. It is true that often change is easier to bring from bottom-up, subject level alterations cumulating into larger ones. But sometimes it is also necessary to use macro-level tools in order to shatter micro-level fascist blockages and free room for new becomings.

Thus, it is possible also to reverse the roles commonly given to law and pluralism. Such a shift of perspective is important as it sheds new light on common phenomena and reveals not only injustices and problems left hidden by the first perspective but also new paths forward. The point is not simply to discard everything we assumed so far but to play the different perspectives against each other in order to provide novel solutions. Existing models of pluralism have many tremendously important aspects to them and may provide a launching ground for further flows of pluralization. This article should therefore not be considered as an attack against those models but rather as a wake-up call that invites scholars and practitioners to think of the possibilities that the models offer, as well as the problems inherent in them, from a fresh perspective. This is the whole point of the radical pluralist project. In Connolly's words, pluralist philosophy is possible only:

> if you admit that the philosophy you adopt... is profoundly and legitimately contestable to others, and if you work upon yourself to overcome resentment of this very condition. When you acknowledge that your philosophical stance is grounded in a complex mixture of contestable faith and porous arguments you take a step toward affirmation of political pluralism, even if the philosophy you embrace is block monism, strong dualism, or mechanical materialism.[39]

[39] Connolly, *William E. Connolly: Democracy, pluralism and political theory*, 96.

Bibliography

Agamben, Giorgio. *Means Without an End*.Translated by Juhani Vähämäki. Tutkijaliitto, 2001.
Balibar, Étienne. *Politics and the Other Scene*. London and New York: Verso, 2002.
Benhabib, Seyla. "Toward a deliberative model of democratic legitimacy." In *Democracy and Difference: Contesting the Boundaries of the Political*, edited by Seyla Benhabib, 67–94. Princeton: Princeton University Press, 1996.
Brown, Wendy. *Regulating Aversion: Tolerance in the Age of Identity and Empire*. Princeton and Oxford: Princeton University Press, 2008.
Capotorti, Francesco. *Study on the Rights of Persons Belonging to Ethnic, Religious and Linguistic Minorities*. UN Working Group on Minorities, doc E/CN.4/Sub.2/384/Rev.1.
Connolly, William E. *Pluralism*. Durham: Duke University Press, 2005.
— *William E. Connolly: Democracy, pluralism and political theory*, edited by Samuel A. Chambers and Terrell Carver. London and New York: Routledge, 2008.
Deleuze, Gilles. *Difference and Repetition*. London and New York: Continuum, 2004.
Deleuze, Gilles, and Felix, Guattari. *A Thousand Plateaus: Capitalism and Schizophrenia*. London and New York: Continuum, 2004.
Douzinas, Costas. "The Paradoxes of Human Rights." *Constellations* 20, no. 1 (2013): 51–67.
Esposito, Roberto. *Communitas: The Origin and Destiny of Community*. Stanford: Stanford University Press, 2010.
Foucault, Michel. *The History of Sexuality, vol. 1: An Introduction*. New York: Penguin Books, 1978.
— "Preface." In *Anti-Oedipus: Capitalism and Schizophrenia* Gilles Deleuze and Felix Guattari. London: Continuum, 2004.
— *Society Must Be Defended: Lectures at the Collège de France*, 1975–1976. New York: Picador, 2003.
Habermas, Jürgen. "Three normative models of democracy." In *Democracy and Difference: Contesting the Boundaries of the Political*, edited by Seyla Benhabib, 21–30. Princeton: Princeton University Press, 1996.
— *Between Facts and Norms*. Cambridge: Polity Press, 1997.
Hobbes, Thomas. *Leviathan*. Oxford: Oxford University Press, 1996.
Lefebvre, Alexandre. *The Image of Law: Deleuze, Bergson, Spinoza*. Stanford: Stanford University Press, 2008.
Mussawri, Edward. *Jurisdiction in Deleuze: The Expression and Representation of Law*. Oxon and New York: Routledge, 2011.
Protevi, John. "The Terri Schiavo Case: Biopolitics, Biopower and Privacy as Singularity." In *Deleuze and Law: Forensic Future*, edited by Rosi Braidotti, Claire Colebrook, and Patrick Hanafin, 59–72. Hampshire and New York: Palgrave Macmillan, 2009.
Rancière, Jacques. "Who Is the Subject of the Rights of Man?" *The South Atlantic Quarterly* 103, no. 2 (2004): 298–310.
— *Disagreement: Politics and Philosophy*. Translated by Heikki Kujansivu. Helsinki: Tutkijaliitto, 2008.

Rawls, John. *Political Liberalism.* New York: Columbia University Press, 1996.
Tanke, Joseph J. *Jacques Rancière: An Introduction.* London and New York: Continuum, 2011.
Žižek, Slavoj. *Living in the End Times.* London and New York: Verso, 2011.

Magdalena Kmak*

'THE UGLY' OF EU MIGRATION POLICY: THE ROLE OF THE RECAST RECEPTION DIRECTIVE IN FRAGMENTATION OF THE REFUGEE SUBJECT

Introduction

On 9 June 2013 the European Parliament and the Council adopted a recast of the Reception Directive, regulating the conditions of reception and detention of those applying for asylum in the EU (2013). Adoption of this directive constitutes completion of part of the second stage of the Common European Asylum System [CEAS]. The aim of CEAS is to narrow down discrepancies between asylum laws and application of the refugee procedure in Member States in order to improve its fairness and quality. This task proved to be difficult due to disagreements among Member States with regard to the content of the directives. Moreover, various analyses of the draft amendments show that recast laws would not require states to considerably raise their protection standards. In consequence, the second stage of CEAS may not significantly differ from the first stage completed in 2008, so that the effort to improve the quality and fairness of the asylum system throughout Europe may not bring the planned effects.[1]

One of the aims of the recast Reception Directive was to adopt "clear and strict rules on detention" of those applying for asylum, which would guarantee that detention is not applied in an arbitrary manner and the fundamental rights of asylum seekers are respected in all cases.[2] It has been claimed, however, that despite this aim the directive, when transposed by the Member States, will contribute to the systematic and prolonged use of detention in asylum cases under the new law.[3] This refers in particular to those categories of migrants who apply for asylum while trying to enter the territory of the EU in an irregular manner, those in the so-called Dublin procedure, asylum seekers whom the authorities consider at risk of absconding or to constitute a security threat.

* PhD, lecturer in International law, post-doctoral researcher, Erik Castrén Institute of International Law and Human Rights, University of Helsinki.

1 Steve Peers, "Analysis: The EU Directive on Reception Conditions: A Weak Compromise" (Statewatch, 2012), www.statewatch.org/analyses/no-184-reception-compromise.pdf.

2 European Commission, "Amended Proposal for a Directive of the European Parliament and of the Council Laying down Standards for the Reception of Asylum Seekers (Recast)," June 1, 2011, para. 3.1.2.

3 ECRE, "Comments from the European Council on Refugees and Exiles on the Amended Commission Proposal to Recast the Reception Conditions Directive (COM(2011)320 Final)," September 2011.

In this chapter I claim after Mezzadra and Neilson that the regulation for detaining asylum seekers in article 8 of the Reception Directive embeds continuous efforts to re-establish the original boundary between asylum seekers and economic migrants, laying the basis of the post-war refugee protection system. This boundary became blurred as a result of escalation of movements by refugees and expansion of the definition of refugee.[4] In the EU these efforts have been increasingly based on managing flows of asylum seekers through the production of subjectivities – or in other words specific positions of agency and identity – of bogus asylum seeker and genuine refugee. The directive, by allowing in practice systematic detention of those asylum seekers entering the EU territory irregularly, or those who are considered to be abusing the asylum systems in other ways, reinforces these subjectivities. In consequence of these efforts the subjectivity of a refugee has become fragmented and consists of two inter-related and inter-dependent subjectivities – the bogus asylum seeker and the genuine refugee. An asylum seeker seeking protection in the EU is caught in the circular relationship between these two subjectivities, which I call a subjectivity trap.

The aim of this chapter is therefore to show the role of the recast Reception Directive in reinforcing the subjectivity trap and to propose ways of resisting it. The next section focuses in more detail on the provisions of the recast Reception Directive. It shows that, despite the intention of the Commission, the directive may contribute to systematic and prolonged detention of numbers of asylum seekers. Section three conceptualises the subjectivity trap by focusing, first on the division of foreign citizens in EU countries into three categories which can be described as the Good, the Bad and the Ugly.[5] It then uses this distinction, in particular the category of the Ugly, in analysing the creation and features of dominant subjectivities: bogus and genuine asylum seekers. Finally, section four deconstructs the subjectivity trap and focuses on ways to resist it. It claims that hegemonic understanding of a nation state in international law creates divisions between the citizen and the foreigner, leading to a distinction between bogus and genuine asylum seekers and in consequence to creation of the subjectivity trap. The chapter then reflects on how subjectivities imposed on migrants and asylum seekers by law are being contested and dismantled by asylum seekers themselves.

The Recast of the Reception Directive

The aim of the Reception Directive is to lay down clear and uniform standards for the reception of those seeking protection in EU Member States, including their detention. Despite wide use of detention of asylum seekers by Member States this matter has not so far been regulated at the EU level. For that reason, the directive introduced four articles laying down a basis for detention of asylum seekers (Article 8), guarantees for detained applicants (Article 9), conditions of detention (Article 10) and provisions referring to

4 Sandro Mezzadra and Brett Neilson, Border as Method, Or, the Multiplication of Labor (Durham, NC: Duke University Press, 2013), 143.

5 Magdalena Kmak, "Limits of Sovereignty?: Rethinking the Conflict between Human Rights and Immigration in the European Union," Finnish Yearbook of International Law 20 (2011): 53–81.

detention of vulnerable persons and those with special needs (Article 11). In particular, the directive obliges Member States not to hold a person in detention for the sole reason of applying for international protection in accordance with EU law, and requires that detention should be in line with the principles of necessity and proportionality.[6] It has been claimed, however, that despite its aim of improving the position of asylum seekers in administrative detention, the directive, when transposed by the Member States, could contribute to proliferation of the institution of detention in the EU. This is because detention is currently regulated in four different binding legal documents, including, beside the recast Reception Directive, also the Returns Directive (2008), the recast Procedures Directive (2013) and the Dublin III Regulation (2013). Such regulation of provisions on detention in numerous documents raises concerns, not only about increasing use of detention towards various categories of immigrants but also about observance of the same standards of detention under the regimes of various directives.[7] In addition, despite the Commission's intention to guarantee respect for the human rights of detained asylum seekers, analysis of the directive, in particular article 8, raises concerns of the possible systematic and prolonged use of detention in asylum cases under the new law.[8]

According to article 8 of the directive, an applicant for asylum may only be detained on a limited number of grounds including the need to determine or verify identity or nationality or the elements of the asylum application, which could not be obtained in the absence of detention, in particular when there is a risk of absconding. An asylum seeker may also be detained in the context of the entry procedure, in a situation when there are reasonable grounds to believe that the asylum seeker is applying for international protection merely in order to delay or frustrate enforcement of a return decision, when protection of national security or public order so requires, or in the context of the Dublin procedure. As the European Council on Refugees and Exiles [ECRE] points out, the provision allowing detention of an asylum seeker in order to determine or verify identity or nationality, due to its vagueness and unspecified character, may contribute to detention becoming systematic in the situation when most asylum seekers arrive in Europe without travel documents.[9] The directive also raises concerns about detention of an asylum seeker for the duration of the entire asylum procedure (not in the initial stages of the asylum procedure only as proposed by the Commission in the initial draft of the directive), in order to determine the elements of the asylum application in case of the risk of absconding. Such regulation is particularly problematic in the context of the UN High Commissioner for Refugees' [UNHCR] guidelines on detention of asylum seekers, which allow for detention only in order to establish the essential facts of the case (whether the applicant has any reasons for claiming asylum). According to the UNHCR, detention

6 Directive 2013/33/EU of the European Parliament and of the Council of 26 June 2013 Laying down Standards for the Reception of Applicants for International Protection (recast), OJ L 180/96, recital 15.

7 Meijers Committee, "Detention Provisions in the Recast Proposals for the Reception Conditions Directive and the Dublin Regulation and the Right to a Remedy with Suspensive Effect," May 16, 2012.

8 ECRE, "Comments from the European Council on Refugees and Exiles on the Amended Commission Proposal to Recast the Reception Conditions Directive (COM(2011)320 Final)."

9 Ibid., para. 2.1.

should not be extended to determination of the merits of the case.[10] Detention for the period of the whole asylum procedure is also against article 5 of the European Convention on Human Rights. In its recent judgments the European Court has confirmed that detention "must be closely connected to the purpose of preventing unauthorised entry of the person to the country."[11] Both the guidelines and the judgment point out that detention which lasts beyond the initial stages of the asylum procedure does not fulfil these requirements. Moreover, the provision of the recast Reception Directive allowing for detention in order for the authorities "to decide on the right to enter the territory" may allow systematic detention of asylum seekers in an entry procedure irrespective of whether the asylum seeker entered the EU regularly or irregularly and whether they applied for protection without delay.[12] Moreover, the provision allowing for detention on the basis of article 27 of the draft Dublin III Regulation is problematic, as it does not require that such detention fulfils the condition of necessity.[13] Finally, article 8.3.d allowing for detention on the basis of protection of national security or public order can allow for very broad application of detention due to lack of definition of security and public order.[14]

As we can see, despite the intention to narrow down the number of instances of detention of those applying for asylum and to guarantee that detention is applied in line with the principles of necessity or proportionality, the provisions described may cause the opposite effect. In particular, what is important in the context of this chapter, the right to detain an asylum seeker in order to determine their identity or nationality without additional requirements possibly allows detention of every person without a travel document or those travelling with false documents. This is particularly problematic because strict migration policies in the EU significantly limit the possibilities of asylum seekers to apply for protection in a regular manner.[15] This often necessitates using alternative channels of reaching EU territory, including use of false identity documents, and may in consequence significantly enhance application of detention in the asylum procedure on the basis of the above-mentioned provision of article 8 of the directive. Other bases for detention enumerated in the directive, such as detention in case of the risk of absconding, in the context of the entry or return procedure as well as in the Dublin procedure, are aimed at guaranteeing control over and expulsion of those who are considered to be using the asylum procedure instrumentally. This happens without taking account of significant discrepancies in refugee recognition rates and levels of

10 UNHCR, "Revised Guidelines on Applicable Criteria and Standards Relating to the Detention of Asylum Seekers," February 1999, guideline 3(ii).

11 Lokpo and Touré v. Hungary, no. 10816/10, judgment of September 20, 2011.

12 ECRE, "Comments from the European Council on Refugees and Exiles on the Amended Commission Proposal to Recast the Reception Conditions Directive (COM(2011)320 Final)."

13 Meijers Committee, "Detention Provisions in the Recast Proposals for the Reception Conditions Directive and the Dublin Regulation and the Right to a Remedy with Suspensive Effect."

14 Ibid.

15 Magdalena Kmak, "Producing Irregularity – Management of Immigrants in the European Union," in Mobilités et Migrations: Figures et Enjeux Contemporains. Pluralité Des Regards et Des Disciplines, ed. Véronique Ancey et al., Collection Presses Universitaires de Sceaux (Paris: L'Harmattan, 2014), 267–79.

protection offered by different EU Member States. In consequence, these provisions may lead to broad or even systematic detention of asylum seekers without providing them with sufficient guarantees.

In what follows I will conceptualise the consequences of the Reception Directive in the context of dominant subjectivities produced by migration discourses in the EU – bogus asylum seekers and genuine refugees. I will show how the provisions of the directive contribute to blurring the distinction between asylum seekers and irregular immigrants and, as a result, to turning the former into the latter. This metamorphosis happens because the provisions of the directive are based on the perception that those applying for protection in the EU in an irregular manner do not fulfil the criteria for refugee status but simply abuse migration laws in order to enter EU territory. In other words, they are bogus asylum seekers. This perception is combined with the image of the genuine refugee as a person who not only fulfils the refugee criteria but who also waits patiently for the possibility to enter EU territory in a regular manner. I will base my analysis on a categorisation of immigrants present in or coming to the EU as the Good, the Bad and the Ugly.

Subjectivity Trap – Genuine Refugee v. Bogus Asylum Seeker

In an article entitled "Limits of Sovereignty?: Rethinking the Conflict between Human Rights and Immigration in the European Union"[16] I referred to Sergio Leone's famous 1966 movie entitled "The Good, the Bad and the Ugly" in order to illustrate various approaches to foreigners in the European Union. In my categorisation, the Good comprise EU citizens and their family members benefiting from their right of freedom of movement, and also academics, students, long-term residents and highly skilled third-country nationals entering the EU for the purpose of work. Those foreigners belong to a privileged group of EU citizens and economically beneficial third-country nationals for whom special legal status, available in simplified procedures, has been designed in EU law. The Bad on the other hand refers to immigrants who are perceived as those abusing EU and national legislation, constituting a security threat or negatively affecting the economy. My analysis showed that EU laws often do not provide effective human rights protection to this group of immigrants but rather focus on both preventing their entry and their effective removal from common territory. Finally, the Ugly refers to asylum seekers or other foreigners towards whom the EU and Member States have international human rights obligations. We can see that EU and national laws, regulating the right to entry and residence of this third group of foreigners, reflect the existing conflict between human rights obligations and States' preferences regarding the design of their immigration policies. States juxtapose their obligation to provide protection to those seeking asylum with their preferences based on a number of interests, including economic, social or security. In consequence, states often treat asylum seekers as economic migrants, offenders, terrorists, or bogus asylum seekers, a.k.a. the Ugly.

[16] Kmak, "Limits of Sovereignty?".

As is clear from the analysis in the previous section, the Reception Directive, and in particular its article 8, is guided by the philosophy of the Ugly and the conflict embedded in it. The conflict is visible at two levels. At the more immediate level, the directive aims to prevent arbitrary detention and improve the treatment of detained asylum seekers in accordance with the human rights obligations of the EU and its Member States. However, in consequence of its design, the directive sanctions systematic detention of asylum seekers in contradiction to the rules developed by the UNHCR or guaranteed by the ECHR. At a more subdued but systemic level, the directive contributes to the process of fragmentation of the refugee subject into the genuine refugee and the bogus asylum seeker. It does so by allowing systematic detention of those asylum seekers entering EU territory irregularly or those whom states consider as abusing asylum systems in other ways, in a situation where EU law makes it very difficult to seek protection in a regular manner. In consequence, the directive blurs the distinction between refugees and irregular or economic migrants. We can see that the fragmented refugee subject is produced by a conflict between state interests on the one hand, and state obligations to protect the human rights of asylum seekers on the other. Whereas focus on control of external borders and placing limitations on those coming to the EU produces the bogus asylum seeker, a focus on human rights obligations produces the genuine refugee.

Bogus asylum seeker is a catch-all concept encompassing various groups of foreigners, including those using irregular means of reaching the country in which they seek protection. Wide use of the concept by states means that numbers of asylum seekers are considered, not as genuine refugees, even if they fulfil the refugee criteria, but as economic migrants without the need for protection who abuse the laws of EU Member States and who should be deterred from doing so. The Recast Reception Directive is not a novel instrument in this respect and it reflects the established approach of the EU and Member States to irregular migration. The perception of asylum seekers arriving in the EU in an irregular manner as economic migrants or bogus asylum seekers has been expressed in a number of instances by EU institutions and Member States, for instance in the 2011 EU Communication on Migration.[17] The image of the economic or irregular migrant, who intends to enter EU territory in an irregular manner in the disguise of an asylum seeker, has hence become a common phantom, haunting the authorities of European states and prompting rapid and fierce responses.

However, turning an asylum seeker into a bogus asylum seeker constitutes only part of the process of fragmentation of the refugee subject. The perception of all asylum seekers as bogus asylum seekers is related to a particular understanding of who can be considered as a genuine refugee. Subjectivation of the genuine refugee happens through human rights law. Since human rights derive from the dignity of the human person, and not from their agency, the subject produced by human rights is not an active

17 According to the Commission, "[i]t is important to differentiate between irregular migrants (economic migrants trying to cross EU borders illegally), refugees or persons who may seek asylum, and people who are temporarily displaced. The legal status of these people, as well as help the EU can provide to them, is different." See also Kmak, "Producing Irregularity."

individual but rather a helpless subject.[18] In consequence, a genuine refugee has to fit into the idea of a passive and traumatised victim of human rights violations "unwillingly impelled by events, whose fate lies in the beneficent hands of the sovereign state."[19] According to Zagor it is exactly the idea of passivity of asylum seekers that gives states the power to exclude from protection those aliens tinted by the "apparent pathology of unauthorised arrivals," in other words, those who cross borders in an irregular manner.[20] This subjectivity of a genuine refugee, based on victimisation and passivity, requires that in order to be considered as deserving international protection, an asylum seeker must not only fulfil the criteria of the 1951 Refugee Convention but also convince the refugee authorities that their story fits the authorities' imagination of an authentic refugee story.[21] This in turn prompts asylum seekers to adjust their story to the required template. In turn, this display of agency and adjustments made by an asylum seeker in their story in order to obtain refugee status creates a perception of the asylum seeker as a liar or opportunist, and therefore a bogus asylum seeker.[22] We can see that as a result of this process, these two subjectivities – bogus asylum seeker and genuine refugee – operate in a circular manner: due to a limited number of places in the resettlement procedure and lack of possibilities to apply for asylum in the EU in a regular manner, asylum seekers are forced to use irregular ways of entering EU territory. This in consequence turns them into bogus asylum seekers. In order to convince the authorities that they are in fact genuine refugees, asylum seekers need to readjust their story, which turns them into liars and opportunists. These two subjectivities appear to reinforce each other, thus keeping the asylum seeker in what I call the subjectivity trap.

In the final section of this chapter I will uncover the processes that lead to creation of the subjectivity trap. I will in particular show how the trap is a consequence of the hegemonic understanding of the nation state as based on effective control over the population inhabiting a particular territory. I will also look at ways in which asylum seekers can challenge the subjectivity trap created by fragmentation of the refugee subjectivity.

Resisting the Subjectivity Trap

This mutual reinforcement of the subjectivities of the bogus asylum seeker and genuine refugee as a result of the conflict between obligations and preferences of states is based on the uneasy attitude of states towards the image of the Ugly, which challenges the national

18 Rene Ureña, No Citizens Here: Global Subjects and Participation in International Law, Academic Dissertation (University of Helsinki Printing House, 2010), 97.

19 Matthew Zagor, "The Oceanic Viking and Australia's Refugee Dilemma," East Asia Forum 26 (2009), www.eastasiaforum.org/2009/12/26/the-oceanic-viking-and-australias-refugee-dilemma/.

20 Ibid.

21 Matthew Zagor, Recognition and Narrative Identities: The Legal Creation, Alienation and Liberation of the Refugee, SSRN Scholarly Paper (Rochester, NY: Social Science Research Network, 2011), http://papers.ssrn.com/abstract=1906507, 24.

22 Ibid.

order of things.[23] In hegemonic legal discourses the concept of the nation state is inherently based on effective control of the population inhabiting a particular territory. This definition of statehood was generally recognised and expressed in article 1 of the 1933 Montevideo Convention on the Rights and Duties of States, which is firmly established as a norm of customary international law. According to article 1 of the Convention, the state as a subject of international law should possess a permanent population, defined territory, effective government and the capacity to enter into relations with other states. The multifaceted relationship between population and territory means that on the one hand, the state is understood as the "original subject of the right over its territory." On the other, the right of the state to territory depends on the original entitlement of the population constituting the state.[24] This means that the state guarantees citizens entitlement to the territory but at the same time the rights of citizens limit states' own right to territory. The absolute sovereign right over territory is therefore juxtaposed to the "reflexive right of the authority exerted over citizens."[25] For that reason, whereas the right of the state is limited by the entitlement of citizens to the territory, states exercise their right without limitations in the case of foreigners.[26] In consequence, international law creates a binary distinction between the citizen and the foreigner, which serves as the foundation for migration laws and policies.

The state's power over population and territory based on the binary distinction between citizens and foreigners operates through a number of technologies, in particular through the technology of citizenship and border technology. The aim of the former, based on the practice of expulsion or deportation of foreigners, is to differentiate between citizens and non-citizens. In the words of Walters: "... seen from an international perspective, deportation represents the compulsory allocation of subjects to their proper sovereigns." Its aim is to sustain an image of the world as divided into national populations.[27] On the other hand, the aim of border technology is to manage such recognised foreignness. According to De Genova, "if there were no borders, there would be no migrants – only mobility." The aim of borders is to turn mobility into migration and through this process to manage human mobility "sorting and ranking the free movement of people around the world into a different hierarchy of more or less permissible and more or less prohibited varieties of mobility."[28]

23 Liisa H. Malkki, "Refugees and Exile: From 'Refugee Studies' to the National Order of Things," Annual Review of Anthropology 24 (1995): 495–523.

24 Enrica Rigo, "Citizens despite Borders: Challenges to the Territorial Order of Europe," in The Contested Politics of Mobility: Borderzones and Irregularity, ed. Vicki Squire (London; New York: Routledge, 2012), 211.

25 Enrica Rigo, "The Right to Territory and the Contemporary Transformation of European Citizenship," in Citizenship Between Past and Future., ed. Engin F. Isin, Nyers Peter, and Bryan S. Turner (London: Routledge, 2008), 154.

26 Ibid., 155.

27 William Walters, "Deportation, Expulsion, and the International Police of Aliens," Citizenship Studies 6, no. 3 (2002): 282.

28 Nicolas De Genova, "Debate: The Free Movement of People around the World Would Be Utopian," n.d., www.nicholasdegenova.net/13.html.

All these concepts contribute to the production of different types of subjects including citizens, desirable foreigners, irregular immigrants or refugees. In other words, those classified as the Good, the Bad or the Ugly. The binary division between the citizen and the foreigner deriving from the territorial sovereignty of states is, however, contested in a number of ways. In particular, this division collapses in the image of a refugee, who through claiming protection based on international human rights instruments, challenges the right of the state to decide who can enter and reside in a territory. In other words it questions the theory of two-tiered authority of the state over the territory and population. This situation is well described by Agamben, according to whom "[i]f the refugee represents such a disquieting element in the order of the nation-state, this is so primarily because, by breaking the identity between the human and the citizen and that between nativity and nationality, it brings the originary fiction of sovereignty to crisis."[29] In order to reinforce sovereign control over the population and the territory the state juxtaposes its human rights obligations with the need to control borders and territory and protect citizens from various security threats and in consequence use the subjectivities of bogus asylum seekers and genuine refugees to manage forced migration.

These examples also show that the relationship between these categories of subjects is in flux and the borders between them are blurred. This means that there are always people, situations or categories that escape the territorial order of citizenship. According to Rigo, "[t]he territorial order of citizenship has always been an artificial construction that is impossible to reduce to natural facts such as geographically determined areas or birth within a given space"[30] This constructed character of citizenship constitutes a point of departure for actions aiming to resist the process of production of irregular immigrants or bogus asylum seekers and in consequence the basis of contemporary asylum and migration policies. Since the subjects of immigration laws are defined generally as persons who do not possess the citizenship of the countries in question, one of the ways of challenging contemporary asylum and migration policies would be through generation of new narratives of citizenship. These narratives need to derive from the process of dismantling the current hegemonic relationship between citizenship and territory and in consequence the binary distinction between citizen/foreigner and legal/illegal. In other words citizenship has to be conceptualised as based on mobility, not borders.[31]

One example of this approach to citizenship and belonging, which is able to challenge the hegemonic understanding of citizenship and go beyond the subjectivity trap, is the movement of Sans-Papiers (irregular immigrants) in France described by Anne Mc Nevin in her book titled "Contesting Citizenship: Irregular Migrants and the New Frontiers of the Political". The Sans-Papiers have been struggling for recognition of their rights in France since 1996. They underlined their important role in the French labour market and demanded recognition of their rights through such actions as strikes,

29 Giorgio Agamben, "Beyond Human Rights," n.d., 93, www.casadosaber.com.br/sabermais/2755/Agamben.BeyondHumanRights.pdf.

30 Rigo, "Citizens despite Borders," 210.

31 Rigo, "Citizens despite Borders."

occupation of a church or the union hall of the General Confederation of Labour. Their demands for recognition were, however, based not only on their importance to the labour market, as they argued for the right to reside to be granted also to those who did not and could not work such as the elderly and the sick. Through those actions Sans-Papiers manifested their presence and belonging regardless of their irregular status and insisted on the right to reside in France.[32] Some of them, for instance the authors of the open letter "To Our Sisters and Brothers in Africa: A Common Struggle for the Freedom of Movement and the Right to Stay," strove to challenge the dominant subjectivities of bogus/genuine asylum seekers. However, they did so by expressing a new subjectivity, deriving from the right to keep their future in their own hands and to move through artificially created borders, rather than insisting on their recognition as refugees.[33] As they wrote in their letter:

> When we, migrants, chosen to leave Africa, we did so as free woman and men. Some used to say that we are victims of hunger, wars, poverty, that we were forced to escape. It is often true. But we always decided to move because we had and we have a project, we want a possibility to keep our future in our hands. When we have chosen migration, we wanted to free ourselves from those who pretend that some are rich and the others poor, some Europeans, the others African, to free ourselves from a system of exploitation which has no borders, while it builds up borders and wars in order to exploit our needs and our projects, in Africa, as well as in Europe.[34]

In this example the Sans-Papiers can be conceptualised, after Rigo, as illegal citizens – those who by informal exercise of citizenship, by their claim to belonging, challenge the closeness and exclusiveness of the existing community based on a territorial understanding of citizenship.[35] This example shows how refugees and asylum seekers are able to resist imposed subjectivities and challenge the hegemonic understanding of belonging deriving from the principle of sovereignty of states and the division between citizen and non-citizen. They leave behind the triangle of the Good, the Bad and the Ugly and detach the discourse on statehood and citizenship from traditionally understood territoriality.

Conclusions

In this chapter I showed how subjectivities of asylum seekers are created and strengthened by legal and political discourses in the European Union. As an example of these processes I analysed the text of the recently adopted Recast Reception Directive, which despite its aim of aligning detention of asylum seekers with human rights requirements, may

32 Anne McNevin, Contesting Citizenship: Irregular Migrants and New Frontiers of the Political (New York: Columbia University Press, 2011), 152–53.

33 Ibid., 113.

34 Ibid., 112.

35 Rigo, "Citizens despite Borders," 204.

achieve the opposite effect when transposed by Member States. This approach is based on the fragmented refugee subject which derives from the conflict between human rights obligations and preferences of states and is based on the one hand, on the perception of those applying for protection in Europe as bogus asylum seekers or in other words, economic migrants who abuse asylum laws in order to enter EU territory and, on the other, on the particular concept of the genuine refugee. I also showed how EU migration policies reinforce these subjectivities, keeping those applying for protection in a subjectivity trap. This chapter also showed how mutual reinforcement of the subjectivities of bogus asylum seekers and genuine refugees is based on the uneasy relationship of states towards the image of "the Ugly," which challenges the national order of things based on territorial exercise of power by states.

But the aim of this paper was also to point out possible modes of resisting these dominant subjectivities. In order to do so, I showed examples of resisting the normalising quality of law and dismantling subjectivities imposed on migrants and asylum seekers by the law. Only through such acts of resistance to the concept of a bogus asylum seeker they are able to challenge the hegemonic understanding of belonging deriving from the principle of territorial sovereignty of states and the division between citizen and non-citizen. Even though the consequences of this approach to immigration go beyond the limits of our own understanding of international law, they allow us to come up with means to circumvent existing mechanisms of management of migration, which may eventually lead to their transformation in the future.

Bibliography

Agamben, Giorgio. "Beyond Human Rights," n.d. www.casadosaber.com.br/sabermais/2755/Agamben.BeyondHumanRights.pdf.

ECRE. "Comments from the European Council on Refugees and Exiles on the Amended Commission Proposal to Recast the Reception Conditions Directive (COM(2011)320 Final)," September 2011.

ECtHR. Lokpo and Touré v. Hungary (ECtHR 2011).

European Commission. "Amended Proposal for a Directive of the European Parliament and of the Council Laying down Standards for the Reception of Asylum Seekers (Recast)," June 1, 2011.

De Genova, Nicolas. "Debate: The Free Movement of People around the World Would Be Utopian," n.d. www.nicholasdegenova.net/13.html.

Directive 2013/33/EU of the European Parliament and of the Council of 26 June 2013 Laying down Standards for the Reception of Applicants for International Protection (recast), EU OJ L 180/96.

Kmak, Magdalena. "Limits of Sovereignty?: Rethinking the Conflict between Human Rights and Immigration in the European Union." Finnish Yearbook of International Law 20, no. 2009 (2011): 53–81.

— "Producing Irregularity – Management of Immigrants in the European Union." In Mobilités et Migrations: Figures et Enjeux Contemporains. Pluralité Des Regards et Des Disciplines, edited by Véronique Ancey, Gérard Azoulay, Chantal Crenn, Daniel Dormoy, André Mangu, and André Thomashausen, 267–279. Collection Presses Universitaires de Sceaux. Paris: L'Harmattan, 2014.

Malkki, Liisa H. "Refugees and Exile: From 'Refugee Studies' to the National Order of Things." Annual Review of Anthropology 24 (January 1, 1995): 495–523. doi:10.2307/2155947.

McNevin, Anne. Contesting Citizenship: Irregular Migrants and New Frontiers of the Political. Columbia University Press, 2011.

Meijers Committee. "Detention Provisions in the Recast Proposals for the Reception Conditions Directive and the Dublin Regulation and the Right to a Remedy with Suspensive Effect," May 16, 2012.

Mezzadra, Sandro, and Brett Neilson. Border as Method, Or, the Multiplication of Labor, 2013.

Peers, Steve. "Analysis: The EU Directive on Reception Conditions: A Weak Compromise." Statewatch, 2012. www.statewatch.org/analyses/no-184-reception-compromise.pdf.

Rigo, Enrica. "Citizens despite Borders: Challenges to the Territorial Order of Europe." In The Contested Politics of Mobility: Borderzones and Irregularity, edited by Vicki Squire, 197–215. London; New York: Routledge, 2012.

— "The Right to Territory and the Contemporary Transformation of European Citizenship." In Citizenship Between Past and Future, edited by Engin F Isin, Nyers Peter, and Bryan S. Turner. London: Routledge, 2008.

UNHCR. "Revised Guidelines on Applicable Criteria and Standards Relating to the Detention of Asylum Seekers," February 1999.

Ureña, Rene. No Citizens Here: Global Subjects and Participation in International Law. Academic Dissertation. University of Helsinki Printing House, 2010.

Walters, William. "Deportation, Expulsion, and the International Police of Aliens." Citizenship Studies 6, no. 3 (2002): 265–292. doi:10.1080/1362102022000011612.

Zagor, Matthew. Recognition and Narrative Identities: The Legal Creation, Alienation and Liberation of the Refugee SSRN Scholarly Paper. Rochester, NY: Social Science Research Network, 2011. http://papers.ssrn.com/abstract=1906507.

— "The Oceanic Viking and Australia's Refugee Dilemma." East Asia Forum, 26 2009. www.eastasiaforum.org/2009/12/26/the-oceanic-viking-and-australias-refugee-dilemma/.

Sanne van de Pol*

WELCOME TO THE MARGINS OF SOCIETY: AN ANALYSIS OF (CIVIC) INTEGRATION POLICY AND THE FUNDAMENTAL RIGHTS OF IMMIGRANTS

Introduction

Legally residing immigrants from third countries[1] are in many ways living on the margins of society in Europe and on the verge of crossing the outside-inside divide. Immigrants have to get used to life in the receiving country and transform themselves from being an "outsider" to being an "insider." This transition, however, does not come about without a struggle. Third country nationals (TCNs) do not hold the same rights as EU citizens, for example when it comes to spheres of immigration, access to the labour market, social benefits and family (re)unification. Besides that, third country nationals are often the object of compulsory civic integration policies in Western Europe. These policies are in place to incorporate immigrants into society and to manage, and as a logical consequence, to control ethno-cultural diversity. Not every migrant is obliged to follow integration courses, which amounts to differentiation and more importantly civic stratification. This chapter seeks to analyse the tensions that implementation of civic integration programmes can bring about when studied from the perspective of fundamental rights. In doing so, predominant focus will be on Flemish civic integration policy.

Flanders, a region of the federal state of Belgium, has full autonomous powers over matters related to immigrant integration. The Federal state of Belgium is in charge of immigration and asylum law (residence permits) and questions of naturalisation. Flanders has decided to focus on integration in multiple ways. On the one hand, broad integration policies exist that focus on several groups in society, specifically on more vulnerable groups such as (descendants of) migrants, caravan dwellers and refugees. This type of policy was fixed by the Minority Decree of 28 April 1998. On the other hand, a policy known as civic integration (*inburgering*) exists that focuses solely on (newly

* PhD candidate, Policy Research Centre on Integration, Government and Law Research Group, University of Antwerp.

1 Nationals of countries not belonging to the EU.

arriving) migrants and their incorporation into society through attending special integration courses. This policy was first introduced by the Flemish government by Decree of 28 February 2003. Recently, the Flemish government adopted a policy combining integration and civic integration. The Decree of 7 June 2013 on Flemish integration and civic integration will be implemented in the future.[2] The philosophy behind this policy largely remains the same. Further in this chapter, a more extensive description follows of civic integration taking into account the new policy. These policies are relevant for research purposes since, par excellence, tensions related to integration and fundamental rights come about. Creation of integration and civic integration policies constitutes the international and national responses of policy makers to increasing diversity. This is also the case in Flanders and leads to the following question: how does civic integration, (i) designed and implemented top-down by the government and supported by the majority, and (ii) made compulsory for some individuals (iii) interfere or conflict with a human rights perspective on freedom and equality? In answering this question tentatively, different tensions related to fundamental rights, migrants and civic integration policy are studied.

The analysis starts with an overview of national and international responses to increasing diversity followed by a more detailed description of integration and civic integration policy in Flanders. The next three parts are focused on predominant tensions related to civic integration and fundamental rights. These tensions are on the one hand situated at the intersection of civic stratification processes and on the other hand related to the migrant perspective of civic integration policy. This chapter explains how civic integration is maintained or even strengthened by civic stratification and how certain migrants are considered to live on the margins of society in both a figurative and a literal sense. From the migrants' perspective, learning the language and core (legal) norms, values and customs of a society helps them to live in the receiving society. Meanwhile, these policies and the framework in which newcomers need to integrate are designed by the majority group in society, which might not match the diverse reality within society. The last set of more general tensions relates to fundamental rights. Before concluding this chapter, a brief note touches on the possible emancipatory power of fundamental rights over integration within society.

(Inter)national Responses to Increasing Diversity

Increased movement of people throughout the world has brought about significant changes in both sending and receiving countries. In traditional migrant receiving countries, e.g. in Western Europe, today's society is characterised by an ever growing ethnic diversification. As a response, European "immigration countries" respond to diversification with campaigns for unity and integration.[3]

2 This might change the practical execution of these policies. At the time of writing, it is too early to foresee these practical changes regarding this policy as its implementation is still awaited.

3 Christian Joppke, *Citizenship and Immigration. Vol. 2* (Cambridge: Polity Press, 2010).

The topic of integration has slowly been pulled to the European policy level, where migration is increasingly regulated. In 1999, at the Tampere summit, the European Council asked for a more vigorous integration policy and more cooperation between countries. This was the first inter-ministerial conference of great importance for integration policy in Europe. At the 2002 Seville summit, the European Council pointed to the need to develop a common policy on the separate, but closely related, issues of asylum and immigration.[4] Under the Dutch presidency, a list of parameters for integration policy was published: the Common basic principles for immigrant integration policy.[5] Later followed the Handbooks on integration for policy-makers and practitioners.[6] In 2005, the Common Agenda for Integration and the Framework for the integration of Third Country Nationals provided a general framework for TCN integration.

Although the European Union faces a rather wide variety of initiatives concerning (civic) integration,[7] some note a convergence between European state policies on immigrant integration.[8] For example, Joppke discerns a focus on obligation as a shared feature of all civic policies.[9] These policies contain a strong focus on duties and a relative neglect of rights. Consequently, different traditional integration models in EU countries are moving towards each other. Others, such as Jacobs and Rea argue that despite some convergence in policy for newcomers, sufficient divergence continues to exist across nation state policies.[10] According to Jacobs and Rea, national models remain important but a strict distinction between multiculturalism and assimilation[11] is not necessarily as valid in the new millennium.[12] However, this again points towards the convergence

4 European Parliament. *European Council Seville Conclusions of the Presidency*, June 21–22, 2002.

5 European Commission. *Common Basic Principles for Immigrant Integration Policy*. ed. Justice and Home Affairs Council. 2004.

6 European Commission, *Handbook on Integration for Policy-Makers and Practitioners*. ed. Freedom and Security Directorate-General Justice, 2004; European Commission, *Handbook on Integration for Policy-Makers and Practitioners*, ed. Freedom and Security Directorate-General Justice, 2007; European Commission, *Handbook on Integration for Policy-Makers and Practitioners*, ed. Freedom and Security Directorate-General Justice, 2010.

7 For a systematic overview see MIPEX, Migrant Integration Policy Index, 2013, accessed June 6, 2013. www.mipex.eu/.

8 Christian Joppke, "Beyond National Models: Civic Integration Policies for Immigrants in Western Europe," *West European Politics* 30, no. 1 (2007): 1.

9 Ibid., 14.

10 Dirk Jacobs and Andrea Rea, "Open Forum: The End of National Models? Integration Courses and Citizenship Trajectories in Europe," *International Journal on Multicultural Societies* 9, no. 2 (2007): 264–83.

11 For more information, see Adrian Favell, *Philosophies of Integration: Immigration and the Idea of Citizenship in France and Britain* (New York: Palgrave Macmillan, 2001). Put simply, multiculturalism and assimilation are two opposing philosophies on immigrant integration. Multiculturalism is an ideology that cherishes diversity within a unified society. Different policies can be developed for different (ethnic) groups. Assimilation is an ideology that wishes to diminish differences between groups for a unified society. This republican ideal is that every citizen is equal, regardless of their (ethnic) background.

12 Jacobs and Rea, "The End of National Models? Integration, Courses and Citizenship Trajectories in Europe" 5.

thesis of Joppke. The development of integration policies strongly connects to the role states and integration philosophies play in the European era of migrant integration. What role do they play today?

This interconnects with the debate on the power and prevalence of the nation state in the context of migration. Joppke summarises two very different positions with a central role for the nation state.[13] One perspective emphasises the enduring power of the nation state, capable of resistance to change through immigration because of immigration and citizenship policies and restrictions.[14] Important in this respect is the influence of official state categories. State choices can become part of social reality by making alternatives hard to think of.[15] In Flanders, the terms *autochthonous* (native) and *allochthonous* (non-native) have influenced ethnic categorisation in society. The term allochthonous today makes the Flemish think of, and has become synonymous for, Turkish and Moroccan migrants, whereas the original term was not ethnically connoted as such.[16] This illustrates the power of state classifications. The second perspective sees migration, and more specifically migrants' rights, as a manifestation of an emergent "post-national" society in which migrants can increasingly draw on transnational rights located outside of the nation state, rendering national citizenship redundant.[17] Joppke opts for a middle position. "Neither is the nation-state simply reaffirmed by recent migratory challenges, nor is it undergoing fundamental transformation."[18] However, according to Morris, neither of these perspectives offers an adequate basis for a full understanding of either the migrant experience or the political responses it has provoked. Instead of "national closure" or "post-national expansion," a differentiated system of rights – civic stratification – aids in understanding the transnational dimension of (citizenship) rights.[19]

Despite the debate on diversification versus convergence and the debate on the power of the nation state in a transnational era, more and more countries are also applying immigration, integration and citizenship trajectories. Responses to increasing diversity through migration can be captured under the heading of civic integration. Below, the focus shifts to Flemish civic integration policy, which is analysed so as to capture the tensions between this policy and a fundamental rights perspective on freedom and equality.

13 Christian Joppke, *Immigration and the Nation-state: the United States, Germany, and Great Britain* (Oxford: Oxford University Press, 1999).

14 See Rogers Brubaker, *Citizenship and Nationhood in France and Germany. Vol. 21* (Cambridge: Cambridge University Press, 1992).

15 Godfried Engbersen, "La misère du monde: sociaal lijden in de hedendaagse samenleving," in *Het oeuvre van Pierre Bourdieu*, ed. Jacques Tacq (Antwerpen/Apeldoorn: Garant Uitgevers, 2003), 135–36.

16 Noel Clycq, *Van keukentafel tot "God": Belgische, Italiaanse en Marokkaanse ouders over identiteit en opvoeding* (Antwerpen/Apeldoorn: Garant Uitgevers, 2009).

17 See: Yasemin Nuhoglu Soysal, *Limits of Citizenship: Migrants and Postnational Membership in Europe* (Chicago: University of Chicago Press, 1994).

18 Joppke, *Immigration and the Nation-state*, 4.

19 Lydia Morris, "Managing Contradiction: Civic Stratification and Migrants' Rights," *International Migration Review* 37, no. 1 (2003): 74–5.

Integration and Civic Integration Policy in Flanders

Civic integration policy has been developed to create awareness and familiarisation with language, societal norms and values, and the Flemish labour market. This must allow "newcomers" to participate and integrate in society. It is based on the Belgian legal system, societal norms and values and fundamental rights as internationally recognised. The Dutch term for this course and policy – *Inburgering* – means no less than the active process of *becoming a citizen*. In Flanders, integration policy comprises four main components: independent and proportional participation, accessibility of regular facilities, active and shared citizenship and strengthening of social cohesion.[20] Independent and proportional participation focuses primarily on (legally resident) people who were born without Belgian nationality or whose parent(s) do not have Belgian nationality at birth. These policies are also directed at persons in a situation of obvious deprivation as well as Travellers. Emancipation of these groups is one policy goal. Secondly, integration policy aims at equal participation in regular facilities, regardless of people's background, and active and shared participation by everyone. Thirdly, active and shared citizenship is a major objective. This entails taking up citizenship rights, responsibilities and engagement with society. The fourth goal is attaining social cohesion through living together in diversity.[21] While this general integration policy gives attention to both migrants and other groups in society, civic integration policy specifically focuses on recent migrants.

The civic integration programme in Flanders is composed of four parts. These are: (i) a basic course in the Dutch language, (ii) societal orientation, (iii) counselling towards work, education or use of free time and (iv) personal general counselling during the entire process. Each person will have a particular coach to guide them and follow-up on their trajectory. Although not everyone is obliged to follow this trajectory, it is obligatory for the following: A) foreigners over 18, registered, living in a municipality of the Flemish Region, who have a first residence permit of more than three months; B) Belgian nationals over 18, born outside Belgium of at least one foreign-born parent who, for the first time, have not been registered in Flanders for more than a year; C) newly arriving minors with a non-Dutch mother tongue who turn 18 in the first year of their residence of minimally three months; D) religious servants/leaders in religious community recognised by the Flemish government.[22]

Integration courses to guide migrants in the process of becoming citizens have been designed to take migrants out of the margins of society. This can be taken both literally and figuratively in terms of immigrants. Some migrants actually live in the margins of society, regularly or irregularly, segregated in a poor urban neighbourhood away from mainstream society. This is, however, not the main reason to use the word margin. Obliging certain – not all – newcomers to take part in a civic integration course suggests that these people are not full citizens so far despite their legal presence on national soil.

20 Vlaamse Overheid, *Decreet betreffende het Vlaamse integratie- en inburgeringsbeleid*, 2013.

21 *Ibid.*

22 *Ibid.*

The very idea of *inburgering*, teaching new migrants how to be a citizen, illustrates this. Civic integration courses are designed to take these migrants out of these margins and to provide them with "tools," enabling them to function in the receiving society. Except for knowledge of the language, these tools are also composed of knowledge of society. A commission of policy makers, scholars and representatives of civic organisations was appointed by the government to develop the ideal material for the course on societal orientation.[23] In this course, the norms and values of Flemish society, as vested in internationally recognised fundamental rights and the Constitution, are central. Special reference is made to both legal and social norms and values. Although the latter are less clear-cut and not really enforceable, according to the Commission migrants can benefit from knowledge of these norms and values.[24] The Commission identified five main norms and values. Firstly, *freedom* is made up of values such as freedom of opinion, freedom of religion, freedom of expression. Secondly, *equality* (and non-discrimination) form part of the most fundamental principles in the legal system. Every form of discrimination or exclusion on the basis of race, skin colour, ethnic or national background is prohibited. Equality between the sexes is also emphasised. A third important value is *solidarity*, based on equality and justice. This is vested in ideologies both religious and secular in nature. Flemish society has both legal and social norms in terms of solidarity. Real-life tensions related to these norms are discussed during the course. Fourthly, *respect*, strongly related to human dignity, is the next value. Since real-life tensions such as racism and xenophobia do exist, tolerance and dialogue are discussed. The fifth central value is *citizenship*. These five most important values within society exist within three "sets of norms and values": democracy, the constitutional state and pluralism.[25] A course established by the Commission and designed in accordance with these principles informs migrants on many aspects relevant to daily life.

Tensions Created by Civic Integration

The civic integration programme has the ability to create multiple tensions within society, endangering integration. Some of these tensions are discussed below. Strengthening civic stratification and classification along the lines of social groups in society that can be enforced by civic integration constitutes the first tension. A second set of tensions connects with the perspective of migrants (in the civic integration programme) and their view on integration. Thirdly, various tensions related to fundamental rights are touched upon.

Civic Stratification

One significant set of tensions arises from a distinction made between citizens. Flanders distinguishes between EU citizens and third country nationals (TCNs). This is not

23 Vlaamse Regering, *Eindverslag: Commissie "ter invulling van de cursus maatschappelijke oriëntatie,"* 2006.

24 *Ibid.*, 16.

25 *Ibid.*, 17–34.

uncommon; other EU countries also make the same distinctions between national citizens, citizens of other EU member states and third country nationals.[26] For citizens of the EU, the right to reside in another member state is automatic (under certain circumstances) and regulated by Directive 2000/38/EC on the right of citizens of the Union and their family members to move and reside freely within the territory of the member states. They are considered to be exempted from the obligation to follow integration courses, as such an obligation might hinder their free movement from one member state to another. Family members of EU citizens enjoy this freedom of movement as well, even if they are TCNs. During or after exercise of free movement by their EU family member, they cannot be subjected to demands with regard to their integration in the host society. Civic integration programmes can only be followed on a voluntary basis.

For other third country nationals, however, states are allowed to create requirements with regard to the "integration" of immigrants. The existence of this differentiation in terms of civic integration therefore indicates that social and legal differences exist between categories of people. These are created by the receiving country and inherent to the concept of the European Union and the free movement of its citizens, a freedom that does not exist for third country nationals. This is closely connected to the important influence of politics and the state in determining the view of society and the consequent division of social reality into groups.[27] Morris has already suggested that an emergent civil stratification sorts migrants into different positions in an inclusory and exclusory manner.[28]

As civic integration has been made compulsory for specific groups of individuals, it needs to comply with the demands of a liberal state and its fundamental rights and liberties. These rights and freedoms protect people's individual identities within the limits of democratic society as well as the rights and freedoms of others. In civic integration programmes, migrants do not officially have to replace their particular cultures and identities with those of the dominant majority in the receiving country. However, migrants have to adapt in a certain way and, as Joppke notes, the emphasis of civic integration programmes lies on the obligations and duties of migrants.[29] In official policy documents and academic publications, the concept of integration is often described as a two-way process. In Flanders, integration is thought of as "a dynamic and interactive process in which individuals, groups, communities and facilities, each departing from a context of enforceability of rights and duties inherent to the democratic legal state, relate to each other and deal with migration and its consequences in a

26 This resonates with the idea of "primordial autochthony" which states that a dominant (majority) ethnic group in society has the primordial right – as native inhabitants of this specific nation – to decide what the rules, policy, legislation, ... are. Eugene Roosens, *Eigen grond eerst? Primordiale autochtonie: dilemma van de multiculturele samenleving* (Leuven: Acco, 1998).

27 Pierre Bourdieu, *Méditations pascaliennes. Vol. 316* (Paris: Seuil, 1997), 44–5; Rogers Brubaker, Mara Loveman, and Peter Stamatov, "Ethnicity as Cognition," *Theory and Society* 33, no. 1 (2004): 34; Clycq, *Van keukentafel tot "God."*

28 Hynes et al., "Sociology and Human Rights: Confrontations, Evasions and New Engagements," *The International Journal of Human Rights* 14, no. 6 (2010): 825; Morris, "Managing Contradiction."

29 Joppke, "Beyond national models," 14.

constructive way."[30] Despite the official definition portraying integration as a two-way process, the question arises: how much room is given to the perspective of newcomers? How do individual identity constructions and civic integration relate to one another? This relationship is important for an understanding of which steps are needed to reach an inclusive society.

Migrant Perspective

A second set of tensions arises from the migrant's perspective towards civic integration policy. This is closely connected to the distinction made between those obliged to follow the trajectory and those who are exempted.

While we can argue that these civic integration programmes have been implemented with the best intentions, offering a possibility to learn about the culture and language of a country in order to facilitate participation and give migrants the opportunity to function within society, another reading is possible. These programmes can also be considered to be restrictive. We can argue that a specific way of life is imposed with norms and values that are said to exist in wider society. Firstly, fundamental rights and the core norms, values, customs and traditions of the receiving country make up the framework according to which one should live in the receiving country. This raises expectations on the part of immigrants about their reception and life in the receiving society that might not tally with their daily experience. In real life, the values portrayed above might be more distant for new immigrants than expected. This is not surprising since people tend to judge their own behaviour differently from that of others. This makes it plausible that at a societal level as well, a discrepancy exists between norms and values, as documented above, and actual practice. Whereas norms and values such as freedom, equality, solidarity, respect and citizenship are deemed central in Flemish society, migrants are likely to experience behaviour contradictory to those values. An illustration of this is provided by the Belgian Equality Body that registers all claims related to discrimination. Racial and religious discrimination claims are most prominent, showing how central values are not always lived up to in reality.[31] Discrimination and xenophobia, for example, make some migrants appeal for rights such as respect for private and family life, freedom of religion and non-discrimination, illustrating existing tensions.

Secondly, integration and civic integration programmes have been created in a desire to control and manage ethno-cultural diversity. In most countries, this integration is thought of as additive acculturation and entails the idea that one can maintain one's original culture and identity and *add* the "new culture and identity."[32] It is supposed to encompass a recognition and appreciation of differences as well. However, in practice, tensions become apparent and civic integration courses are mostly designed top-down

30 Vlaamse Overheid, *Kernbegrippen en opdrachten van het integratie- en inburgeringsbeleid*, 2012.

31 Centrum voor Gelijkheid van Kansen en Racismebeschrijding, *Jaarverslag 2012 discriminatie en diversiteit* (Brussels: Centrum voor Gelijkheid van Kansen en Racismebeschrijding, 2013), 65.

32 Roosens, *Eigen grond eerst?*, 162–4.

and one-way. They disregard the fact that integration is a multi-way and multilateral process. Civic integration policy has been designed to control and manage "otherness," which could be defined as ethnic, national, cultural, religious and linguistic differences within society.[33] Trying to characterise civic integration, we see that it has been designed to introduce "others" to a specific way of life, and to specific norms and values.

Thirdly, civic integration strongly emphasises duties while to a certain extent neglecting rights. Migrants are obliged to follow integration courses but duties are also emphasised in the course. The content of the course seems to focus more strongly on duties than (fundamental) rights. This is all the more surprising since central values identified by the Commission on Civic Integration are said to provide the basis for policy. In real terms, as portrayed in the course, daily life in society entails more practical duties and responsibilities than abstract (fundamental) rights.

Fourthly, despite policy and academic definitions of integration being a multi-way process, migrants remain the target group of such policy. Although migrants play a pivotal role in the wider societal integration process, the receiving society should not be put aside. The question remains how to incorporate the (dominant) majority of the receiving society in this process, not just as the designer of civic integration courses but also as the recipient of new ways of life and perspectives provided by newcomers.

Civic Integration and Fundamental Rights

Other and different kinds of tension can arise that directly relate to fundamental rights. Steiner and Alston recognise two distinct kinds of tension. On the one hand, an asserted (allegedly) universal norm can be challenged. This happens when a norm itself is said to be non-universal or conflicting with certain (religious) traditions. In the Flemish case, that would mean that one of the central norms and values identified is not as widely accepted within society after all. For example, the central value of solidarity is challenged by attempts to refrain from paying taxes, or by budget cuts that mainly infringe on the lives of the weakest in society. Such acts do not seem to be compatible with the idea of solidarity. On the other hand, a conflict could arise between rights that are all recognised in leading human rights instruments, which makes it an internal conflict. Tensions are then often linked to the boundaries of certain rights in certain contexts.[34] When the rights of one person conflict with the rights of others, as is often the case with relative rights such as freedom of speech and freedom of religion, a balance needs to be found.

Gender is another pre-eminent source of tension between different fundamental rights. Gender roles can be inspired by certain traditions, customs and religion and this could interfere with the commonly accepted framework of norms and values in Flanders. This should be acknowledged during the civic integration course.

33 Sergio Carrera, *Integration of immigrants in EU law and policy*, March 7, 2013, at Université Libre de Bruxelles, Brussels, 2013.

34 Henry J. Steiner and Philip Alston, *International Human Rights in Context: Law, Politics, Morals: Text and Materials* (New York: Oxford University Press, 2000), 403.

Furthermore, civic integration might create an even larger stratification within society. Not only is not every migrant obliged to participate but there is also the question whether a migrant manages to pass a (non-obligatory) test that might be implemented in the future. It remains to be seen whether this test will indeed be installed and what consequences this will have, but it has already sparked fierce and worrisome reactions. Through this non-obligatory test, migrants could run the risk of being excluded from facilities such as social housing and professional education on the basis of their formal level of civic integration. Whereas legally, migrants who are obliged to participate in civic integration programmes only have to be present at a considerable amount of classes to comply with civic integration requirements, migrants could, if they so wish, also pass a test. Aside from proof of participation that shows the efforts the student has gone to, there is now a possibility to obtain a certificate of civic integration (*inburgeringsattest*). In order to receive this certificate, one needs to meet the requirements prescribed by the education system dealing with societal orientation and mastery of Dutch at a sufficient level (*Niveau richtgraad 1, Waystage*). The Flemish Council of Education (VLOR) understands that this certificate can be useful for some migrants but that it could also turn into a measure of exclusion. For most illiterate or weakly literate people, the level to be achieved (in terms of writing skills) is too high so that they would never be able to obtain a certificate. Therefore, the VLOR states that the certificate should be prevented from becoming a requirement for further (social) facilities such as social housing and further education possibilities.[35]

In Flanders, attention should be paid to tensions like these since civic integration policy might not only be about enabling migrants to participate in society. As to integration policies, Henrard stresses that integration without assimilation would entail effective integration of certain groups and the possibility or permission to maintain their particular characteristics. This system would have to be based on two pillars, namely prohibition of discrimination on the one hand and measures to protect and promote a specific identity (of minority groups) on the other.[36] This is vitally important for the well-being of people in society as a whole, regardless of being a migrant or not. Below, the possible emancipatory power of fundamental rights will be considered within the context of civic integration.

Civic Integration and Fundamental Rights as an Emancipatory Tool

In this chapter, much emphasis has been put on tensions and restrictions and so far an emancipatory function has been left aside. This is because human rights of migrants and the possible emancipatory effect of rights in the western world have been under-studied. Most sources refer to people outside the western world or women in general who could

35 Vlaamse Onderwijsraad, *Advies over het voorontwerp van decreet betreffende het Vlaamse integratie- en inburgeringsbeleid*, 2012.

36 Kristin Henrard, "The interrelationship between individual human rights, minority rights and the right to self-determination and its importance for the adequate protection of linguistic minorities," *The Global Review of Ethnopolitics* 1, no. 1 (2001): 43.

benefit from human rights. Bond provides an overview of women's human rights violations and treaties covering gender from an intersectional perspective.[37] Henrard focuses on minority protection and human rights and interestingly notices that most states, and some scholars also, see long-standing ties with the country of residence and/or nationality a necessary condition in order to be considered a minority.[38] Minority rights are a branch of human rights, albeit limited in scope for migrant minorities. The strict definition of a minority would, for example, entail that in the Netherlands, the Friesians (who are of non-migrant origin), would be considered a minority whereas Moroccan and Turkish migrant groups would not. Migrant groups, even if already present for decades, would fall outside this narrow reading of the minority concept focusing on *original* minorities. This is particularly important in terms of social, economic and cultural rights and minority entitlement to benefits accordingly. This approach may in principle exclude "new" or immigrant minorities, in turn entailing that legally residing (third country) immigrants are kept outside of the fundamental rights debate. Moreover, within Europe less public attention seems to be focused on human rights in relation to integration. Policies have been elaborated for fundamental rights and it seems to be widely assumed that Western European countries do not have fundamental rights issues when it comes to immigrant integration. A civil and political rights approach to these tensions could clarify the position. Since EU nationals and some third country nationals to a certain extent have voting rights, it could be presumed that the democratic process ensures their rights sufficiently. However, full enjoyment of all fundamental rights for everyone is still a utopia.

In this discussion, I would like to raise the question as to the enabling side of human rights in terms of integration policy. In civic integration policy, the duties and rights of migrants are central, whereas the receiving society is largely left aside. Civic integration focuses on the migrant's integration into the receiving society while integration is a societal (not individual) multi-way process. The receiving society should also be incorporated in civic integration. In Madsen and Verschraegen, an analysis of Durkheim's work is provided which emphasises this enabling side of rights.[39] Whereas the liberal concept of rights, state and law is merely negative, entailing removal of arbitrary legal impediments, Durkheim also stressed the positive, enabling side of rights. This idea can be beneficial for migrant integration and should be explored further. One could imagine a civic integration policy emphasising both the rights and duties of migrants in close connection with the rights and duties of all members of society. Awareness of human rights among migrants is important but general awareness within society is even more crucial to the smooth functioning of society. Especially when it comes to relative rights, such as freedom of expression and freedom of religion, interaction between actors

37 Johanna E. Bond, "International Intersectionality: A Theoretical and Pragmatic Exploration of Women's International Human Rights Violations," *Emory Law Journal* 52 (2012): 71–186.

38 Kristin Henrard, "Charting the gradual emergence of a more robust level of minority protection: Minority specific instruments and the European Union," *Netherlands Quarterly of Human Rights* 22, no. 4 (2004): 561.

39 Mikael Rask Madsen and Gert Verschraegen, *Making Human Rights Intelligible* (Oregon: Hart Publishing, 2013), 67.

determines what rights and duties people have. The right of one person can be restricted legitimately by the rights of another. Creating general awareness about this among migrants and wider society could have an important emancipatory effect, not only on migrants but also on society as a whole. This deserves further academic attention.

Conclusion

This chapter has explored the tensions between (civic) integration policy and fundamental rights. An overview has been given of what integration policy entails and how certain TCN migrants are both in a literal and figurative sense living on the margins of society. On the one hand it has been shown how civic integration policy is of an ambiguous nature in that it enables migrants to function within society after having been introduced to its central norms and values. On the other hand, civic integration policy also has its restrictive side leading to tensions. Not all (TCN) migrants are obliged to follow such a trajectory which insists upon a certain framework according to which one should live. In real life, tensions are likely to arise in terms of these values. Discrimination, racism and xenophobia could also be part of migrants' lives, which makes the focus of the programme on central norms and values in society a distant story. The tensions explored in this chapter relate to civic stratification, the migrant perspective and fundamental rights in relation to civic integration. The last section of this work, dedicated to discussion, has shown how a focus on fundamental rights in (civic) integration policy might result in empowerment. However, this catalyst function of fundamental rights for integration needs a change in the philosophy of integration, focusing not solely on migrants but on society as a whole.

Bibliography

Bond, Johanna E. "International Intersectionality: A Theoretical and Pragmatic Exploration of Women's International Human Rights Violations. " *Emory Law Journal* 52 (2012): 71–186.

Bourdieu, Pierre. *Méditations pascaliennes. Vol. 316.* Paris: Seuil, 1997.

Brubaker, Rogers. *Citizenship and Nationhood in France and Germany. Vol. 21.* Cambridge: Cambridge University Press, 1992.

Brubaker, Rogers, Mara Loveman and Peter Stamatov. "Ethnicity as Cognition." *Theory and Society* 33, no. 1 (2004): 31–64.

Carrera, Sergio. *Integration of Immigrants in EU Law and Policy,* March 7, 2013, at Université Libre de Bruxelles, Brussels, 2013.

Centrum voor Gelijkheid van Kansen en Racismebeschrijding. *Jaarverslag 2012 discriminatie en diversiteit.* Brussels: Centrum voor Gelijkheid van Kansen en Racismebeschrijding, 2013.

Clycq, Noel. *Van keukentafel tot "God": Belgische, Italiaanse en Marokkaanse ouders over identiteit en opvoeding.* Antwerpen/Apeldoorn: Garant Uitgevers, 2009.

Engbersen, Godfried. "La misère du monde: sociaal lijden in de hedendaagse samenleving." In *Het oeuvre van Pierre Bourdieu,* edited by Jacques Tacq, 131–44. Antwerpen/Apeldoorn: Garant Uitgevers, 2003.

European Commission. *Common Basic Principles for Immigrant Integration Policy.* edited by Justice and Home Affairs Council, 2004

— *Handbook on Integration for Policy-Makers and Practitioners.* edited by Freedom and Security Directorate-General Justice, 2004.

— *Handbook on Integration for Policy-Makers and Practitioners.* edited by Freedom and Security Directorate-General Justice, 2007

— *Handbook on Integration for Policy-Makers and Practitioners.* edited by Freedom and Security Directorate-General Justice, 2010.

European Parliament. *European Council Seville Conclusions of the Presidency* 21 and 22 June 2002.

Favell, Adrian. *Philosophies of Integration: Immigration and the Idea of Citizenship in France and Britain.* 2 ed. New York: Palgrave Macmillan, 2001.

Henrard, Kristin. "The interrelationship between individual human rights, minority rights and the right to self-determination and its importance for the adequate protection of linguistic minorities." *The Global Review of Ethnopolitics* 1, no. 1 (2001): 41–61.

— 2004. "Charting the gradual emergence of a more robust level of minority protection: Minority specific instruments and the European Union." *Netherlands Quarterly of Human Rights* 22, no. 4 (2004): 559–84.

Hynes, Patricia, Michele Lamb, Damien Short and Matthew Waites. "Sociology and Human Rights: Confrontations, Evasions and New Engagements." *The International Journal of Human Rights* 14, no. 6 (2010): 811–32.

Jacobs, Dirk, and Andrea Rea. "The End of National Models? Integration Courses and Citizenship Trajectories in Europe." *International Journal on Multicultural Societies* 9, no. 2 (2007): 264–83.

Joppke, Christian. *Immigration and the Nation-state: the United States, Germany, and Great Britain*. Oxford: Oxford University Press, 1999.

— "Beyond National Models: Civic Integration Policies for Immigrants in Western Europe." *West European Politics* 30, no. 1 (2007):1–22.

— *Citizenship and Immigration. Vol. 2*. Cambridge: Polity Press, 2010.

Madsen, Mikael Rask, and Gert Verschraegen. *Making Human Rights Intelligible*. Oregon: Hart Publishing, 2013.

MIPEX. *Migrant Integration Policy Index*. 2013. [cited June 6, 2013]. Available from www.mipex.eu/.

Morris, Lydia. "Managing Contradiction: Civic Stratification and Migrants' Rights." *International Migration Review* 37, no. 1 (2003): 74–100.

Roosens, Eugene. *Eigen grond eerst? Primordiale autochtonie: dilemma van de multiculturele samenleving*. Leuven: Acco, 1998.

Soysal, Yasemin Nuhoglu. *Limits of Citizenship: Migrants and Postnational Membership in Europe*. Chicago: University of Chicago Press, 1994.

Steiner, Henry J., and Philip Alston. *International Human Rights in Context: Law, Politics, Morals: Text and Materials*. New York: Oxford University Press, 2000.

Vlaamse Onderwijsraad. *Advies over het voorontwerp van decreet betreffende het Vlaamse integratie- en inburgeringsbeleid*. 2012.

Vlaamse Overheid. *Kernbegrippen en opdrachten van het integratie- en inburgeringsbeleid*. 2012.

— *Decreet betreffende het Vlaamse integratie- en inburgeringsbeleid*. 2013.

Vlaamse Regering. *Eindverslag: Commissie "ter invulling van de cursus maatschappelijke oriëntatie."* 2006.

Sam Bennett*

PERFORMING CITIZENSHIP AND INTEGRATION IN THE UK

Introduction

It is only since the end of the Second World War that certain European countries, such as the United Kingdom, have witnessed large scale immigration, which was brought about by certain processes including decolonisation and European integration. As well as changes to the extent, there have also been changes in the reasons for migration. Initially, in the post-war period migrants moved to the UK to fill short-term labour needs and it was not expected that they would settle for good. As a result, migrants were not seen as potential future citizens[1] and so immigration and nationality legislation did not deal with integration. More recently though there has been a shift in migration patterns to one of more permanent migration which has been precipitated by pull factors (greater economic opportunity and an overall better quality of life) as well as traditional push factors (conflicts or environmental disasters). Combined, this greater level of migrants and the shift towards permanent migration and settlement has called into question and disrupted the dominant expressions of national identity and community which had hitherto been held to be solid and self-explanatory. New migration trends also forced states to confront whether, and how, to integrate newcomers.

As DaLomba argues, a migrant's legal status can greatly influence the breadth and depth of their integration into their new country of residence.[2] Likewise, whether or not a person has citizenship of their country of residence (COR) can affect access to services and democratic rights (to vote) as well as delineating what activities they can participate in and therefore also imposes limits to integration. As such, migrants are left in a situation whereby potential integration into a new country's society is blocked, or at the very least, hindered, by their legal status. The integration of migrants though rests not only on their legal status but is further complicated by how the issue is discursively constructed by politicians in policy documents and in the media. In the UK public sphere, integration is

* Department of Cognitive Linguistics, Faculty of English, Adam Mickiewicz University, Poznań.

1 Marco Martinelli, "Political Participation, Mobilisation and Representation of Migrants and Their Offspring in Europe," in *Migration and Citizenship: Legal Status, Rights and Political Participation*, ed. Rainer Bauböck (Amsterdam: Amsterdam University Press, 2006).

2 Sylvia Da Lomba, "Legal Status and Refugee Integration: A UK Perspective," *Journal of Refugee Studies* 23, no. 4 (2010): 415–36.

constructed as a two-way process whereby the responsibility for integration is shared between incoming migrants, who must adapt, and existing populations who should welcome the diversity that migration brings and facilitate easier integration. In reality though, this rhetoric hides the assimilatory nature of integration policies and legislation which coerce newcomers into becoming like those already "inside" the nation-state. As such, both integration and citizenship policies can be seen as "technologies of corrective citizenship."[3] Within this framework, I argue that citizenship, understood as a discursively constructed, normative, conception of how to act and interact, plays an important normative role in directing integration. I argue that migrants are increasingly being asked to "act out" integration via displays of "good citizenship" before they are given legal citizenship. I term this *"performative integration."* The sites of these performances are legal, social, cultural and political and can often be ritualised, as in the case of citizenship ceremonies, but they also appear in how newcomers are expected to act.

In this paper I will initially explain the connections between integration and citizenship. I will then argue for a discursive interpretation of integration within the UK public sphere which moves between political, media and wider social sites and that the current discursive construction of integration is based upon an understanding of citizenship that revolves around neo-liberal concepts of self-sufficiency and not relying on the state. This underpins my proposition that integration is a performative act, that is, that migrants need to act as good neo-liberal citizens in order to integrate into British society. Finally, in order to give my theoretical argument some grounding via some discursive evidence, I will critically analyse two extracts from a local British newspaper which, together, indicate this neo-liberal conception of citizenship and the pressure to perform a specific formulation of integration.

Citizenship and Integration

Citizenship is a difficult concept to pin down; it is certainly more traditionally associated with the official legal status of membership of a given (national) community as opposed to inclusion into a society and societal norms, although there are obviously a number of overlaps. Nation states "reify belonging into formal citizenship"[4] and it is certainly true that formal citizenship is where migration and integration intersect with the law. As argued above, a person's legal status theoretically reflects a person's position regarding the state and brings with it assumptions as to allegiances and commitment to the (national) community.[5] The "achievement" of citizenship also serves a normative function by indicating the level of integration which is expected (for example, linguistic proficiency) of migrants. Moreover, the conditions set for citizenship also indicate how

3 Anne-Marie Fortier, "The Politics of Scaling, Timing and Embodying: Rethinking the 'New Europe'," *Mobilities* 1, no. 3 (2006): 320.

4 Deborah Reed-Danahay and Caroline Brettell, "Introduction," in *Citizenship, Political Engagement and Belonging: Immigrants in Europe and the US*, ed. Deborah Reed-Danahay and Caroline Brettell (London: Rutgers University Press, 2008), 10.

5 Da Lomba, "Legal Status and Refugee Integration."

willing a government is to allow certain types of migrant to join the "national" community.

This legal-political conception notwithstanding though, within the social sciences there is now a general acceptance that there is more to citizenship than merely formal membership of a state and that there also exists an active element to it which, I would argue, overlaps with integration. Various writers have forwarded conceptions of citizenship that go beyond the simply legal question of which state a person belongs to. For example distinctions have been made by Neveu[6]: horizontal relations (relations among citizens) vs vertical relations (relations with the state and its institutions); Stewart[7]: "state citizenship" vs "democratic citizenship" and Balibar[8]: a strict sense of citizenship (political rights) vs a "broad sense" i.e. the "cultural initiative or effective presence in the public sphere (the capacity to be 'listened to' there)." However, most relevant for this paper is Kymlicka and Norman's differentiation between "citizenship-as-legal-status and citizenship-as-desirable-activity."[9] As will become clear later on, this conception fits well with a theory of performative integration because it highlights both the normative nature of non-formal citizenship and the assimilatory nature of this integration.

UK governmental policy throughout Labour's time in power, and under the coalition government today, has constructed citizenship as one of the foundations of the integration process.[10] The two areas often overlap so that policy provisions for encouraging citizenship are sometimes replicated in integration and immigration policy papers. Indeed, it would not be possible to fully understand the British government's approach to integration without also investigating their policies on citizenship.

Citizenship has been spoken of in government policy as a "privileged bond"[11] whereas immigration status involves a more distant relationship with the country of residence. Yet despite governmental policy pronouncements during the 2000s that "continuity and sense of purpose" aid integration,[12] the government proceeded to introduce a number of measures that arguably created barriers to integration and to acquiring citizenship. One such example was the removal the right of Indefinite Leave to Remain (ILR) for those granted refugee status. Instead, nearly all refugees were now given Limited Leave to Remain (LLR) and their status was subject to five-year reviews. This new review system reduced the chances of permanence and a settled future (via acquiring British citizenship) which provides a substantial motivation to integrate as there is logically little compulsion to integrate if there is a real risk of having to return to the country of origin. As well as a

6 Catherine Neveu, "European Citizenship, Citizens of Europe and European Citizens," in *The Anthropology of the European Union*, ed. Irene Bellier and Thomas Wilson (Oxford: Berg Publishers, 2000).

7 Angus Stewart, "Two Conceptions of Citizenship," *British Journal of Sociology* 46, no. 1 (1995): 63–78.

8 Etienne Balibar, "Propositions on Citizenship," *Ethics* 98, no. 4 (1988): 724.

9 Will Kymlicka and Wayne Norman, "Return of the Citizen: A Survey of Recent Work on Citizenship Theory," *Ethics* no. 104 (1994): 353.

10 Da Lomba, "Legal Status and Refugee Integration."

11 Ibid., 420.

12 Home Office, *Indicators of Integration: Final Report* (London: Stationery Office, 2004).

less settled short-term future, those with LLR status also have fewer rights and have less access to state support.[13]

This difficulty in acquiring citizenship is further compounded by two other factors, firstly the need for language proficiency, despite a simultaneous cutting of the budget for English as a Second Language (ESOL) lessons and further eligibility restrictions for asylum seekers and refugees in terms of access to lessons. Secondly, the requirement to take and pass a citizenship test was introduced.[14] The combination of LLR and more restricted access to ESOL lessons, combined with the governments' belief that integration can only start after the grant of refugee status, produces further barriers to integration.[15] Together, I would argue that these measures indicate a confused government message on the place of citizenship in integration and the place of integration in citizenship. On the one hand citizenship is increasingly harder to acquire, and on the other hand integration is expected before citizenship can be acquired.

Like citizenship, the term "integration" is a distinctly ambiguous one, which is indeed part of the reason why its use is so widespread and accepted within public discourse over immigration in the UK. Favell has argued that the need for maintaining order within a polity leads to and necessitates a "social inclusive unity," the basis of which are certain terms with which everyone can align within mainstream politics.[16] These terms allow for a political and social consensus and therefore provide both a framework and justification for certain policies. Similarly for Stråth, the value of "integration" as a term around which policies and politicians can coalesce lies in this ambiguity which facilitates the realisation of the "goals of holistic unification."[17] According to McPherson, the term's broad uptake and usage across political and media fields in Australia "inhibits articulation of an alternative perspective" and the same can be said for the United Kingdom.[18] As McPherson notes, the lexical unit "integration" has a neutral or even positive semantic load. It can be seen as an acceptable discursive middle ground between; on the one hand the concept of multiculturalism which according to some politicians has failed[19] and, on the other hand, the term assimilation which since WWII has lost much of its legitimacy. As such, use of the term is acceptable for nearly all political persuasions because of its emptiness and potential for

13 Gareth Mulvey "When Policy Creates Politics: The Problematizing of Immigration and the Consequences for Refugee Integration in the UK," *Journal of Refugee Studies* 23, no. 4 (2010): 437–62.

14 Nationality, Immigration and Asylum Act 2002.

15 Steve Kirkwood, "'It Is about Integration': The Discursive Construction of Integration among Professionals Who Work with Asylum Seekers and Refugees in Scotland" presented at the Migration: Economic change, social challenge, April 6, 2011, University College London.

16 Adrian Favell, *Philosophies of Integration: Immigration and the Idea of Citizenship in France and Britain* (London: Palgrave Macmillan, 1998).

17 Bo Stråth, "Multiple Europes: Integration, Identity and Demarcation of the Other," in *Europe and the Other and Europe as the Other*, ed. Bo Stråth (Brussels: Peter Lang, 2010), 395.

18 Melinda McPherson, "'I Integrate, Therefore I Am': Contesting the Normalizing Discourse of Integrationism through Conversations with Refugee Women," *Journal of Refugee Studies* 23, no. 4 (2010): 550.

19 David Cameron, "PM's speech at Munich Security Conference," February 5, 2011, accessed October 15, 2013, www.gov.uk/government/speeches/pms-speech-at-munich-security-conference.

representing many policy options or perspectives on how the state manages new entrants.

There are then a number of overlaps between citizenship and integration. A country's approach to citizenship will greatly influence integration policies, in particular who is allowed to enter and what hurdles they have to meet before legal citizenship is granted. Discursively, the two policy fields are also linked in terms of intertexual reference to one policy in documents of the other policy and in the type of wording used.

Discursive Constructions of Integration

Though rhetorically held up as a beacon of reasonable reaction to the issue of immigration, the discursive construction of integration, of which citizenship is a major part in UK governmental policy, points to a more assimilatory understanding of the term.

Integration and citizenship policies, either separate documents or contained within immigration policy, are highly normative. They express official government opinion and indicators to the intended recipients (the electorate, the media and, more obliquely, migrants themselves) of what is expected of newcomers, what is deemed as acceptable/unacceptable behaviour, and what the process of integration includes. The normative nature of these policies is linguistically evidenced by the use of modal verbs indicating necessity ("need to"), recommended behaviour ("should"/"ought to"), obligation ("must"/"have to") and impermissibility ("can't") throughout the documents. Integration and citizenship policies therefore also pronounce, explicitly or otherwise, what type of member of society and what type of citizen new migrants are expected to become, or as Fortier writes, these policies and their practical application, can be seen as "technologies of corrective citizenship."[20]

According to Lewis, UK policies purportedly promote tolerance of cultural difference but only within quite narrowly defined boundaries, which actually belies a "normalising discipline" contained within the provisions and language of the policies.[21] Lewis points to a pamphlet written by Tony Blair in 1998 entitled *The Third Way* in which he wrote that the government would seek to promote "tolerance *within agreed norms*" (emphasis added) and that "strong communities" depended on "shared values and a recognition of the rights and duties of citizenship not just the duty to pay taxes and obey the law, but the obligation to bring up children as competent, responsible citizens."[22] Discursively we see a movement whereby the positive liberal democratic concepts of tolerance, rights and citizenship are qualified by caveats such as "within agreed norms" or "obligation to bring up children as... responsible citizens." A similar move is present in *Building Cohesive Communities*, a report from the ministerial Group on Public Order and Community Cohesion published in the wake of the disturbances in Bradford and Oldham in 2001:

20 Fortier, "The Politics of Scaling," 320.

21 Gail Lewis, "Welcome to the Margins: Diversity, Tolerance and Policies of Exclusion." *Ethnic and Racial Studies* 23, no. 8 (2005): 536.

22 Tony Blair, *The Third Way: New Politics for the New Century* (London: Fabian Society, 1998), 12.

> Our society is multicultural, and it is shaped by the interaction between people of diverse cultures. There is no single dominant and unchanging culture into which all must assimilate. The public realm is founded on negotiation and debate between competing viewpoints, at the same time as it upholds inviolable rights and duties. Citizenship means finding a common place for diverse cultures and beliefs, *consistent with our core values…*[23]

As with the first examples from Tony Blair, in this paragraph diversity is first praised and constructed as a positive feature of modern British life (though in reality, much of the UK remains relatively homogenously white) and again mitigated by the claim that there is only space for diverse cultures and beliefs with the scope of "our core values." Here the possessive pronoun "our" is (intentionally) vague. It can be read inclusively as pertaining to the core values of everyone living in the UK, or can be read exclusively as relating to a more parochial/nationalist conception of British identity. When the first part of the sentence, "finding a common place for," is included in the analysis it appears to lean more towards the second reading. "Finding a place" for something implies insertion into a pre-existing object, much like a children's toy where blocks of certain shapes need to be placed into the correct holes and only those shapes (or migrants) who fit the mould will be successful.

This assimilationist, or at best, narrow definition of tolerance and integration became more pronounced after the disturbances in Bradford and Oldham and 9/11 in 2001. Whereas previously integration had focussed on new immigrants, those awaiting a decision or those trying to enter the country (asylum seekers, refugees and economic migrants), government policy was now enlarged to include a focus on settled Muslim communities, some of whom had lived in the UK for multiple generations. Indeed, McPherson argues that the integration policies post 9/11 conceived of social cohesion as being only possible via greater levels of conformity.[24] Connected to this, within the UK, there has historically been a widespread and commonly accepted strategy of discursively linking black families to social pathologies. That is, readers or recipients of a discourse are already "primed" via familiar schema and stereotypes so that explicit racialisation is no longer needed.[25] This is evident within the UK discourse on integration where there has been a notable de-racialisation of language via a focus on "communities" which enables discourse participants to avoid explicitly naming specific ethnic and minority groups whilst at the same time ensuring that their subject matter is clear, for example "those communities that continue the practice of arranged marriages."[26]

There is also a secondary dual discursive move in play whereby firstly certain migrant cultures, and by extension migrants themselves, are problematised as a barrier to integration and secondly, the "native" culture is privileged. Within policy and professional

23 Home Office. *Building Cohesive Communities: Report of the Ministerial Group on Public Order and Community Cohesion* (London: Stationery Office, 2001), 3.12, emphasis added.

24 McPherson, "I Integrate, Therefore I Am."

25 Claire Worley, "It's Not about Race. It's about the Community: New Labour and Community Cohesion," *Critical Social Policy* 25, no. 4 (2005): 483–96.

26 Home Office, Secure Borders, Safe Haven: Integration with Diversity in Modern Britain. (London: Stationery Office, 2002), 18; following Worley, "It's Not about Race," 488.

research, integration is often constructed as a two-way process in which the government, the (undefined) "wider community," and migrants all need to work together in order for integration to be successful.[27] This is often bound up in a language of rights and duties, i.e. the right of refugees to work and live where they want[28] and the "duty to integrate."[29] However, as noted above, this works to obfuscate the more assimilatory nature of integration and citizenship policies. Within discourses of integration, whether in the press, by politicians or wider society, migrants, and indeed sometimes foreigners in general, are constructed as a problem to be dealt with[30] and the inside is presumed to be unproblematic.[31] For example, for Hughes, the language in the UK government's immigration policies constructs secure borders as a precondition for harmonious social relations.[32] If correct, then it can be inferred that increased entry will upset societal harmony. Consequently the responsibility for a failure to integrate is placed with newcomers or sometimes, as with post-2001 UK, settled communities who were also British citizens.[33] Thus, despite being "advertised" as integrationary, migration policy will necessarily be assimilatory in terms of its provisions because they, *a priori*, privilege the receiving community.

In addition to this, in many migration policies refugees and other migrants are constructed as deficient and backward and in need of changing or even civilising.[34] Discursively, two archetypal migrants are constructed: on the one hand there are "good" migrants; ones that need protecting, are "like us" or can contribute economically and therefore deserve to be civilised. On the other hand, there are "bad" ones who need treating harshly because they present a threat or are so different from "us" that it is impossible to integrate them. The "good migrants" will be constructed as having minimal differences, whereas bad ones will be constructed as being radically different. As noted above this racialisation of certain migrants is discursively masked behind an outward commitment to tolerance[35] and the deracialised language of community cohesion.[36] Likewise, racialised differences might be couched in terms of culture or a failure to adhere to vaguely defined shared values rather than race.

27 Alison Ager and Alistair Strang, "Understanding Integration: A Conceptual Framework," *Journal of Refugee Studies* 21, no. 2 (2008): 166–91; McPherson, "I Integrate, Therefore I Am."

28 Home Office, *Building Cohesive Communities.*

29 Tony Blair, "Speech on Multiculturalism and Integration," December 8, 2006. www.itnsource.com/shotlist/ITN/2006/12/08/R08120603/?v=1&a=0.

30 Kristine Horner and Jean-Jacques Weber, "Not Playing the Game: Shifting Patterns in the Discourse of Integration," *Journal of Language and Politics* 10, no. 2 (2011): 139–59.

31 Jan Blommaert and Jef Verschueren, *Analysing the Rhetoric of Tolerance* (London: Routledge, 1998).

32 Gordon Hughes, "Community Cohesion, Asylum Seeking and the Question of the Stranger," *Cultural Studies* 21, no. 6 (2007): 931–51.

33 Arun Kundnani, "Integrationism: The Politics of Anti-Muslim Racism," *Race and Class* 48, no. 4 (2007): 24–44.

34 McPherson, "I Integrate, Therefore I Am." Blommaert and Verschueuren, *Analysing the Rhetoric of Tolerance.*

35 Blommaert and Verschueren, *Analysing the Rhetoric of Tolerance.*

36 Worley, "It's Not About Race."

A Neo-Liberal Understanding of Citizenship and Performing Integration

The section above attempted to explain the issues surrounding citizenship-as-legal-status and their implications for integration and section 3 introduced a discursive understanding of integration. At this juncture, though, I would like to return to the ideas of citizenship-as-desirable-activity and policies as technologies of corrective citizenship. I will elaborate the idea of a neo-liberal construction of citizenship which was introduced earlier. Moreover, I will argue that it plays a major role in the modelling of what migrants are expected to do in order to "successfully" integrate and furthermore that such an understanding of citizenship is also useful in making clear both the discursively constructed and assimilatory nature of integration policy in the UK.

Since the introduction of neo-liberal politics and economics under firstly Margaret Thatcher and later Blair, the provision of social welfare has slowly declined in the UK, and indeed the same is true for most EU states. There is now greater political emphasis from all the major parties on individual responsibility and success and a move away from reliance on the state that stems more generally from liberal capitalism and the privileging of the market place as the dominant domain of action within society. The same holds true for how citizenship is now construed and talked about. For Ong the "neo-liberal technologisation of government" means that citizens' well-being is now down to themselves and their own capacities to "confront globalised insecurities."[37] Thus, being a good citizen includes being at the very least both a minimal burden on the state (and your fellow citizens) and an active participant in the economy.[38] Politicians increasingly speak of the responsibility to self-improve and help the country grow (via action in the economy). This is especially evident in UK political discourse since the most recent economic crisis and the "strivers vs shirkers" debate in the public sphere in which British residents are crudely categorised into those that work hard and contribute to the economy and those that do not and instead rely on government aid.[39] Via explicit discursive processes, "the good citizen" is bestowed with certain qualities such as producer, consumer and tax-payer. In opposition to this, to be dependent on state assistance via benefits somehow precludes a person from being conceived of as a full citizen. For Ong, those who "can't climb the ladder or self govern" are labelled as deviant or risky and therefore transgress the market-oriented norms of society.[40] However, I would go one step further than Ong and argue that it is not just about the ability to climb the ladder, but also it is about the (discursive) exclusion of some people from the means to climb the ladder that leads to them being labelled as second class citizens.

For migrants, and especially asylum seekers and refugees, who at least initially work generally in low-paid jobs or rely on welfare, the situation is therefore even more difficult.

37 Aihwa Ong, "(Re)Articulations of Citizenship," *Political Science and Politics* 38, no. 4 (2005): 698.

38 Aihwa Ong, "Cultural Citizenship as Subject-Making: Immigrants Negotiate Racial and Cultural Boundaries in the United States. Comments and Reply," *Current Anthropology* 37, no. 5 (1996): 737–62.

39 Anna Coote and Sarah Lyall, "Strivers vs Skivers: Real Life's Not like That at All," *Guardian*, April 11, 2013. www.guardian.co.uk/commentisfree/2013/apr/11/strivers-v-skivers-divisive-notion?CMP=twt_gu.

40 Ong, "(Re)Articulations of Citizenship," 698.

For example, the right for asylum seekers to undertake paid work was withdrawn in 2002. They thus have to rely on welfare and as a result are seen as less capable, less self-dependent and a greater burden on the taxpayer. More recently, new UK immigration policy has stipulated a minimum income before visas and permanent stays for family members are accepted.[41] This is a possible explanation for why some asylum seekers, and by the process of conceptual slippage, some refugees and migrants, are not accorded full citizenship status. This is clearly partly due to the fact that they are not permanent residents but it is also down to them being legally stopped from being productive participants in the market place and reliant on state benefits. It is a short conceptual move from this position to their discursive construction as "scroungers" who "skive off the state."

The current debate over citizenship thus includes a normative assessment of the extent and type of economic activity of potential applicants. However, this is but one facet of the concept and there is also a racialised, gendered and familial side to the neo-liberal understanding of citizenship. Lepofsky and Fraser argue that this normative element has a white middle class family as its focal point.[42] Likewise, for Ong notions of self sufficiency and consumer power, which are central to being a good citizen, are associated with a masculinised whiteness.[43] Certainly, within political discourse, the potential for success is not outwardly precluded by membership of any cultural or racialised group. However, these successes, and subsequent integration and acceptance into the community, necessitate the migrant subject "whitening" themselves and conversely, if success is whitened, then, in the US context on which Ong writes, welfare dependency is blackened.[44] This may not be fully applicable to the UK situation but it should be remembered that welfare reliance is one of the dominant features within representation of asylum seekers, refugees and other migrants.

The arguments presented in this paper so far lead us to the point where it appears clear that for a migrant to become a fully accepted member of society (Kymlicka and Normans' citizenship-as-desirable-activity), they have to act "like" other "good" citizens, at least in public. To be clear, I am arguing that acceptance within a given society is only possible via performative acts. Citizenship has for a long time been about both legal status and performance but there has been a recent shift in emphasis to the latter in terms of policy and discourse to the extent that legal status is only guaranteed after performative acts.[45] A number of authors provide similar arguments: With reference to the Dutch context, Roggeband and Verloo note that whereas previously social and economic integration was a precondition for cultural integration, nowadays new migrants are expected to be culturally similar and integrated before entry into social and economic

41 United Kingdom Borders Agency, "Immigration Directorate Instructions. Annex FM Section FM 1.7. Financial Requirement," (United Kingdom Borders Agency, 2012). www.ukba.homeoffice.gov.uk/sitecontent/documents/policyandlaw/IDIs/chp8-annex/section-FM-1.7.pdf?view=Binary.

42 Jonathan Lepofsky and James Fraser, "Building Community Citizens: Claiming the Right of Place-Making in the City'," *Urban Studies* 40, no. 1 (2003): 127–42.

43 Ong, "Cultural Citizenship as Subject-Making."

44 Ibid.

45 Lepofsky and Fraser, "Building Community Citizens."

sites of life.[46] Likewise, in the USA Roxworthy argues that there is a common belief that citizenship will be bestowed "based simply upon the performance of a codified repertoire of speech acts and embodied acts, ranging from the recitation of the Oath of Citizenship to public participation in patriotic pageantry and even enlistment in the armed services."[47] For Kostakopolou the obligation to show a sufficient degree of integration is deeply embedded in certain symbolic practices.[48] These may be institutionalised, such as citizenship ceremonies, but integration also includes an expectation of "smaller" performances which occur in various situations. Indeed, potential migrants are often expected to be better citizens than the current population. For example, in the UK, the threat from government ministers that taking part in certain legal activities such as demonstrations might jeopardise citizenship applications[49] and the policy that if migrants undertake fifty hours of voluntary community service, their citizenship application can be dealt with more swiftly.[50] The alternative view of this is that, if one does not undertake voluntary work, the application will be delayed by a year, which might place applicants who cannot volunteer (the sick, elderly or those caring for children) at a disadvantage. Following Butler, Roxworthy proposes a vital component of the performance of citizenship as the "performativity of the gaze" that forces the migrant into becoming like the "inside."[51] The way in which migrants are looked at, discursively constructed and projected necessitates this performativity and decides upon whether they are deemed integrated or even able to integrate. If migrants, especially asylum seekers, are discursively constructed culturally as radically different, and legally restricted from being economically self-sufficient, then in order to be accepted into society, that is, in order to integrate, they will be expected to alter this state. In effect they have to be, or at least act like, the dominant in-group by performing integration. Some of these expectations are of course unreasonable given that a migrant's legal status will greatly impact on their potential actions.

This "performative integration" reflects Butler's theory of performativity and the externally established decided conditions in which a person constructs their identity. Individuals do not invent social, economic and cultural practices.[52] Rather, "we are outside ourselves, constituted in cultural norms that precede and exceed us."[53] Power, and here I mean discursive power, to establish the "performativity of the gaze," not only

46 Conney Roggeband and Mieke Verloo, "Dutchwomen Are Liberated, Migrant Women Are a Problem," *Social Policy and Administration* 41, no. 3 (2007): 271–88.

47 Emily Roxworthy, *The Spectacle of Japanese American Trauma: Racial Performativity and World War Two* (Honolulu: University of Hawai'i, 2008), 13.

48 Dora Kostakopolou, "Why Naturalisation?" *Perspectives on European Politics and Society* no. 4 (2003): 85–115.

49 Andrew Sparrow and Vikram Dodd, "Immigrants Will Have to 'Earn' Citizenship, Says Phil Woolas," *Guardian*, August 3, 2009. www.guardian.co.uk/uk/2009/aug/03/immigrations-citizenship-points-phil-woolas.

50 Borders, Citizenship and Immigration Act 2009.

51 Roxworthy, *The Spectacle of Japanese American Trauma*, 14.

52 Bronwyn Davies, "Subjectification: The Relevance of Butler's Analysis for Education," *British Journal of Sociology of Education* 27, no. 4 (2006): 425–38.

53 Judith Butler, *Precarious Life: The Powers of Mourning and Violence* (London: Verso, 2004), 45.

forms the migrant subject but also creates and sets the conditions for their continued presence in their country of residence.

In order to highlight instances of the pressure to perform integration and the consequences of not doing so, I now turn to two excerpts from a local newspaper in the UK, the *Brighton and Hove Argus*. The first excerpt pertains to Mohammed Samad, an asylum seeker living in the area, and his battle against extradition, and the second to the case of Delshad Aziz, also an asylum seeker, found guilty of causing death by dangerous driving.[54]

> He has paid his taxes in full and become a hugely popular member of the community and a key player for Henfield Cricket Club.[55]

> Aziz, 28, had no driving license and no insurance and was living on benefits in Britain while he appealed a decision not to grant him asylum.[56]

In the first example, within this short sentence there are a number of indicators of successful performative integration and the main protagonist is constructed as being very much part of the community. Firstly, with regard to a neo-liberal construction of integration, Mr Samad is described as paying his taxes "in full," which is something that is expected of all "good" citizens. Thus, it can be deduced that the opposite would be true, namely that non-payment of taxes is an undesirable action and something that might preclude membership from the community. Secondly, Mr Samad's character is constructed by modifying the nominative and predicative "popular member" with an intensifying adverb, "hugely." Finally, his already positive standing is further augmented by reference to his participation in the symbolic, almost ritualised activity of local cricket which is a quintessentially British event so that highlighting this facet of his life cements his successful integration into British life. This is maybe an alternative to Norman Tebbit's infamous "cricket test" for migrants.[57] It is also worth noting that this sentence was repeated verbatim twice more in articles about Mr Samad's situation, and so through this repetition readers could have been left in no doubt that he was located positively within the community.

In stark contrast, in the second excerpt Mr Aziz is constructed as multiply deficient. Firstly, he failed to possess certain things that are expected of reasonable, law-abiding

54 For a more extensive linguistic exploration of the construction of integration in the *Brighton Argus*, see Samuel Bennett et al., "The Representation of Third Country Nationals in European News Discourse: Journalistic Perceptions and Practice," *Journalism Studies* 7, no. 3 (2013): 248–265.

55 Miles Godfrey, "'Perfect Citizen' Faces Being Kicked out," *Brighton Argus*, April 11, 2007. www.theargus.co.uk/news/1321021._Perfect_citizen__faces_being_kicked_out/?ref=arc.

56 Nigel Freedman, "Family of Portslade Victim Slam Death Crash Driver's Sentence," *Brighton Argus*, April 13, 2010. www.theargus.co.uk/news/8094859.Family_of_Portslade_victim_slam_death_crash_driver_s_sentence/.

57 This was a comment made by the Conservative MP, Norman Tebbit about the loyalty of migrants to the UK: "A large proportion of Britain's Asian population fail to pass the cricket test. Which side do they cheer for? It's an interesting test. Are you still harking back to where you came from or where you are?" Darcus Howe, "Tebbit's Loyalty Test Is Dead," *New Statesman*, July 3, 2006.

citizens (driving license and insurance). Secondly, the neo-liberal conception of citizenship is evident in his construction as "living on benefits" and therefore, not only not contributing to the community but actively taking from it. This is extra information that is not relevant to his driving at all and therefore we can assume that it was a deliberate lexical choice that this description of him was included in the article. Finally, he is described by using the nominative "asylum seeker," who, as argued above, are constantly portrayed as outside the community. In a further move, asylum seeking is linked to crime, which is a common theme within media reporting.[58] Taken together, Mr Aziz could not be more different from Mr Samad: One has performed integration successfully and as a result is discursively constructed as very much on the "inside," whereas the other due to the foregrounding of his reliance upon benefits and immigration status, has "failed" to integrate.

Conclusion

In this paper I first highlighted the connection between integration and citizenship. I then argued that integration is discursively constructed in UK governmental policy. Following this, I forwarded a neo-liberal construction of citizenship, that acts as a technology of corrective citizenship and then I proposed my concept of "performative integration." Finally, in an attempt to give some textual evidence to support the argument constructed throughout this paper, I offered two brief excerpts of media discourse on integration.

When migrants arrive into the UK and intend to settle they are to all intents and purposes "auditioning" for permanent roles in British society in order to be successful. There is a "tension" between, on the one hand, how the Labour government constructed integration as two-way and, on the other hand, the actual policy, laws and public discourse. They need to be seen as authentic and similar to the existing members of the group as well as not possessing any (cultural) threat. In order to be accepted, they are expected to perform certain identities, the parameters of which are set by the country of residence via governmental policy (especially immigration policy and community cohesion) and the media. Migrants are increasingly being asked to "perform" integration by acting in certain ways that are characterised by a gendered and racialised neo-liberal understanding of citizenship-as-desirable-activity which privileges economic activity and rewards self-sufficiency.

These markers of integration are not objective but are constructed within the mediated public sphere. The conditions of integration (language requirements, formal citizenship, cultural similarity and an adherence to "common values") are set by the "inside."[59] It is then the responsibility of those on the outside to perform what is required of them. Given this, the idea of "successful integration" can therefore be seen to be a false goal as there is not necessarily any clear endpoint where migration is seen as authentic or even complete.[60]

58 Bennet et al., "The Representation of Third Country Nationals."
59 Horner and Weber, "Not Playing the Game," 146.
60 Ibid.

Bibliography

Ager, Alison, and Alistair Strang. "Understanding Integration: A Conceptual Framework." *Journal of Refugee Studies* 21, no. 2 (2008): 166–91.

Balibar, Etienne. "Propositions on Citizenship." *Ethics* 98, no. 4 (1988): 723–30.

Bennett, Samuel, Jessika Ter Wal, Artur Lipiński, Małgorzata Fabiszak, and Krzyzanowski, Michał. "The Representation of Third Country Nationals in European News Discourse: Journalistic Perceptions and Practice." *Journalism Practice* 7, no. 3 (2013): 248–265.

Blair, Tony. *The Third Way: New Politics for the New Century.* London: Fabian Society, 1998. — "Speech on Multiculturalism and Integration." December 8, 2006. www.itnsource.com/shotlist/ITN/2006/12/08/R08120603/?v=1&a=0.

Blommaert, Jan, and Jef Verschueren. *Analysing the Rhetoric of Tolerance.* London: Routledge, 1998.

Butler, Judith. *Gender Trouble: Feminism and the Subversion of Identity.* New York: Routledge, 1990.

— *The Psychic Life of Power.* Stanford: Stanford University Press, 1997.

— *Precarious Life: The Powers of Mourning and Violence.* London: Verso, 2004.

Cameron, David. "PM's speech at Munich Security Conference." February 5, 2011. Accessed October 15, 2013. www.gov.uk/government/speeches/pms-speech-at-munich-security-conference.

Coote, Anna, and Lyall Sarah. "Strivers vs Skivers: Real Life's Not like That at All." *Guardian*, April 11, 2013. www.guardian.co.uk/commentisfree/2013/apr/11/strivers-v-skivers-divisive-notion?CMP=twt_gu.

Da Lomba, Sylvia. "Legal Status and Refugee Integration: A UK Perspective." *Journal of Refugee Studies* 23, no. 4 (2010): 415–36.

Davies, Bronwyn. "Subjectification: The Relevance of Butler's Analysis for Education." *British Journal of Sociology of Education* 27, no. 4 (2006): 425–38.

Favell, Adrian. *Philosophies of Integration: Immigration and the Idea of Citizenship in France and Britain.* London: Palgrave Macmillan, 1998.

Fortier, Anne-Marie. "The Politics of Scaling, Timing and Embodying: Rethinking the 'New Europe'." *Mobilities* 1, no. 3 (2006): 313–31.

Freedman, Nigel. "Family of Portslade Victim Slam Death Crash Driver's Sentence." *Brighton Argus*, April 13, 2010. www.theargus.co.uk/news/8094859.Family_of_Portslade_victim_slam_death_crash_driver_s_sentence/.

Godfrey, Miles. "'Perfect Citizen' Faces Being Kicked out." *Brighton Argus*, April 11, 2007. www.theargus.co.uk/news/1321021._Perfect_citizen__faces_being_kicked_out/?ref=arc.

Home Office. *Building Cohesive Communities: Report of the Ministerial Group on Public Order and Community Cohesion.* London: Stationery Office, 2001.

— *Secure Borders, Safe Haven: Integration with Diversity in Modern Britain.* London: Stationery Office, 2002.

— *Indicators of Integration: Final Report.* London: Stationery Office, 2004.

Horner, Kristine, and Jean-Jacques Weber. "Not Playing the Game: Shifting Patterns in the Discourse of Integration." *Journal of Language and Politics* 10, no. 2 (2011): 139–59.

Howe, Darcus. "Tebbit's Loyalty Test Is Dead." *New Statesman*, July 3, 2006.

Hughes, Gordon. "Community Cohesion, Asylum Seeking and the Question of the Stranger." *Cultural Studies* 21, no. 6 (2007): 931–51.

Kirkwood, Steve. "'It Is about Integration': The Discursive Construction of Integration among Professionals Who Work with Asylum Seekers and Refugees in Scotland" presented at the Migration: Economic change, social challenge, April 6, 2011, University College London.

Kostakopolou, Dora. "Why Naturalisation?" *Perspectives on European Politics and Society* no. 4 (2003): 85–115.

Kundnani, Arun. "Integrationism: The Politics of Anti-Muslim Racism." *Race and Class* 48, no. 4 (2007): 24–44.

Kymlicka, Will, and Wayne Norman. "Return of the Citizen: A Survey of Recent Work on Citizenship Theory." *Ethics* no. 104 (1994): 352–81.

Lepofsky, Jonathan, and James Fraser. "Building Community Citizens: Claiming the Right of Place-Making in the City'." *Urban Studies* 40, no. 1 (2003): 127–42.

Lewis, Gail. "Welcome to the Margins: Diversity, Tolerance and Policies of Exclusion." *Ethnic and Racial Studies* 23, no. 8 (2005): 536–58.

Martinelli, Marco. "Political Participation, Mobilisation and Representation of Migrants and Their Offspring in Europe." In *Migration and Citizenship: Legal Status, Rights and Political Participation*, edited by Rainer Bauböck, 52–64. Amsterdam: Amsterdam University Press, 2006.

McPherson, Melinda. "'I Integrate, Therefore I Am': Contesting the Normalizing Discourse of Integrationism through Conversations with Refugee Women." *Journal of Refugee Studies* 23, no. 4 (2010): 546–70.

Mulvey, Gareth. "When Policy Creates Politics: The Problematizing of Immigration and the Consequences for Refugee Integration in the UK." *Journal of Refugee Studies* 23, no. 4 (2010): 437–62.

Neveu, Catherine. "European Citizenship, Citizens of Europe and European Citizens." In *The Anthropology of the European Union*, edited by Irene Bellier and Thomas Wilson, 119–36. Oxford: Berg Publishers, 2000.

Ong, Aihwa. "Cultural Citizenship as Subject-Making: Immigrants Negotiate Racial and Cultural Boundaries in the United States. Comments and Reply." *Current Anthropology* 37, no. 5 (1996): 737–62.

— "(Re)Articulations of Citizenship." *Political Science and Politics* 38, no. 4 (2005): 697–99.

Perching, Bernard. "EU Citizenship and the Status of Third Country Nationals." In *Migration and Citizenship: Legal Status, Rights and Political Participation*, edited by Rainer Bauböck, 67–82. IMISCOE Reports. Amsterdam: Amsterdam University Press, 2006.

Reed-Danahay, Deborah, and Caroline Brettell. "Introduction." In *Citizenship, Political Engagement and Belonging: Immigrants in Europe and the US*, edited by Deborah Reed-Danahay and Caroline Brettell, 1–17. London: Rutgers University Press, 2008.

Roggeband, Conney, and Mieke Verloo. "Dutchwomen Are Liberated, Migrant Women Are a Problem." *Social Policy and Administration* 41, no. 3 (2007): 271–88.
Roxworthy, Emily. *The Spectacle of Japanese American Trauma: Racial Performativity and World War Two.* Honolulu: University of Hawai'I, 2008.
Sparrow, Andrew, and Vikram Dodd. "Immigrants Will Have to 'Earn' Citizenship, Says Phil Woolas." *Guardian*, August 3, 2009. www.guardian.co.uk/uk/2009/aug/03/immigrations-citizenship-points-phil-woolas.
Stewart, Angus. "Two Conceptions of Citizenship." *British Journal of Sociology* 46, no. 1 (1995): 63–78.
Stråth, Bo. "Multiple Europes: Integration, Identity and Demarcation of the Other." In *Europe and the Other and Europe as the Other*, edited by Bo Stråth, 385–420. Brussels: Peter Lang, 2010.
United Kingdom Borders Agency. *Earning the Right to Stay: A New Points Test for Citizenship.* London: United Kingdom Borders Agency, 2009.
— "Immigration Directorate Instructions. Annex FM Section FM 1.7. Financial Requirement." United Kingdom Borders Agency, 2012. www.ukba.homeoffice.gov.uk/sitecontent/documents/policyandlaw/IDIs/chp8-annex/section-FM-1.7.pdf?view=Binary.
Worley, Claire. "It's Not about Race. It's about the Community: New Labour and Community Cohesion." *Critical Social Policy* 25, no. 4 (2005): 483–96.

PART II

RELIGION, AGENCY AND MINORS

Sanna Mustasaari*

LAW, AGENCY AND THE INTIMATE RELATIONSHIPS OF YOUNG PEOPLE: FROM RIGHTS TO DUTIES AND BACK?

Introduction: The Intimate Sphere, "Normality" and Law

In the intimate sphere, the power of the law to prescribe the rights and duties of individuals is often outweighed by norms other than (state) law. Examining moral obligations in personal relationships, Eekelaar and Maclean emphasize the diversity of sources for perceptions of personal obligations.[1] Social, cultural, religious or moral norms that govern the family cover, for instance, gender relations, sexual behaviour and conceptions of duties and responsibilities within personal relationships. The emergence of research themes such as "family law and religion," "unofficial law," or "multiculturalism and family law" shows that legal studies on the family increasingly encounter issues arising at the intersections of religious, cultural, and legal norms.[2] Passing on fundamental values, which these norms represent, to the next generation is of crucial importance to any normative discourse about the family, be it legal, religious or cultural. The significance of preserving and determining values that prescribe relationships in the family sphere implies that young people inevitably symbolize a threat to the continuity of these values and thus a threat to the social order.[3] Hardly surprising, young people are subjected to control through various discourses, such as welfarist discourses defining the "normal" or the "healthy," religious or ideological discourses defining the "good" and the "sacred," cultural discourses defining belonging and identity, and legal discourses defining, for instance, the best interests of the child. The debate over who gets the final say about "best interests" is, at least partly, an issue of balancing the interests of the minority and the majority.

* LLM, PhD Candidate, Faculty of Law, University of Helsinki.

1 John Eekelaar and Mavis Maclean, "Marriage and the Moral Bases of Personal Relationships," *Journal of Law and Society* 31, no. 4 (2004): 510–38; John Eekelaar and Maclean, Mavis, "The Obligations and Expectations of Couples within Families: Three Modes of Interaction," *Journal of Social Welfare and Family Law* 26, no. 2 (2004): 117–30.

2 See for example the work of Shaheen Sardar Ali, John Eekelaar, Ann Laquer Estin, Marie-Claire Foblets, Maarit Jänterä-Jareborg, Marthe Minow, Anne Phillips and Ayelet Shachar, to name but a few.

3 Catriona Macleod, *"Adolescence," Pregnancy and Abortion. Constructing a Threat of Degeneration* (New York: Routledge, 2011), 31.

As the central principle in child and family law, the best interests of the child is often perceived as equal to the public interest and is, thus, closely connected to prevailing ideas about "normality." After all, as Eekelar reminds us, the duty to advance the interests of the vulnerable comes with the power to determine what those interests are.[4] This chapter discusses legal regulation of the intimate sphere and examines how the law shapes the agency of young people through attempts to secure autonomy by interpretations of the public interest and limitations such as incapacity to consent. The argument advanced in this chapter is that in a world of increasing plurality, regulation of intimate relationships ought to be grounded on recognition of agency and autonomy, for instance through placing more emphasis on sexual rights. Young people who lack complete legal capacity are subjects of the public interest, which inherently includes constructions of "normality." This conception of what is "normal" forms the matrix of the autonomy of a young person. The risk here is that a far too narrow conception of autonomy is accepted, one that disregards both the relational reality of personhood and the importance of critical autonomy and critical citizenship to the concept of sexual autonomy. Critical autonomy here refers, simply put, to the ability to receive and assess information and make judgments, to inquire and to evaluate knowledge claims about reality, both external as well as internal to the self. Critical citizenship may then be viewed as a political element of critical autonomy, one that emerges as participation in the public domain.

After this introductory section the text will proceed as follows. Section 2 discusses the issues of autonomy and agency in the context of intimate relationships. The conceptual category of sexual rights is introduced in order to grasp the centrality of the act of consent to notions of sexual autonomy and agency in the personal sphere. Section 3 then moves on to reflect the centrality of notions of "normality" to the best interests of the child. The ability to exercise sexual rights and sexual autonomy requires sufficient information on sexuality and rights. In this section, the debated issue of sexual education is examined through a case example from the European Court of Human Rights. The point made in this section is that the question of sexual education is problematic in relation to autonomy and agency of the child, because once we view the issue as a conflict between private interest and public interest or as a conflict between the family and the state, we lose sight of the particular child involved. Section 4 returns to ideas about autonomy. Through approaching the Finnish discussion about the absolute age limit to marry from the perspective of "normality," it is suggested that the notion of sexual autonomy is, at least to a certain extent, applied to reinforce the majority's view of "normal youth." The final section brings the focus back to the conditions of agency in the personal sphere. Drawing on the notion that assuming duties is central to agency, this chapter concludes by suggesting that the rights of young people ought to be viewed from a perspective that embraces a plurality of values and accepts culture and religion as integral to critical autonomy and critical citizenship.

4 John Eekelaar, *Family Law and Personal Life* (Oxford: Oxford University Press, 2007), 13.

Intimate Relationships, Autonomy and Human Agency

Human agency, i.e. the capacity of an individual to make choices and to act in the world, is respected throughout the legal system, most apparently through fundamental rights. Despite the fact that respecting human agency is also one of the key elements in contemporary family law, recognition of intimate relationships still rests largely on statuses. Since traditions of recognition of intimate relationships vary across the globe, rights connected to any particular status, such as the freedom to marry, lack efficiency in the quest for common ground in recognizing human agency within intimate relationships. Such overarching structures might, instead, be found in rights that address personal relationships regardless of their form or the tradition according to which they have been established.[5] With regard to marriage and other intimate relationships, cross-culturally salient rights could be found in sexual rights emphasizing the notion of sexual autonomy.

The right to sexual self-determination is based on human rights, such as the rights to integrity and private life.[6] The term "sexual rights" refers to a variety of rights, of which only some are necessarily and essentially legal rights in the positivistic sense. The term is emerging especially in the field of studies on human rights and health, and it is used, for example, by the World Health Organization.[7] One of the many possible ways of sub-categorizing sexual rights is to place them into three groups that consist, firstly, of rights that are conduct -based (such as the right to participate in sexual activity, the right to sexual pleasure and expression, and the right to sexual and reproductive self-determination, which includes rights to bodily integrity, autonomy, control and safety); secondly, rights that are related to identity (such as the right to the self-definition of sexual identity, and the right to public and social recognition of sexual identity); and thirdly, rights that are essential in relationships (such as the right to consent to sexual practices, the right to freely choose one's sexual partners, and the right to have one's sexual relationships publicly recognized).[8]

Despite the legal vagueness of the notion of sexual rights and the debatable nature of sexual rights as a distinct group of rights, the category of sexual rights is clearly useful. Seen as an analytical tool, it enables us to focus attention on conditions of agency within intimate relationships, regardless of their form or status. This category also interlocks various rights that are reflected in national laws as well as in international law.[9] Furthermore, sexual rights carry the potential to operate as overarching structures

5 See also Lisa Glennon, "The Limitations of Equality Discourses on the Contours of Intimate Obligations," in *Rights, Gender and Family Law*, ed. Julie Wallbank et al. (Abingdon and New York: Routledge, 2010), 170, who argues that instead of solely focusing on relationship forms the law should provide far greater recognition of caregiving in personal relationships.

6 Ilsa L. Lottes, "Sexual Rights: Meanings, Controversies, and Sexual Health Promotion," *Journal of Sex Research* 50, no. 3/4 (2013): 367–91.

7 WHO, "Defining sexual health. Report of a technical consultation on sexual health," Geneva, January 28–31, 2002. About the historical development of sexual rights, central international players on the field, and discussion over defining sexual rights see Lottes, "Sexual Rights."

8 Lottes, "Sexual Rights," 374–375.

9 See for example the UN Convention on Elimination of the Discrimination Against Women, as well as the requirement of free and full consent to marry, expressed in several international treaties.

between different normative orders. If intimate relationships are examined from the perspective of sexual rights, they concern the rights to physical and psychological integrity, the rights to family life and private life, and personal autonomy.

As the close connection between sexual rights and norms concerning the free and full consent to marry shows, sexual rights are essentially perceived as self-determination rights. They thus concern the idea of consent, which is essential to how law recognizes human agency in the private sphere. Consent works to create or change normative relationships between people. Beyleveld and Brownsword even go as far as to suggest that consent is, in fact, a morally universal principle.[10] Consent, and the centrality of the role it plays in legal reasoning, can best be understood within a rights-based conceptual framework. In Beyleveld and Brownsword's view, rights (understood essentially as choice and will) mark respect for the individual and, thus, instead of creating binary positions, frame the space for agency.[11]With regard to young people and their intimate relationships, the concept of consent as a requirement for agency is problematic. For consent to be informed, a person needs to have the capacity to make a decision and at least a certain degree of independence from others. Children, due to their stage of psychological development, are often perceived as incapable of forming a sufficiently informed opinion and, consequently, cannot effectively consent.[12] The sexual rights of minors are, thus, incomplete, and the scope of the sexual autonomy of a minor changes according to their cognitive and moral development. Furthermore, sexual autonomy and the exercise of sexual rights involve a critical dimension, as education and knowledge about sexuality and sexual rights are preconditions for exercising these rights. Hence, the possibility to receive information about sexuality and sexual rights is crucial to the sexual rights of young people.

The UN Convention on the Rights of the Child (UNCRC, the Convention on the Rights of the Child) promotes children's active citizenship and agency through advocating children's equal rights despite their vulnerability and need for protection. On the whole, the UNCRC also protects the right to receive education and information about sexuality, health and sexual rights.[13] According to Art 29 education about rights includes sexual rights.[14] But while states are under an obligation to promote the health of

10 Deryck Beyleveld and Roger Brownsword, *Consent in the Law* (Oxford: Hart Publishing, 2007). The authors view consent as an essentially procedural concept, which makes it more universal than if it were understood only as a justificatory concept.

11 The quest for overarching structures is of course challenging, because it inevitably requires a universalist approach to at least some elements about law. Cane points out that Beyleveld and Brownsword's problem lies precisely in their effort to create a universal account of consent in law, which results in rejection of normative and moral pluralism. Peter Cane, "Review on Consent in the Law," *Law and Politics Book Review* no. 7 (2007): 577–81.

12 Fauzia Ahmad, "British Muslim Perceptions and Opinions on News Coverage of September 11," *Journal of Ethnic and Migration Studies* 32, no. 6 (2006): 44, 46, 50. See also Helen Holgate and Roy Evans, "Sexuality and Young Motherhood," in *Teenage Pregnancy and Parenthood. Global Perspectives, Issues and Interventions*, ed. by Helen Holgate et al. (K.O., 2006), 20.

13 See Articles 13, 19, 24 and 29. The new Istanbul convention (Council of Europe, the Convention on Preventing and Combating Violence Against Women and Domestic Violence) also includes important norms that are relevant to sexual rights, see Articles 13 and 14.

14 See general comments no 1 of the Committee on the Rights of the Child, CRC/GC/2001/1, 2, 3 and 6.

young people and children, it is nevertheless clear that education concerning sexuality and sexual rights can never be completely value neutral.[15] The notion of "normality" thus plays a crucial role in determining who has authority over minors if the values of their parents are in conflict with those upheld by society. The interplay between the notion of "normality," the public interest and the best interests of the child, and the effect this interplay has on the space provided for agency, will be addressed in the next section.

Autonomy, Notions of "Normality" and Sexual Education

Family practices are regulated by social norms in all cultures. These norms define what is considered to be "normal" and, consequently, "permissible" and "good." Even though the process of individualization has decreased the impact of the so-called normal biography on the life course,[16] the choices that young people make are still often evaluated in the light of what is perceived as ordinary, common and normal. Education, care arrangements and common conceptions about parenting all support and shape perceptions both of normal youth and of rationalities relating to founding a family and reproduction. Early marriage and having children at a young age, for example, do not fit well with the general conception about "normal" youth.

The power borne by this imagined "normality" invokes questions about freedom of choice relating to family practices and reproduction. While a consensus might be achievable that the sexual rights of young people require adequate information, the content of that information is subject to value conflicts. The right to choose the information passed on to minors is a classic field of tension between the interests and convictions of parents and definitions of public interest by society. The European Court of Human Rights (ECtHR, the Court) has pinned down general principles concerning sexual education and the obligation of the State to respect the right of the parents to ensure that that education is in conformity with their religious convictions, provided in Article 2 of the First Protocol of the European Convention on Human Rights (P1–2).[17]

In *Kjeldsen, Busk Madsen and Pedersen v. Denmark*, the applicants claimed that their rights in (P1–2) had been violated as their children were not exempted from school during sexual education lessons that they considered to be against their religious views. The ECtHR stated that (P1–2) does not prevent States from imparting information or knowledge of a directly or indirectly religious or philosophical kind in education, nor does it permit parents to object to the integration of such education in the school curriculum. The Court also noted that many subjects taught at school are necessarily

15 General comments no 4 of the Committee on the Rights of the Child, CRC/GC/2003/4 on health of young people, sections 26 and 39.

16 About the normal biography, see for example Ulrich Beck and Elisabeth Beck-Gernsheim, *Individualization. Institutionalized Individualism and its Social and Political Consequences* (Los Angeles, London, New Delhi and Singapore: Sage Publications, 2002), 88.

17 Article 2 of the First Protocol of the ECHR (P1–2): "No person shall be denied the right to education. In the exercise of any functions which it assumes in relation to education and to teaching, the State shall respect the right of parents to ensure such education and teaching in conformity with their own religions and philosophical convictions."

based on some philosophical account of moral values. According to the Court, the obligation to respect the religious convictions of parents means that the State must see that information or knowledge included in the curriculum is conveyed in an objective, critical and pluralistic manner. The State is thus forbidden to pursue an aim of indoctrination that might be considered as not respecting parental religious and philosophical convictions. In this case, the Court considered the moral underpinnings of the education in question to be very general in character and did not go beyond what a democratic State may regard as the public interest.[18]In the more recent case of *Dojan and others v. Germany*,[19] the applicants claimed a similar infringement of their rights as the teaching staff did not exempt their children from sexual education classes, which included a workshop called "My body is mine," aimed to combat sexual abuse. Since the exemption was not granted, the applicants kept their children off school during sexual education lessons. Consequently, they were sanctioned with penal fines. The applicants asserted that their children did not have the necessary maturity to receive the envisaged sex education, as they had been raised without the influence of the media, which the parents considered to have a negative impact on them, and had been used to modest and chaste sexual behaviour at home.

The parents objected in particular to the educational material, which in their opinion was partly pornographic and contrary to Christian sexual ethics requiring that sex should be limited to matrimony. In their view, it set forth a liberal, emancipatory image of sexuality, which was not consistent with their religious and other moral beliefs. In their view such an approach to sexuality would lead to premature "sexualisation" of their children. In this case, the Court viewed the application as manifestly ill-founded, on the basis that it had previously solved similar issues and no genuine question arose about whether the State had exceeded its margin of appreciation.

These cases give rise to difficult questions about the moral dimensions of public interest, as well as culturally and religiously informed definitions of sexual rights. The cases demonstrate how the conflict between the public interest concerning sexual education and values and the religious convictions of individuals becomes a conflict between parental authority and state authority over the children in question. Discretion regarding the rights of children, their opinions (participatory rights) or their individual best interests is absent in these decisions. The right to information, which is a key element of sexual rights, thus seems to work to legitimize certain understandings of "normality," which then seem to translate as the public interest.[20]

18 Kjeldsen, Busk Madsen and Pedersen v. Denmark, no. 5095/71, 5920/72, 5926/72, judgment of 7 December 1976, paras 53, 54.

19 Dojan and Others v. Germany, no. 319/08, 2455/08, 7908/10, 8152/10, 8155/10, decision of 13 September 2011.

20 For more detailed discussion on these cases, see Sanna Mustasaari and Sanna Koulu, "State curriculum and parents' convictions under the European Convention on Human Rights" in *Families, Faith and Functions: The Child in the Intersections between Family, Society and Culture*, ed. by Maarit Jänterä-Jareborg and Anna Singer (Cambridge: Intersentia, 2015), in press; Frankie McCarthy, "Prayers in the Playground: Religion and Education in the United Kingdom and Beyond," in *The Place of Religion in Family Law: A Comparative Search*, ed. by Jane Mair and Esin Örücü (Cambridge: Intersentia, 2011), 235–63.

Autonomy and Exemptions of Age Limits: the Finnish Case of Child Marriage?

The importance of sexual autonomy and the insufficient capacity of a child to consent are the main reasons why the law on intimacy builds so substantively on age limits. In Finland, as in many other countries, the minimum age for marriage is 18. For a special reason, however, the Ministry of Justice may grant a special permit for a minor to marry.[21] This exemption, too, is a rather common mechanism in laws on marriage. Recently this provision of the Marriage Act, which has been said to effectively enable child marriages, has been subject to fierce criticism as, according to critics, the marriage of a minor always signifies a gross violation of human rights.[22] The Swedish Marriage Act used to contain a similar provision, which was repealed as of 1 July 2014.[23]

For sure, sound reasons support the suggestion to make the age limit to marry an absolute one. It is true, of course, that age limits for maturity are necessary, as the capacity to marry has to be defined and set clearly by the law. Nor can age limits, being general by definition, correspond to individual circumstances in every case.[24] Age limits are a classic example of how a formally universal subject is created. The choice to regulate through an absolute age limit is a choice made in favour of structuralism rather than personal experience, and the possible problems that come with it merely reflect the tension between personal experience and the structural critique of false consciousness, namely that it is difficult to rely on the participant's own interpretation of a situation, e.g. the stage of their psychological development.[25]

Moreover, harmonizing marriage ages internationally might be a practically efficient way to combat child marriages, which would indeed call for abolishing any exemptions to the age of maturity with regard to marriage. The Parliamentary Assembly of the Council of Europe, for instance, in its Resolution 1468 (2005), emphasizes "the need to take the requisite legislative measures to prohibit child marriage by making 18 years the minimum marriageable age. Thus, persons not having reached this age would not be able to lawfully contract marriage."[26] Why then, do I find the Finnish discussion about the exemption for marriage age problematic? The answer has to do with the image of autonomy, which seems to underlie public discussion in Finland.

For me, the concept of autonomy in the context of the age limit/special permit discussion is questionable, as it pays too much heed to the formal status of the relationship and too little to relational reality in the intimate sphere. Marriage as such is not, any more than other type of relationship, necessarily in breach of "the best interests of the

21 Section 4 of the Finnish Marriage Act, Avioliittolaki 234/1929, 4§.

22 About the Finnish discussion see for example the blog by Anna Kontula, a leftist politician on 16 February 2013, accessed February 17, 2014. www.aamuposti.fi/blogit/anna-kontula/222661-sivistyneen-lannen-lapsiavioliitot; and "Lapsena alttarille: Onko Suomen avioliittolaki vanhentunut?" *Helsingin Sanomat, NYT* 25 January 2013.

23 Chapter 2, Section 1 of the Swedish Marriage Act, Äktenskapsbalken 1987: 230, 2 kap 1§.

24 Toni M. Yetano, "The Constitutionalisation of Party Autonomy in European Family Law," *Journal of Private International Law* 6, no. 1 (2010): 168–9.

25 James Boyle, "Is Subjectivity Possible? The Post-Modern Subject on Legal Theory," *University of Colorado Law Review* 62 (1991): 493–4.

26 Resolution 1468 (2005): Forced marriages and child marriages, Section 12.

child." If the concern was genuinely over the best interests of those young people who wish to marry, then surely their situation ought to be compared to their peers establishing other types of intimate relationships. The rationale of rejecting child marriages is that they involve abuse, not that society has a legitimate reason to regulate intimate relationships between adolescents.

Furthermore, childhood, adolescence and maturity are culturally defined social constructions, as both adulthood and childhood reflect ideas about the interrelationship between the individual and the community.[27] In fact, the age limits of legal capacity to marry do vary notably even between European countries. The Convention on the Rights of the Child, which defines "child" to mean "every human being below the age of 18 years (unless, under the law applicable to the child, majority is attained earlier," Article 1), also requires states to take measures to secure the physical, emotional and psychological well-being and equality of all children as well as to protect them from all forms of abuse (Article 3, Article 19, Article 34). The point of providing age limits for maturity is precisely to provide protection from abuse.

Marriage ages have risen all around Europe and an increasing number of children are born to unmarried mothers.[28] The most plausible explanation for this development is that marriage no longer marks the necessary legitimization of sexual relationships. If the "illegitimate" status of a child still bore shame for mother and child, it would of course be logical to allow young people to marry in the case of pregnancy, as marriage would decrease the stigma of unwanted or unplanned pregnancies. The social changes of recent decades have signified a change in the values of the majority, but this change might just as well be interpreted to mean that the value marriage has in contemporary Northern European societies is mainly symbolic and thus carries deep personal, cultural or religious significance. This account of marriage would emphasize personal experience over structuralist concerns about the absolute unacceptability of child marriages.

My point here, however, extends beyond mere personal experience. The ideas of the majority about what is considered "normal" carry power to define the scope of agency especially with regard to those who lack full autonomy. Inevitably, ideas about "normality" operate as a legitimation of the exercise of power over those defined abnormal and lacking agency. Macleod refers to this as a means of "othering," which derives from the socially constructed sharp distinction between adolescence and adulthood.[29] Of course, the range of "normal" never includes everyone and "adolescents" in reality are different people in diverse life situations. Discourses that emphasize economic rationalities as "normal," for instance, might operate poorly in meeting the needs and pursuits of those young people who, for one reason or another, refuse to follow the values expressed through assumptions about "normality." Similarly, for some young people education or labour do not necessarily seem like prospective routes to success.

Furthermore, as Macleod points out, the way that young parents, especially women, are represented in public speech through social problems, decadence and degeneration,

27 David Archard, *Sexual Consent* (Boulder and Oxford: Westview Press, 1998), 40–48.

28 On the Finnish development, see Eva Gottberg, *Perhesuhteet ja lainsäädäntö* (Turku: Turun yliopiston oikeustieteellisen tiedekunnan julkaisuja, 2010), 133–4.

29 Macleod, *"Adolescence," Pregnancy and Abortion*, 31.

is a mechanism of exercising power and control over them.[30] The same could be said, for example, about representations of the young Muslim woman; concern over her autonomy also denies her agency and represents her through a variety of threats, such as those caused by religion, migration or culture.[31] Social problems and threats legitimize intervention by society, so that invoking the question about autonomy and incompetence necessarily involves the potential to restrict agency. Although there is no doubt that the wellbeing of adolescents is a question of public interest, the notion of sexual autonomy may also be invoked to reinforce the majority's view of the "normal."

Finally, the rhetoric of sexual autonomy may, in fact, obscure how inconsistently sexual autonomy is applied as a principle. In a recent article on rape law, Rubenfeld argues that the rhetoric of sexual autonomy may be harnessed to promote traditional sexual morality. He accuses modern rape law of inconsistency, as it tries to ground the criminalization of rape on violations of sexual autonomy and particularly lack of consent, and yet fails to punish deceptive behaviour that creates false consent to a sexual act.[32] With regard to minors, we have already seen that the scope of sexual autonomy and sexual rights is explained as changing according to the physical and psychological development of the individual child or adolescent. This offers a waterproof, if somewhat question-begging, explanation of inconsistencies in the scope of sexual autonomy of a young person.

I have argued above that disputes over sexual education are conflicts of authority between the state and the family and do not necessarily add to the empowering idea of the autonomy of the child involved. In the example cases of the European Court any sight of the children whom the cases concerned was indeed lost, for their individual circumstances played no role in the discretion of the Court. By reflecting the Finnish discussion about the marriage age my criticism was aimed towards the power of "normality" in determining the "right" way of life. But the criticism above still leaves us with the intractable challenge of conjoining two needs: to promote the autonomy of young people and to provide protection for them. The question that follows, then, is what kind of approach would support and recognize the agency of young people while still acknowledging their possible vulnerability. The final section of this chapter explores the conditions of agency embedded in relatedness and interdependency.

Agency and Critical Autonomy: from Rights to Duties and Back?

Despite the critical observations above, broader recognition of sexual rights and sexual autonomy is indeed needed as a basis for legal regulation of intimate relationships.

30 *Ibid.*, 57, 64.

31 Ahmad, "British Muslim Perceptions and Opinions."

32 Jed Rubenfeld, "The Riddle of Rape-By-Deception and the Myth of Sexual Autonomy," *Yale Law Journal* 122, no. 6 (2013): 1372–443. Here I only wish to highlight the inconsistent and sometimes rhetoric use of 'sexual autonomy' in legal reasoning. For the reasons comprehensively articulated by e.g. Corey Rayburn Young, Tom Dougherty, Deborah Tuerkheimer, Patricia Falk and Gowri Ramachandran, I do not support Rubenfeld's conclusions regarding what should follow from this doctrinal inconsistency to legal responses to sexual violence.

However, autonomy seems to be a particularly difficult concept not only as it is difficult to choose whether to approach it through personal experience or through more general knowledge. In the personal sphere characterized by inter-dependence and personal, affective relationships the concept of autonomy faces yet other challenges. The problem of notions of autonomy and, consequently, a rights-based framework in the personal sphere is that relatedness seems to erode autonomy, partly because the relational aspects of autonomy are difficult to recognize in legal discourse.

Relatedness threatens the atomistic idea of an independent, autonomous subject. It might even be said that the only type of relatedness the idea of autonomy seems to cohere with is the type of romantic love that can be perceived as a symbiotic relationship with the other – fulfilling and thus liberating.[33] This kind of relatedness is possessive and consuming by nature – almost as if the only way to see relatedness as part of freedom and autonomy would require a contractual relation that balances contributions made within the relationship.[34] Needless to say, the centrality of romantic love as a source of empowerment in relational reality echoes ethnocentricity, as it embraces a cultural and mythical fantasy as the norm or ideal.

Agency is not, however, inevitably in conflict with relatedness even in the absence of romantic love. Instead, relatedness is often a necessary condition for agency, as autonomy and relatedness are both basic human needs, so that being able to respond to others in personal relationships adds to competence and agency.[35] Indeed, it is possible simultaneously to be high in autonomy and high in relatedness.[36] Eekelaar and Maclean have shown that rights in the personal sphere are commonly experienced as responsibilities: as rights of the other person and as duties that one individual owes towards another that they deeply care about.[37] Duties thus appear to be more verifiable than rights in the day-to-day experience of personal relationships, which signals the constant presence of moral reasoning in personal relationships.

The ordinary evaluation of needs and duties, present in everyday life and in personal relationships, brings cultural rights into the personal sphere. This is the case not only regarding the idea of the liberal equality of individuals and groups or their lifestyles, cultures or value systems. More importantly, this refers to the necessity of cultural frameworks for the functioning of moral reasoning. For whereas rights claim to be universal, duties seem to be highly specific and local, because they are, as Brennan puts

33 See for example Ulrich Beck and Elisabeth Beck-Gernsheim, *The Normal Chaos of Love* (Cornwall: Polity Press, 1995).

34 An interesting point of comparison is the relationship between the child and the parent, which also seems to reflect possessiveness as the child is traditionally thought to belong to the parents. By exercising parental authority the autonomy of the parent remains intact and in fact also includes the autonomy of the child.

35 Jonathan Herring, "Relational Autonomy and Family Law," in *Rights, Gender and Family Law*, ed. by Julie Wallbank et al. (Abingdon and New York: Routledge, 2010), 257–75.

36 Cigdem Kagitcibasi, "Adolescent Autonomy-Relatedness and the Family in Cultural Context: What is Optimal?," *Journal of Research on Adolescence* 23, no. 2 (2013): 223–35.

37 Eekelaar and Maclean, "Marriage and Moral Bases."

it, "inevitably discovered and implemented locally in community and tradition."[38] In addition, duties invoked by personal conscience are also recognized through affections, through the experience of caring.

For Brennan, it is a fact of human nature to strive for the real and the good, and this "moves the subject beyond his subjectivity to what is and to what is good. More acutely stated, satisfaction of this desire has as its consequence nothing short of transcendence."[39] It is this evaluation of the good, of duties, that requires respect for cultural rights, such as freedom of religion. This raises the issue of critical citizenship, the necessity of culture and religious tradition as a framework for understanding, for exercising both the autonomy and moral reasoning required by the relationality of autonomy in the personal sphere. As "ought" implies "can," it is the need for critical reflection – evaluation of duty – that tradition, culture and religion respond to. Autonomy in the political or moral field requires the capability of autonomous thought, to which culture gives resources.[40] Culture thus creates autonomy, but the autonomy referred to here is different from autonomy as in the claims of the autonomy of a cultural community to preserve the existence of a group or a specific way of life or cultural practice. Autonomy, as aptly expressed by Roberts and Wood, is "not a matter of sheer independence but of what one does with one's dependence,"[41] and thus it is future -oriented and reflective, aiming beyond the community of today.

But while critical citizenship and intellectual autonomy are inevitably connected to community through intellectual and value traditions as sources of understanding, and relational autonomy is connected to communities through duties, the call for assessment of these duties, the call for transcendence, is nevertheless individual and cannot be carried out by parents, the community or the state. Supporting the agency and autonomy of young people requires respect for all of these rights that enable assumption of responsibilities. Sexual autonomy, properly understood, cannot exist without critical autonomy and cultural rights.

Conclusions

In internally plural contemporary societies, attempts to accommodate diversity in an inclusive manner depend on finding rights that can be accepted as cross-culturally salient. Such rights provide for diversity, for instance, by protecting identity claims, minority ways of life, freedom of religion and rights to culture, but also by protecting respect for private life and family life. In the sphere of marriage and sexual relationships, these rights need to be interlocked with rights that protect autonomy, especially sexual autonomy. Rights rest on the idea of the autonomous subject who is capable of consenting, i.e. expressing free and full consent. People under the age of majority do not have that

38 Patrick M. Brennan, "The 'Right' of Religious Liberty of the Child: Its Meaning, Measure, and Justification." *Emory International Law Review* 20, no. 1 (2006): 138.

39 Ibid., 146.

40 Robert C. Roberts and W. Jay Wood, *Intellectual Virtues: An Essay in Regulative Epistemology* (Oxford: Oxford University Press, 2007), 257–8.

41 *Ibid.*, 266.

capacity, so their agency is in practice shaped by competing interpretations of their best interests.

Recognizing the agency of young people remains an intractable challenge, as the "best interests of the child," "normality," "good" and "right" are often debated among those who claim to have authority over young people. Young people thus risk being represented as passive subjects of concern, restrictions or action. As important as it is to find cross-culturally acceptable rights in the sphere of intimate relationships, autonomy or rights alone fail meaningfully to address agency in the personal sphere. Legal recognition of the agency of young people thus requires focusing attention on the conditions of agency, autonomy and relatedness. This recognition does not necessarily gain its empowering force by focusing on classic notions of consent and autonomy, but instead on critical autonomy, which is necessary in evaluating and assuming duties in the personal sphere. Recognition of agency thus rests significantly on cultural rights, such as freedom of religion. Consequently, it is a question of fundamental political importance – as to how critical citizenship is enabled in society.

Bibliography

Ahmad, Fauzia. "British Muslim Perceptions and Opinions on News Coverage of September 11." *Journal of Ethnic and Migration Studies* 32, no. 6 (2006): 961–82.
Archard, David. *Sexual Consent*. Boulder and Oxford: Westview Press, 1998.
Balkin, Jack M. "Understanding Legal Understanding: The Legal Subject and the Problem of Legal Coherence." *Yale Law Journal* 103, no. 1 (1993): 105–76.
Beck, Ulrich, and Elisabeth Beck-Gernsheim. *Individualization. Institutionalized Individualism and its Social and Political Consequences*. Los Angeles, London, New Delhi and Singapore: Sage Publications, 2002.
— *The Normal Chaos of Love*. Cornwall: Polity Press, 1995.
Beyleveld, Deryck, and Roger Brownsword. *Consent in the Law*. Oxford: Hart Publishing, 2007.
Boyle, James. "Is Subjectivity Possible? The Post-Modern Subject on Legal Theory." *University of Colorado Law Review* 62 (1991): 489–524.
Brennan, Patrick M. "The 'Right' of Religious Liberty of the Child: Its Meaning, Measure, and Justification." *Emory International Law Review* 20, no. 1 (2006): 129–55.
Cane, Peter. "Review on Consent in the Law." *Law and Politics Book Review*, no. 7 (2007): 577–81.
Eekelaar, John. *Family Law and Personal Life*. Oxford: Oxford University Press, 2007.
Eekelaar, John, and Mavis Maclean. "Marriage and the Moral Bases of Personal Relationships." *Journal of Law and Society* 31, no. 4 (2004): 510–38.
— "The Obligations and Expectations of Couples within Families: Three Modes of Interaction." *Journal of Social Welfare and Family Law* 26, no. 2 (2004): 117–30.
Glennon, Lisa. "The Limitations of Equality Discourses on the Contours of Intimate Obligations." In *Rights, Gender and Family Law*, edited by Julie Wallbank, Shazia Choudhry and Jonathan Herring, 167–98. Abingdon and New York: Routledge, 2010.
Gottberg, Eva. *Perhesuhteet ja lainsäädäntö*. Turku: Turun yliopiston oikeustieteellisen tiedekunnan julkaisuja, 2010.
Herring, Jonathan. 2010. "Relational Autonomy and Family Law." In *Rights, Gender and Family Law*, edited by Julie Wallbank, Shazia Choudhry and Jonathan Herring, 257–75. Abingdon and New York: Routledge, 2010.
Holgate, Helen, and Roy Evans. "Sexuality and Young Motherhood." In *Teenage Pregnancy and Parenthood. Global Perspectives, Issues and Interventions*, edited by Helen Holgate, Roy Evans and Francis Yuen, 7–21. K.O., 2006.
Kagitcibasi, Cigdem. "Adolescent Autonomy-Relatedness and the Family in Cultural Context: What is Optimal?" *Journal of Research on Adolescence* 23, no. 2 (2013): 223–35.
Lottes, Ilsa L. "Sexual Rights: Meanings, Controversies, and Sexual Health Promotion." *Journal of Sex Research* 50, no. 3/4 (2013), 367–91.
Macleod, Catriona. *"Adolescence," Pregnancy and Abortion. Constructing a Threat of Degeneration*. New York: Routledge, 2011.

McCarthy, Frankie. "Prayers in the Playground: Religion and Education in the United Kingdom and Beyond." In *The Place of Religion in Family Law: A Comparative Search*, edited by Jane Mair and Esin Örücü, 235–63. Cambridge: Intersentia, 2011.

Mustasaari, Sanna, and Sanna Koulu. 2014. "State curriculum and parents' convictions under the European Convention on Human Rights." In *Families, Faith and Functions: The Child in the Intersections between Family, Society and Culture*, edited by Maarit Jänterä-Jareborg and Anna Singer. Cambridge: Intersentia, 2015. In press.

Roberts, Robert C., and W. Jay Wood. *Intellectual Virtues: An Essay in Regulative Epistemology*. Oxford: Oxford University Press, 2007.

Rubenfeld, Jed. "The Riddle of Rape-By-Deception and the Myth of Sexual Autonomy." *Yale Law Journal* 122, no. 6 (2013): 1372–443.

WHO. 2002. *Defining sexual health. Report of a technical consultation on sexual health.* Geneva, January 28–31, 2002.

Yetano, Toni M. "The Constitutionalisation of Party Autonomy in European Family Law." *Journal of Private International Law* 6, no. 1 (2010): 155–93.

Ryan Hill

RESPECTING RELIGIOUS FREEDOMS AND FREEDOM ITSELF: HOW "ON EARTH" DO WE RAISE OUR CHILDREN?

Introduction

For some time now political debate has been taking place in a number of European states over the place of religion in public spaces. Religious dress – for the purpose of this chapter defined as forms of dress specifically associated with religions but not necessarily strictly prescribed by religions – has attracted considerable attention in this debate. Concern is voiced that the most ostentatious forms of religious dress may impact negatively on social cohesion within wider society.[1] However, particular attention has been paid to religious dress associated with the Islamic faith and worn by women, most notably the *niqab* (face veil) and *burqa* (full body covering). One explanation for this attention can be found in a supplemental concern that this specific dress signifies the subordination of women in Islam, including the subordination of those women choosing to wear these garments.[2]

States seeking to act to try to remedy this perceived subordination by interfering with the choices some women make in terms of a visible manifestation of their religious commitment would face a number of problems. Besides confronting the protected right to freedom of religion, there are principled reasons for respecting people's choices. Equality is clearly a value to promote and ensure in any democratic state. But equality encapsulates equality of choice. Therefore, even where one may suspect that an individual's choice is insufficiently authentic or insufficiently freely chosen, – and there are certainly serious academics that believe this to be the case with women,[3] interfering with choices by consenting adults runs the risk of denying these adults their autonomy and downgrading their individual moral worth. As the intervener's tool (limitation or prohibition) is to circumscribe equality according to the acceptability of the substance of the choice as judged by the intervener, the implication is that one cannot leave certain

1 See Nadirsyah Hosen and Richard Mohr, *Law and Religion in Public Life: The Contemporary Debate* (Abingdon: Routledge, 2011).

2 See discussion in Dawn Lyon and Debora Spini, "Unveiling the Headscarf Debate," *Feminist Legal Studies* 12 (2004): 333.

3 See for example Susan M. Okin, "Feminism and Multiculturalism: Some Tensions," *Ethics* 108 (1998): 678.

individuals to make a balanced choice over their competing commitments from a position of equality.[4] This disempowers the chooser, making an argument based on protecting their equality somewhat patronising. This would apply not only to women in Islam but to any interference with an individual's adoption of a strong commitment to a religious or even a cultural doctrine that seems to compel them to subjugate themselves to what might be considered illiberal practices or a status that seems to severely restrict their equality of opportunity within wider society. Cases brought to the courts over dress limitations therefore largely turn on arguments relating to collective social goods, such as social cohesion and public order, or for the protection of the rights and freedoms of others which the wearer's manifestation might negatively impact upon.

But is there an argument for supporting a limitation on religious dress to apply to children that might specifically draw on the notion of protecting the individual child from their choices or from choices made for them by adults on their behalf? One might suggest that where children are concerned the issues are different. States have an obligation to protect children, including protecting children's welfare and children's rights. This will often result in limits being set on what children are allowed to do. Some of these obligations may extend to parents as it is parents who are often making choices on their child's behalf, or at least influencing their children's choices. Where children's choices are concerned, a significant consideration for both the state and the parents should be the child's best interests. But assessing the child's current best interests seems to require at least some consideration of their future best interests. That is to say, the concept of the "rights of others" might be considered as having some value when considering how we are to protect the rights of the emerging adult that the child will become. Prioritising a future form of equality of choice and of opportunity over a current particular manifestation of choice for a child might therefore seem appropriate. This is especially where the choice one may be denying the current child is of a controversial nature, such as with regard to the most controversial forms of religious dress. This is not to say that the child will be denied the choice to adopt religious dress as they see fit but rather that the decision for the child will be delayed until that child is deemed old enough to fully understand and appreciate the commitment they are making. After all, it does not seem unreasonable to suggest that children adopting particularly orthodox forms of religious dress prompts questions of authenticity and sufficiency of freedom of choice perhaps more than is the case with adults adopting such dress, both in terms of the child and of the adult the child is yet to become.

With the above in mind, this chapter will set out an argument that supports interfering in children's religious dress codes that matches some of the concerns over religious dress some states are raising with regard to impacts on the chooser. It will then show some of the problems this argument would confront at law, finishing with some suggestions on how states might best envision their obligations to children.

4 See discussion in Maleiha Malik, "Complex Equality: Muslim Women and the 'Headscarf'," *Droit et société* 68 (2008): 127.

The Nature of the Argument over Interfering in Religious Dress Code for Adults

Before presenting a specific argument for limiting religious dress for children in the name of protecting their equality, it is worth trying to tease out why certain religious dress has provoked concern over people's equality. It should be pointed out at the outset that arriving at a clear and definitive answer for why certain religious dress triggers a strong reaction in some people is not easy to pin down.[5]An example of the problem in fully identifying the reasons for people's reactions to religious dress can be seen in the somewhat ambiguous way in which France has approached religious dress limitations. The French government, when considering bans on face coverings, was reported as describing face veils thus: "[T]he face-covering veil undermines the basic standards required for living in a shared society while also relegating its wearers to inferior status incompatible with French notions of equality."[6] These concerns have been echoed in other European states debates over, in particular, dress associated with Islam.[7] The 2010 legislation that brought the ban into effect[8] built on, but also departed from, a 2004 prohibition on all forms of ostentatious dress associated with religion.[9] This 2004 legislation was primarily directed at limitations within the public school environment and it captured dress associated with Islam and also the Jewish kippa and large Christian crosses. The 2010 legislation applied to face coverings in all public places but notably did not include the hijab or any other non-face covering forms of what might qualify as ostentatious religious dress.

Concerns over social cohesion naturally arise where difference is manifested and are seen captured in the French government's statement cited above. Fragmentation or parallelism within society threatens to undermine a cultural community that many European states appear to feel that they should either maintain or construct.[10] The greater the degree of perceived "difference" the greater the reaction, one might assume; hence the increased reaction to veils and not headscarves and extension of the limitation to all public spaces rather than solely areas of public engagement which are conducted or regulated by the state. Thus it seems safe to say that social cohesion is one factor that may be driving the religious dress debate. However, the worry that some people are being relegated to an inferior status within society, either voluntarily or involuntarily, suggests more than a state interest in protecting and ensuring a collective value in social cohesion.

5 See Ralph Grillo and Prakash Shah, "Reasons to Ban? The Anti-Burqa Movement in Western Europe," *MMG Working Paper* 12–05 (Göttingen: Max Planck Institute for the Study of Religious and Ethnic Diversity, 2012).

6 "Women in face veils detained as France enforces ban," editorial, *BBC News online*, 11 April 2011, accessed 21 December 2013, www.bbc.co.uk/news/world-europe-13031397.

7 See Dominic McGoldrick, *Human Rights and Religion: The Islamic Headscarf Debate in Europe* (Portland: Hart, 2006).

8 Loi no 2010–1192 du 12 octobre 2010, interdisant la dissimulation du visage dans l'espace public.

9 Loi n° 2004–228 du 15 mars 2004, encadrant, en application du principe de laïcité, le port de signes ou de tenues manifestant une appartenance religieuse dans les écoles, collèges et lycées publics.

10 See discussion in Alana Lentin and Gavan Tiltley, "The Crisis of 'Multiculturalism' in Europe: Mediated Minarets, Intolerable Subjects," *European Journal of Cultural Studies* 15, no. 2 (2012): 123.

It implies that enforcing a certain basic "equality" standard is of direct individual benefit to the person on whom it is being enforced and that it is the state's obligation to ensure this benefit for all within its polity. This might reflect the view that fragmentation generates socio-economic impediments and the state should therefore act to reduce such impediments.[11] The increased focus on the veil might make sense against this view in that its exclusionary nature effectively places a barrier between wearer and non-wearer. But it may go further and portray a perfectionist liberal polemic that views choice options that appear to leave the chooser in some way accepting a subjugated status as needing to fall outside the domain of choice in a liberal democratic society. It is possible therefore that a negative perception of certain choices in people's minds is also impacting on the debate.[12]

Although the idea that some choices might need to be placed outside the domain of choice in a liberal society in order to ensure equality may have focused on women and Islam, the idea need not be limited to this particular group of people, as mentioned in the introduction to this chapter. For example, French political scientist Denis Lacorne has described the French response to religious dress as a clash of principles that can be reduced to a number of key questions that apply beyond niqabs and burqas and even beyond the issue of gender: "[I]s freedom of religion fully compatible with the principle of equality? Is the search for a common conception of the good society compatible with sectarian religious beliefs? Are authentic or strongly held religious convictions compatible with secular reason?"[13] Lacorne's suggestion certainly helps account for the wider debate over religious symbols in Europe and this is perhaps a more appropriate backdrop against which to frame concerns over certain religious dress than a concern over social cohesion or over gender inequality. Lacorne may be right in directing us away from focusing too narrowly on voiced concerns driving limitations on religious dress. Rather we might consider the current debate over the place of religious diversity as a variant of a European struggle between liberalism and religious dogma that can be traced back to at least the Enlightenment period. That struggle appeared to have been settled with the spread of secularism across Europe. The more religious identity visibly manifests itself, however, the more some people may feel their secular world of freedom *from* religion threatened.[14] Constraining religion therefore becomes the underlying aim, whether legitimate or not, and the process starts with attacks on the most visible and most alien manifestations of religion within the dominant cultural community.

11 A view popular in the 1960s, see John Porter, *The Vertical Mosaic* (Toronto: University of Toronto Press, 1965).

12 Ryan W Hill, "The French Prohibition on Veiling in Public Places: Rights Evolution or Violation?" *Oxford Journal of Law and Religion* 2, no. 2 (2013): 417.

13 Corrie Goldman, "*Burqas? Veils? Stanford visiting scholar Denis Lacorne speaks on secularism in France and the U.S.*" (Stanford Report, 2013), accessed December 21, 2013, http://news.stanford.edu/news/2013/february/lacorne-france-secularism-022213.html.

14 See Peter L Berger, *The Desecularization of the World: Resurgent Religion and World Politics* (Washington DC: Ethics and Public Policy Center, 1999).

An Equality Based Argument for Interfering in a Child's Religious Dress Codes

Interfering with the religious dress code of children does not confront the same problems as does interfering with adult choices over their dress, for a number of reasons. Firstly, interfering in children's lives is a natural feature of the law. States owe a special obligation to protect children by virtue of their immaturity and corresponding vulnerable status as minors.[15] Secondly, in terms of children's rights status, children are recognised as "incomplete" rights holders when contrasted with adults.[16] This means that, as agents, their ability to act on their rights is legitimately subject to considerations that would not apply to an adult.

The UN Convention on the Rights of the Child 1989 elaborates on the rights children have and goes some way towards showing how those rights interrelate with the duties states, parents and others have towards children. The limitations applied to a child's agency correspond to the degree to which the child is considered as having developed sufficient capacity to determine how to act on their rights.[17] This developmental notion, described in the CRC as "evolving capacity," refers to "processes of maturation and learning whereby children progressively acquire knowledge, competencies and understanding, including acquiring understanding about their rights and about how they can best be realized."[18] The child's status, along with recognition that children mature, means that children's agency is therefore directly coupled to their development. They are rights holders in one sense but, at the same time, they are at a stage of "becoming" rights holders in another sense. As they are undergoing a continual maturing process, parents and others should therefore concede decision making power to each child in accordance with that child's stage of maturity and in relation to what the issue is that they are being tasked with deciding.[19] However, as Smolin points out, as long as parents and the state are duty holders accountable for the child's wellbeing, they must have a correlate authority over the child that can limit the child's autonomy.[20] Circumscribing the whole parent/state/child relationship is the proviso that all choices concerning children should give primary consideration to what is in that *child's* best interests.[21]

As they can be considered to be on a journey towards being full rights holders in their own right, children are not only current "incomplete" rights holders but also future "complete" rights holders. Thus states must not only consider the child's present interests and rights but also the future adult's interests and rights that relate to the "complete" rights holder the child will become. These are not only implicit in the protection of the

15 UN International Covenant on Civil and Political Rights 1966, Article 24(1).

16 Committee on the Rights of the Child, *CRC General Comment No. 12: The right of the child to be heard,* (UN Doc. CRC/C/GC/12, 2009), para.1.

17 UN Convention on the Rights of the Child (CRC), 1989, Article 5.

18 Committee on the Rights of the Child, *CRC General Comment No. 7 (2005): Implementing child rights in early childhood* 20/09/2006, UN Doc. CRC/C/GC/7/Rev.1, para. 17.

19 Geraldine Van Bueren, *The International Law on the Rights of the Child* (The Hague: Martinus Nijhoff, 1995), 152.

20 David M Smolin, "Overcoming Religious Objections to the Convention on the Rights of the Child," *Emory International Law Review* 20 (2006): 91.

21 CRC Article 3.

child's current rights but also incorporated through a comprehensive right to education directed towards, among other things, development of the child's "talents and mental and physical abilities to their fullest potential,"[22] preparation for "a responsible life in a free society,"[23] and acquisition of understanding about their rights and about how they can best be realized. If it can be shown, therefore, that allowing the child to adopt certain forms of religious dress risks impacting negatively on that child's future rights, either in later childhood or as a full adult, a case can be made for justifying a limitation on the child's present manifestation of religion in the name of protecting those future rights.

It might be possible to construct such a case by drawing on a proposition set out in an article by Joel Feinberg in 1980 entitled *[T]he Child's Right to an Open Future.*[24] Feinberg provides an argument for ensuring that the rights of "future adults" be protected by ensuring that parents and communities are prevented from closing down too many future choice options while raising their children. The child is viewed as being in a fiduciary relationship with their parents who hold in trust a large body of rights that belong to the child but also to the future adult that the child will become. What would follow from this is an obligation on parents to act as trustees for the benefit of both the present *and* the future rights holder, and an obligation on the state to ensure this is the case. The premise is that rights are "saved" for the child but can be violated in advance, for example by effectively depriving the child of their full rights potential through unduly prejudicing the child with restrictive views and understandings. This violation cannot always be established by checking the child's present interests, desires or preferences due to the unknowable future dimension. A degree of determination of the child's interests – the future dimension – must therefore be left to the adult that the child will become.

Feinberg's argument provides at least a basis for differentiating between adults and children when it comes to "choice." It also might lend itself to supporting differentiation between forms of dress for children, dependent on how far they accord with what should be left to a future adult choice. For example, niqabs and burqas might be considered too "narrowing" on a female child's future ability to enjoy all the rights that she is entitled to, while hijabs might be seen as "acceptable." Similarly, another religion's dress might also be captured as unacceptable for children, such as clothing worn by some very young children of Orthodox Jewish parents. Determining where the thresholds lie and at what ages would of course present problems. But perhaps not insurmountable problems, provided that religious groups themselves were adequately consulted on what constitutes appropriate attire to satisfy a minimum or generally acceptable requirement for their faith and at what age.[25]

Showing that allowing a child to adopt certain forms of religious dress risks impacting negatively on that child's future rights is, of course, a difficult task. Nonetheless, the idea that some form of mitigation may be needed on excesses of religious interpretation

22 CRC Article 29(1)(a).

23 CRC Article 29(1)(d).

24 Joel Feinberg, "The Child's Right to an Open Future," in *Freedom and Fulfilment: Philosophical Essays*, Joel Feinberg (Princeton NJ: Princeton University Press, 1992), 77.

25 For an example of where this worked in arriving at a dress code for children within a specific school in the UK, see *R (Begum) v. Governors of Denbigh High School* [2006] UKHL 15.

impacting on children in order to protect the child's future "choice" is certainly arguable. For example, Elizabeth Odio Benito, the former Special Rapporteur on Freedom of Religion and Belief, now Vice President of the International Criminal Court, has noted that "[A]ttitudes learned in childhood from parents, teachers, Churches or assemblies have a lasting and profound influence upon their whole approach to life, and it is almost impossible to set them aside, to be convinced that they are in error, or to adopt new ones."[26] Some religions seem to have made use of this realization. The Bible's Book of Proverbs for example states "train the child the way he should go and when he is old he will not turn from it."[27] Similarly within Islam, the 11th century Islamic scholar Al Ghazali saw the importance of getting to the child at an early age as what was learnt then was as engraved in stone.[28] Neither of these religious examples fit altogether comfortably with the notion of a truly open future.

With the above in mind, an approach to children along the lines suggested by Feinberg might seem a sensible one to adopt, certainly for those who see the "freedom" dimension of choice rights as paramount. Restrictions on the outward manifestation of stricter interpretations of a faith in children would interfere relatively little with the parents' task of child-rearing whilst ensuring that some degree of secularization of the child's world exists and that equality of future choice and of opportunity is prioritized. In many ways adopting such an approach aligns with contemporary understandings of the requirements of education in states with a non-homogenous social landscape.[29] The European Court of Human Rights, for example, recently asserted the view that "in a democratic society, only pluralism in education can enable pupils to develop a critical mind with regard to religious matters in the context of freedom of thought, conscience and religion."[30] It has further accepted that "enabling children to deal critically with influences from society instead of avoiding them" constitutes a legitimate aim when limiting parental rights.[31] The suggestion appears to be that the very nature of freedom of religion requires the ability to fully reflect on and even critically challenge one's own and others' religious understandings or beliefs from a variety of perspectives. Keeping the child's world sufficiently open to difference rather than overly narrowly defined by, or dictated to, by dogma, be it religious or non-religious, might be considered to best satisfy the child's best interests.

The pluralism in education debate throws up serious questions, including over the degree to which private schools should be allowed to follow heavily doctrinal religious or

26 Elizabeth Odio Benito, *Study of the Current dimensions of the problems of intolerance and of discrimination on grounds of religion or belief* (UN Doc. E/CN.4/Sub.2/1987/26, 1986), para. 169.

27 Proverbs 22:6 (Holy Bible: The Tudor Translations 1611, Vol. III).

28 Nabil Nofal, "Al Ghazali (Vol. 1058–1111; A.H. 450–505)," *Prospects: The Quarterly Review of Comparative Education* 23, no. 3/4 (1993): 524.

29 John Keast, *Religious Diversity and Intercultural Education: A Reference Book for Schools* (Strasbourg: Council of Europe, 2007), 16.

30 *Hasan and Eylem Zengin v. Turkey,* no. 1448/04, judgment of 9 October 2007, para. 50. See also Council of Europe Parliamentary Assembly, *Recommendation 1396, Religion and Democracy* (1999), paras 13(ii), 14; Council of Europe, *Recommendation 1720,* (2005) paras 26, 27.

31 *Dojan and Others v. Germany,* no. 319/08, 2455/08, 7908/10, 8152/10, 8155/10, decision of September 13, 2011), para. 2(a).

ideological curriculums.[32] Constraining the degree to which children can become effectively marginalised from wider society through the most isolating forms of religious dress simply represents another dimension of the pluralist approach to the child's upbringing. Furthermore, if the child's choice options are kept sufficiently open, concern over the authenticity of any later choices these children might make in adulthood becomes less relevant, irrespective of whether or not they go on to adopt more orthodox dress and lifestyles. But the constraining state would need to accept that individuals, once adults or of sufficient maturity, must be free to wear the dress they may have been denied in childhood. The equality of choice dimension that intervention would be seeking to ensure for the child's future could not be allowed to deny that adult's choice. To do so we would once again confront the problems already identified in determining what choices adults are permitted to make over their relationship to religion in order to protect them from that religion.

Barriers to Interfering in Children's Adoption of Religious Dress Codes

Although circumscribing what religious dress code might apply to children might have merit for the reasons given, there are of course problems with adopting an interventionist approach, both in terms of the degree to which that intervention truly satisfies equality of choice and opportunity and in relation to existing human rights law.

When thinking about equality of choice and opportunity, Feinberg's argument presents a dilemma pointed out by Alexander and Carr.[33] On the one hand, and in support of Feinberg's approach, Alexander and Carr warn that failing to protect choice prior to a child reaching majority may leave the child with little possibility of challenging or rejecting the value to which they have been exposed. On the other hand, they point out that interfering with the process of upbringing may leave the individual insufficiently well exposed for full appreciation of the religion of their parents, leaving them inclined to reject it or reject parts of it. Whichever approach is taken, therefore, choice potentials can be said to be constrained for the child. And it is this that creates perhaps the greatest challenge for those who might favour intervention. As Feinberg identifies in his paper, and as Alexander and Carr's point alludes to, what one seems unable to do is ascertain in advance what a child's future interests are. That is to say, the chief problem for the interventionist is not about determining what dress or what education or upbringing for that matter leaves sufficient space for future choice options and opportunities and what does not. Rather the question to ask is what future options to protect and what weight these options are to be given when confronted by the claims of competing options and competing rights?[34] And this brings us to the crux of the problem and the salience of

32 See for example James G Dwyer, *Religious Schools v. Children's Rights* (New York: Cornell University Press, 1998).

33 Hanan A. Alexander and David Carr, "Philosophical Issues in Spiritual education and Development," in *The Handbook of Spiritual Development in Childhood and Adolescence*, ed. Eugene C. Roehkepartain et al. (London: Sage Publications, 2005), 81.

34 See the criticisms raised by Claudia Mills, "The Child's Right to an Open Future?" *Journal of Social Philosophy* 35, no. 4 (2003): 499.

Lacorne's point referred to earlier. Barker sets it out in this way: the perspective being taken to justify intervention seems inevitably to be coloured by one's approval or disapproval of the end state.[35] That end state may be a veiled female, a strict orthodox religious adherent, or the proliferation of a certain faith or faiths. Unless one can truly escape accusation of bias, intervention will always be considered suspect by those who are being subjected to it against their will, either for themselves or their children, and its equality justification seen as merely a chimera.

In law it is the protection of a variety of "end states" that seems to receive most support rather than protection of an abstract concept of equality. Where children are concerned, this is reflected in the weight given to parents over their child's religious education, along with their right to privacy and family life. These rights provisions, set out in Article 2 Protocol 1 European Convention on Human Rights (ECHR) and Article 8 ECHR respectively, are not merely about the function of education, the role of the family and the role of the state. They recognise that people's interpretations of what is a value on which to base their lives may vary, that passing judgment on these values is not the task of the state, and that pluralism *as a value worthy of protection in law*[36] implies support for protection of intergenerational relations through transmission from parent to child of, amongst other things, the parents' religion or belief.[37] This is even where a parent's views might be irrational and are being imposed on the child.[38] As such, these rights protect the child's religious socialisation as a feature of protecting pluralism. This protection of pluralism is not about creating children with no strong affiliations who can see all religious and belief perspectives and yet attach to none. It is about protecting diversity through what is effectively protection of a series of monisms, bounded by features such as the need to ensure toleration but not by some overriding ideological belief that certain beliefs or religious commitments or interpretations must be off limits. The parent asserting that adoption of certain religious dress by their child constitutes a feature of the child's religious socialization in accordance with the parent's convictions would have a significant body of law on which to draw.[39]

However, this is not to say that no limits can be set on transmission of religion from parent to child, including in relation to protecting the rights of the child. As the child matures, the weight of their own opinion may add to any parental objection to intervention or may stand in opposition to the parent's wishes. Although courts have, in the past, erred in favour of parents' rights as these are clearly protected under the ECHR,[40] obligations to the child as an emerging rights' holder cannot simply be ignored

35 Eileen Barker, "Misconceptions of the Religious "Other": The Importance for Human Rights of Objective and Balanced Knowledge," *International Journal for the Study of New Religions* 1, no. 1 (2010): 18.

36 See for example *Kokkinakis v. Greece,* no. 14307/88, judgment of May 25, 1993, para. 31.

37 Tore Lindholm et al., "Introduction," in *Facilitating Freedom of Religion or Belief: A Deskbook*, ed. Tore Lindholm, W. Cole Durham Jr. and Bahia G. Tahzib-Lie (Leiden: Martinus Nijhoff, 2004), xl. *Campbell and Cosans v. the United Kingdom*, no. 7511/76, 7743/76, judgment of 25 February 1982, para. 33.

38 *Vojnity v. Hungary,* no. 29617/07, judgment of 12 February 2013, para. 37.

39 See for example Anne Quennerstedt, "Balancing the Rights of the Child and the Rights of Parents in the Convention on the Rights of the Child," *Journal of Human Rights* 8, no. 2 (2009): 162.

40 Rex Ahdar and Ian Leigh, *Religious Freedom in the Liberal State* (Oxford: Oxford University Press, 2005), 203.

due to their substantive absence from the ECHR. Obligations to the child become concrete through the commitment states have made to "respect and ensure" CRC rights to each child without discrimination of any kind, irrespective of the child's or parents' religion, political or other opinion.[41] As the child matures, naturally the kind of considerations that states must pay attention to begin to take the form of the kind of considerations owed to adults. That is to say, the state will need to take into account what the child itself says and what weight should be given that view in light of their stage of maturity and the implications for the child of acting on that view.[42] Circumscribing the whole balancing exercise is the need to consider what is in the child's best interests, not only in the short term but also in the long term.

A Brief Suggestion on How States Might Best Envision Their Obligations to Children over Religious Dress Codes

Intervening in a child's religious dress code on the basis of protecting equality of choice where either parent, child or both parent and child object to intervention may, on the basis of the argument offered in this chapter, have a strong principled justification. However, at law it is difficult to see how one might act on this principled justification. One might attempt to argue that as states are now clearly assigned obligations towards the child,[43] they are now duty bound to consider the child's rights as related to but also uncoupled from the family. The requirements of children's rights cannot therefore be based simply on the views of parents. But they also cannot solely be determined by asking the child due to the child's limited comprehension of their future potential. Nor can they simply be derived from comparative adult rights due to the role parents and children are clearly assigned in the CRC. How children's and adults' rights interrelate therefore needs to be fleshed out in more detail than the CRC provides. The debate over how we are to raise our children should not therefore be seen as purely a matter for one party to decide where the child's rights are a point of issue. Parents' views, the legislator's views, the child's own views and possibly the views of the child's immediate community must all be taken into consideration.

Feinberg's argument presented briefly in this paper clearly leaves many questions unanswered on how we might reconcile what may well be several competing views. And, admittedly, even trying to extend Feinberg's argument to limiting religious dress of children may appear weak. Placing limitations on children's religious dress may have little impact on the child's equality of choice or opportunity in any case. But if there is a legitimate concern over the equality of choice of adults adopting certain forms of religious dress, and if this concern is further legitimised when some form of direct or indirect coercion is suspected, then a discussion on children and religious dress codes seems apposite. This debate need not be considered in isolation but can run parallel with

41 CRC Article 2(1).

42 CRC Article 12(1).

43 UN General Assembly, *Report of the World Conference on Human Rights* (UN Doc. A/CONF.157/24, 1993), para. 5.

debates over children's education, in particular debates taking place over religious education. Balancing competing claims and interests is paramount in this debate. But the focus must remain with serious consideration of what is in the child's best interests on their journey towards full equality as rights holders.

Conclusion

This chapter has suggested that interfering with choices over religious dress codes of children can be considered differently from similar choices made by adults. Children are subject to levels of control over their choices by both parents and the state in recognition of their minor status, their correlate lack of maturity and their status as individuals in a process of evolving as "complete" rights holders on achieving legal majority. A case has therefore been made for protecting children's ability to fully utilise the array of rights available to them as adults by limiting the choices available to them as children. In particular, choices made in childhood that might unduly prejudice the child / future adult should be actively opposed. Keeping the child's domain of choice bounded so as to allow full exercise of free choice in adulthood therefore constitutes a legitimate human rights objective. Anything that falls into an extreme category outside the boundary set can therefore be subject to limitations. Certain religious dress can be suggested as falling within the extreme category and therefore should be outside the child's domain of choice.

This chapter has revealed, however, that although a principled argument can be made for interfering with a child's religious dress code, the parent/child/state relationship at law, and the protection given to pluralism within religiously, culturally, ethically or socially non-homogenised states, seems to favour non-intervention. But with the advent of children's rights, states should not simply accept that a child's best interests, both current and future, necessarily correspond to the subjective interpretations given those interests by either the child themselves, the child's parents or the religious or non-religious immediate community in which the child is being raised. The larger problem though is to arrive at a satisfactory evaluation of exactly what a child's current and future interests are within pluralist societies where protecting religious beliefs, including protecting transmission of those beliefs from parent to child, are strong. The debate over how to raise our children within non-homogenised societies is yet to be fully explored. But it is a debate that deserves greater attention within the wider contemporary debate over accommodating diversity within Europe.

Bibliography

Ahdar, Rex and Ian Leigh. *Religious Freedom in the Liberal State*. Oxford: Oxford University Press 2005.

Alexander, Hanan A., and David Carr. "Philosophical Issues in Spiritual Education and Development." In *The Handbook of Spiritual Development in Childhood and Adolescence,* edited by Eugene C. Roehkepartain, Pamela Ebstyne King, Linda M. Wagener, and Peter L. Benson, 73–91. London: Sage Publications, 2005.

Barker, Eileen. "Misconceptions of the Religious 'Other': The Importance for Human Rights of Objective and Balanced Knowledge." *International Journal for the Study of New Religions* 1, no. 1 (2010): 5–25.

BBC News Online. "Women in face veils detained as France enforces ban." Editorial, 11 April 2011. Accessed 21 December 2013. www.bbc.co.uk/news/world-europe-13031397.

Berger, Peter L. *The Desecularization of the World: Resurgent Religion and World Politics.* Washington DC: Ethics and Public Policy Center, 1999.

Committee on the Rights of the Child, *CRC General Comment No. 12: The right of the child to be heard.* UN Doc. CRC/C/GC/12, 2009.

Dwyer, James G. *Religious Schools v. Children's Rights.* New York: Cornell University Press, 1998.

Feinberg, Joel. "The Child's Right to an Open Future." In *Freedom and Fulfilment: Philosophical Essays*, Joel Feinberg, 77–97. Princeton NJ: Princeton University 1992). Goldman, Corrie. "Burqas? Veils? Stanford visiting scholar Denis Lacorne speaks on secularism in France and the U.S." *Stanford Report*, 21 February 2013. Accessed 21 December 2013, http://news.stanford.edu/news/2013/february/lacorne-france-secularism-022213.html.

Grillo, Ralph, and Prakash Shah. "Reasons to Ban? The Anti-Burqa Movement in Western Europe." *MMG Working Paper* 12–05. Göttingen: Max Planck Institute for the Study of Religious and Ethnic Diversity, 2012.

Hill, Ryan W. "The French Prohibition on Veiling in Public Places: Rights Evolution or Violation?" *Oxford Journal of Law and Religion* 2, no. 2 (2013): 417–39.

Hosen, Nadirsyah, and Richard Mohr. *Law and Religion in Public Life: The Contemporary Debate.* Abingdon: Routledge, 2011.

Keast, John. *Religious Diversity and Intercultural Education: A Reference Book for Schools.* Strasbourg: Council of Europe, 2007.

Lentin, Alana, and Gavan Tiltley. "The Crisis of 'Multiculturalism' in Europe: Mediated Minarets, Intolerable Subjects." *European Journal of Cultural Studies* 15, no. 2 (2012): 123–38.

Lindholm, Tore, W. Cole Durham Jr., Bahia G. Tahzib-Lie and Nazila Ghanea. "Introduction." In *Facilitating Freedom of Religion or Belief: A Deskbook*, edited by Tore Lindholm, W. Cole Durham Jr., and Bahia G. Tahzib-Lie, xxvii–lxxiv. Leiden: Martinus Nijhoff, 2004.

Lyon, Dawn, and Debora Spini. "Unveiling the Headscarf Debate." *Feminist Legal Studies* 12 (2004): 333–45.

Malik, Maleiha. "Complex Equality: Muslim Women and the 'Headscarf'." *Droit et société* 68 (2008): 127–52.
McGoldrick, Dominic. *Human Rights and Religion: The Islamic Headscarf Debate in Europe*. Portland: Hart, 2006.
Mills, Claudia. "The Child's Right to an Open Future?" *Journal of Social Philosophy* 35, no. 4 (2003): 499–509.
Nofal, Nabil. "Al Ghazali (Vol.1058–1111; A.H. 450–505)." *Prospects: The Quarterly Review of Comparative Education* 23, no. 3/4 (1993): 519–42.
Odio Benito, Elizabeth. "Study of the Current dimensions of the problems of intolerance and of discrimination on grounds of religion or belief." UN Doc. E/CN.4/Sub.2/1987/26, 1986.
Okin, Susan M. "Feminism and Multiculturalism: Some Tensions." *Ethics* 108 (1998): 661–84.
Porter, John. *The Vertical Mosaic*. Toronto: University of Toronto Press, 1965.
Quennerstedt, Anne. "Balancing the Rights of the Child and the Rights of Parents in the Convention on the Rights of the Child." *Journal of Human Rights* 8, no. 2 (2009): 162–76.
Smolin, David M. "Overcoming Religious Objections to the Convention on the Rights of the Child." *Emory International Law Review* 20 (2006): 81–110.
Van Bueren, Geraldine. *The International Law on the Rights of the Child*. The Hague: Martinus Nijhoff, 1995.

PART III

RESPECT AND MEMORY

Jernej Letnar Černič*

DEMOCRACY AS A TRUMP CARD? COMBATING HATE SPEECH IN PLURALISTIC SOCIETIES

Backdrop

Freedom of expression is a human right which protects the important democratic values of pluralism, free thinking, tolerance and broadmindedness. The European Court of Human Rights has stated that freedom of expression "is a prerequisite for the functioning of democracy."[1] The maturity of a society can be judged by the level of its culture, speech and dialogue. Freedom of expression, of course, is not an all-encompassing right that would protect even the most extreme forms of expression in a democratic society. When society allows for hatred, intolerance and violence, it is neither liberal nor mature. An exchange of hostile words is often just the tip of the iceberg in societies where their ethical layer has been crippled. The use of offensive words for *ad personam* attacks on individuals and different ethnic, religious, political and other groups illustrates a deep dehumanization of individuals who employ hate speech for disqualification of different social groups and individuals. The role of law in relation to forms of hate speech can be permissive, giving societies the primary role of moving hate speech to their periphery.[2] However, freedom of expression is not unlimited and carries with it corresponding obligations. As such, freedom of expression may need to be balanced with other considerations, such as prevention of crime or protection of national security. These situations illustrate the dilemma encountered by states in reconciling two conflicting values in contemporary democratic societies. This is whether prevention of crime and protection of national security may undermine protection of freedom of expression and democratic processes, and whether protection of society's rights impedes prosecution of hate speech. In response to that dilemma, this chapter will therefore explore regulation of hate speech in contemporary democratic societies by examining recent case law of the European Court of Human Rights (ECtHR or "the Court"). The balancing exercise

* Assistant Professor of Human Rights Law and Vice-Dean, The Graduate School of Government and European Studies, Brdo pri Kranju, Slovenia.

1 Özgür Gündem v. Turkey, no. 23144/93, judgment of March 16, 2000, para. 43.

2 James Weinstein, "Extreme Speech, Public order, and Democracy: Lessons from The Masses," in *Extreme Speech and Democracy*, ed. Ivan Hare and James Weinstein (Oxford: Oxford University Press, 2009), 23–61.

between, for example, legitimate national security concerns and protection of freedom of expression as two of the fundamental pillars of a proper democracy has been and will remain delicate. Which approach a society chooses depends on its maturity, historical experience and culture of hate speech.[3] Therefore, the United States legal order[4] provides much more extensive protection to hate speech than the system of the European Convention on Human Rights and Fundamental Freedoms.[5]

This chapter is divided into five steps. Section 2 discusses the theoretical reach and limitations of freedom of expression under the European Convention on Human Rights and Fundamental Freedoms. Section 3 thereafter examines the case law of the European Court of Human Rights on hate speech and identifies its common principles. Section 4 analyses the relationship between prohibition of hate speech and democracy. It does so in three stages: first, by discussing and analysing the two-tiered approach of the ECtHR towards prohibition of hate speech, and second, by discussing the mutual importance of democracy and pluralism for freedom of expression. On the basis of this analysis, the conclusion argues in section 5 that the ECtHR and national courts must be mindful of both protection of freedom of expression and of the pluralistic democratic process, and must act within those limits.

The Reach of Freedom of Expression

Freedom of expression stands at the heart of any democratic state based on the rule of law. The right to freedom of expression allows for exchange of different views and opinions, which are a prerequisite for the development of a society that is plural, tolerant and free. However, this right is not absolute; it must be protected in relation to other human rights. The ECHR provides in Article 10(1) that "everyone has the right to freedom of expression. This right shall include freedom to hold opinions and to receive and impart information and ideas without interference by public authority and regardless of frontiers," whereas Article 10(2) states that "the exercise of these freedoms, since it carries with it duties and responsibilities, may be subject to such formalities, conditions, restrictions or penalties as are prescribed by law and are necessary in a democratic society, in the interests of national security, territorial integrity or public safety, for the prevention of disorder or crime, for the protection of health or morals, for the protection of the reputation or rights of others, for preventing the disclosure of information received in confidence, or for maintaining the authority and impartiality of the judiciary." The ECtHR noted in the historic case of *Handyside v. the United Kingdom* that freedom of expression applies "to information or ideas that are favourably received or regarded as inoffensive or as a matter of indifference, but also to those that offend shock or disturb the state or any sector of the population. Such are the demands of that pluralism, tolerance and broadmindedness without which there can be no democratic society."[6]

3 Weinstein, "Extreme Speech, Public order, and Democracy."
4 Weinstein, "Extreme Speech, Public order, and Democracy," 81–91.
5 (213 U.N.T.S 222, 3.9. 1953).
6 *Handyside v. the United Kingdom*, no. 5493/72, judgment of 7 December 1978, para. 49.

The right to freedom of expression is especially protected against institutions of the three branches of state government and individuals who perform public functions.

Freedom of expression clearly protects the right to harsh criticism of persons occupying public positions and participation in public debate.[7] Politicians and other public figures may be subject to harsher criticism than individuals who do not occupy public positions, or do not participate in the public sphere, as it is a critique of the holders of public positions in the public interest.[8] Anyone can participate in discussion of matters of public interest and may exaggerate or provoke but subject to respect for the reputation and rights of others. The right to freedom of expression does not protect false statements and records. In totalitarian societies one can often trace statements or posts that aim to denigrate or destroy an individual, an institution or an entire country, even though such statements or records are often not corroborated by documentary evidence. In non-democratic societies such statements represent *objective* truths, whereas in democratic societies they are quickly swept away to the periphery of social space.

Of course, freedom of expression in public space is not unlimited. Nonetheless, freedom of expression is a right which is beneficial to society as a whole. It is not simply an individual human right, such as the right to property. It is a constitutional value which should influence the whole of the law. Protection of freedom of expression in Article 10 also protects political expression, due to its connection with democracy. This is because members of the public must have information in order to decide which politician or political group they wish to support but not be coerced into supporting one. This suggests that everyone should be able to make free and conscious choices between different candidates and different parties, which is essential for the proper functioning of democracy and good governance in a democracy. The Court has explained the nature of political parties as follows:

> It is in the nature of the role they play that political parties, the only bodies which can come to power, also have the capacity to influence the whole of the regime in their countries. By the proposals for an overall societal model which they put before the electorate and by their capacity to implement those proposals once they come to power, political parties differ from other organisations which intervene in the political arena.[9]

Political expression as a form of freedom of expression is important and must be closely protected. It follows that states do not have *carte blanche* to unjustifiably curtail the right to freely choose between different candidates and different parties.[10] All in all, the right

7 See Jernej Letnar Černič, "Freedom of press in the European context: Klein v. Slovakia," *Edinburgh Law Review* 11, no. 3 (2007): 444–446.

8 *Castells v. Spain*, no. 11798/85, judgment of 23 April 1992, para. 46; *Otegi Mondragon v. Spain*, no. 2034/07, judgment of 15 March 2011, para. 50.

9 *Refah Partisi v. Turkey* [GC], no. 41340/98 41342/98 41343/98 41344/98, judgment of 13 February 2002.

10 *United Communist Party and Others v. Turkey* [GC], no. 19392/92, judgment of 30 January 1998, para. 42–43; *The Socialist Party and Others v. Turkey* [GC], no. 21237/93, judgment of 25 May 1998, para. 41; *Freedom and Democracy Party (ÖZDEP) v. Turkey* [GC], no. 23885/94, judgment of 8 December 1999, para. 37.

to freedom of expression must be balanced against protection of national security and each must be recognised and enforced with due respect to the other. The next section moves from a general analysis of freedom of expression to an analysis of hate speech in the jurisprudence of the European Court of Human Rights.

Hate Speech in the Jurisprudence of the European Court of Human Rights

The case law of the ECtHR on prohibition of hate speech is quite extensive. Although the jurisprudence of the ECtHR does not provide a complete all-encompassing definition of hate speech, it does offer some basic principles. The ECtHR defines speech that promotes and propagates racial and religious discrimination as completely prohibited, without exception. What is more, the ECtHR agrees that glorification of totalitarian regimes and denial or trivialization of the crime of genocide, crimes against humanity, war crimes and the Holocaust are excluded from protection of freedom of expression. The ECtHR does not in such cases employ the proportionality test on the basis of Article 10(2), but it declares a complaint inadmissible on the basis of Article 17 of the ECHR concerning prohibition of abuse of rights. More specifically, Article 17 of the ECHR provides: "Nothing in this Convention may be interpreted as implying for any State, group or person any right to engage in any activity or perform any act aimed at the destruction of any of the rights and freedoms set forth herein or at their limitation to a greater extent than is provided for in the Convention." If an expression falls outside the category of the most extreme forms of hate speech, the ECtHR examines the complaint on the basis of the principle of proportionality in relation to Article 10(2).

The ECtHR first employed Article 17 of the ECHR in the case of *Glimmerveen and Hagenbeek v. the Netherlands*, where the European Commission of Human Rights had rejected the complaint of the applicant that intended to distribute fliers with racist content.[11] The Commission has stated that "the general purpose of Article 17 is to prevent totalitarian groups from exploiting in their own interests principles enunciated by the Convention."[12] In the case of *Pavel Ivanov v. Russia*, the complainant published anti-Semitic articles and called for the exclusion of Jews from social life, for which reason the ECtHR dismissed the complaint as inadmissible.[13] In the case of *Lehideux and Isorni v. France*, the daily *Le Monde* of 18 July 1985 published a bulletin post describing Marshal Pétain, head of Vichy France, in a positive light.[14] The Court of Appeal in Paris thereafter criminally convicted the president of the organization that commissioned the contribution and the contributor himself.[15] It ordered them to pay a symbolic fine of one franc and to publish the judgment in *Le Monde*.[16] The ECtHR found that the case "... does not belong to the category of clearly established historical facts – such as the Holocaust – whose negation or revision would be removed from the protection of

11 *Glimmerveen and Hagenbeek v. the Netherlands*, no. 8348/78, 8406/78, decision of 11 October 1979.
12 *Ibid.*, point 11, 195.
13 *Pavel Ivanov v. Russia*, no. 35222/04, decision of 20 February 2007.
14 *Lehideux and Isorni v. France* [GC], no. 24662/94, judgment of 23 September 1998, paras. 9–10.
15 *Ibid.*, para. 21.
16 *Ibid.*

Article 10 by Article 17."[17] The ECtHR judgment then pointed to "the seriousness of a criminal conviction for publicly defending the crimes of collaboration, having regard to the existence of other means of intervention and rebuttal, particularly through civil remedies."[18] The judges ruled the applicants' criminal conviction to be unnecessary in a democratic society and found 10 violations of the ECHR.[19]

In the case of *Garaudy v. France* the author of "Fundamental myths of modern Israel" was sentenced to a suspended prison term and fined for denying crimes against humanity and the Holocaust.[20] The Court stated that "denying crimes against humanity is therefore one of the most serious forms of racial defamation of Jews and of incitement to hatred of them. The denial or rewriting of this type of historical fact undermines the values on which the fight against racism and anti-Semitism are based and constitutes a serious threat to public order."[21] The ECtHR declared his complaint inadmissible on the basis of Article 17, stating that "the applicant attempts to deflect Article 10 of the Convention from its real purpose by using his right to freedom of expression for ends which are contrary to the text and spirit of the Convention. Such ends, if admitted, would contribute to the destruction of the rights and freedoms guaranteed by the Convention."[22] The Court ruled similarly in the case of *Norwood v. the United Kingdom* in respect of religious discrimination against the Muslim community in England and dismissed the complaint.[23] However, the Court recently held that denial of the Armenian genocide does not constitute abuse of rights under Article 17.[24]

In the case of *Ibrahim Aksoy v. Turkey,* concerning publication of an article advocating self-determination for the Kurds within Turkey, the ECtHR stated that "the promotion of racial hatred and the idea of a superior race does not enjoy the protection of Article 10 of the ECHR."[25] The ECtHR held in the case of *Janowiec and Others v. Russia* that "speech that denies the Holocaust and war crimes opposes the values of the ECHR."[26]

Some cases deal with hate speech based on racial discrimination, where Article 17 of the ECHR does not apply. In the case of *Balsyte-Lideikiene v. Lithuania* the Court did not find violations in the case of conviction of the applicant that published "the Lithuanian calendar" that promoted hatred and intolerance towards Jewish, Polish and Russian ethnic groups.[27] The case of *Jerslid v. Denmark* concerned racist statements against immigrants in Denmark, made by a group of young boys in a television programme. A Danish court on 24 April 1987 fined three boys and journalist Jersild who produced the programme. Jersild argued before the ECtHR that the Danish courts had violated his

17 *Ibid.*, para. 47.
18 *Ibid.*, para. 57.
19 *Ibid.*, para. 58.
20 *Garaudy v. France*, no. 65831/01, decision of 24 June 2003, 2–12. See also *Honsik v. Austria*, no. 25062/94, decision of 18 October 1995 and *Marais v. France*, no. 31159/96, decision of 24 June 1996.
21 *Ibid.*, 23.
22 *Ibid.*, para. 1.
23 *Norwood v. the United Kingdom,* no. 23131/03, decision of 16 November 2004.
24 *Perinçek v. Switzerland*, no. 27510/08, judgment of 17 December 2013.
25 *Ibrahim Aksoy v. Turkey,* no. 28635/95, judgment of 10 October 2000, para. 63.
26 *Janowiec and Others v. Russia*, no. 55508/07, 29520/09, judgment of 16 April 2012, para. 119.
27 *Balsyte-Lideikiene v. Lithuania*, no. 72596/01, judgment of 4 November 2008, para. 80.

right to freedom of expression. The ECtHR did not rely in this case on Article 17, but on Article 10 of the ECHR. The Court agreed as the measure was not in accordance with the objective pursued and was not necessary in a democratic society.[28] In the case of *Kühnen v. Germany* concerning the spread of neo-Nazi propaganda, the ECtHR stated that the applicants could not rely on the protection of Article 10 as they had abused their rights and therefore dismissed the appeal under Article 17 of the ECHR.[29] In this context, some academics and practitioners strongly criticized use of Article 17 of the ECHR for the most extreme forms of hate speech, because such an approach is not the most necessary and appropriate in a democratic society.[30] However, their proposals are not very convincing as will be explained in the next sections.

In contrast, the ECtHR did not establish a violation of Article 8 (right to private and family life) of the ECHR in the case of *Aksu v. Turkey* regarding publication of government documents that discriminated against Roma communities in Turkey since the applicants had access to the Turkish courts. Although the Turkish court refused the applicant's requests[31] the ECtHR found that Turkey had thus fulfilled its positive obligations to the private life of Roma individuals under Article 8 of the ECHR.[32]

The ECtHR's case law has also developed a doctrine of prohibiting the use of hate speech in public and political debate. In the case of *Feret v. Belgium*, the ECtHR considered whether the criminal conviction of Mr Feret for the offence of solicitation of racial discrimination fell within Article 10 of the ECHR. Feret promoted hatred and xenophobia against members of the Muslim community in Belgium during an election campaign. The Belgian Court of Appeal sentenced him to 250 hours of charitable work in non-governmental organizations that help immigrants and prohibited him for ten years from exercising his right to be elected.[33] The ECtHR held that the convictions and restrictions on his freedom of expression did not exceed the limits of what is necessary in a democratic society.[34]

The EtCHR noted in the case of *Faruk Temel v. Turkey*, where the Turkish courts convicted Farouk Temel because he criticized the conduct of the Turkish authorities in relation to detainees from Kurdish political organizations,[35] that his "statements taken as a whole did not encourage the use of violence or armed conflict... The main findings thus did not constitute hate speech. The content of statements did not encourage violence by creating a deep and irrational hatred. It therefore follows that a criminal conviction

28 *Jerslid v. Denmark* [GC], no. 15890/89, judgment of 23 September 1994.

29 *Kühnen v. Germany*, no. 12194/86, decision of 12 May 1988, p. 4.

30 See David Keane, "Attacking hate speech under article 17 of the European Convention on Human Rights," *Netherlands Quarterly of Human Rights* 25, no. 4 (2007): 641–664; Hannes Cannie and Dirk Voorhoof, "The Abuse Clause and Freedom of Expression under the European Human Rights Convention: an Added Value for Democracy and Human Rights Protection?," *Netherlands Quarterly for Human Rights* 27, no. 1 (2011): 54–83.

31 *Aksu v. Turkey* [GC], no. 4149/04, 41029/04, judgment 15 March 2012, paras. 25, 35.

32 *Ibid.*, para. 76.

33 *Feret v. Belgium*, no. 15615/07, judgment of 16 July 2009, para. 34.

34 *Ibid.*, paras. 80–82.

35 *Faruk Temel v. Turkey*, no. 16853/05, judgment of 1 February 2011, paras. 23–25.

does not meet a 'pressing social need'."[36] The ECtHR added that the government should have been hesitant in relation to starting criminal proceedings, especially if there were other alternative ways to deal with unjustified attacks and criticisms of its political opponents. The authorities of a democratic state should tolerate criticism, even if statements are highly critical.[37] For this reason, the restriction on freedom of expression of the applicant was not necessary in a democratic society.[38]

The ECtHR decided in the case of *Leroy v. France* that the right to freedom of expression does not protect an individual against a conviction for the offence of incitement to hatred, because the applicant published in a local newspaper after the terrorist attacks of 11 September 2001 a caricature of the demolition of skyscrapers with the words "we are all dreaming about it ... Hamas did it."[39]

Such intervention of the French courts in the applicant's right to freedom of expression was justified for reasons of public order and the rights of others. In the case of *Vejdeland and Others v. Sweden*, the ECtHR stated that Sweden had not infringed the right to freedom of expression where a Swedish court had sentenced four applicants for the offence of incitement to hatred and intolerance because at a high school they distributed hundreds of leaflets with content hostile to homosexuals.[40] Similarly, the ECtHR held in the case of *Le Pen v. France* that a criminal conviction of Mr Le Pen for words spoken against the Islamic community in France in an interview with the newspaper *Le Monde* was necessary in a democratic society.[41]

Freedom of expression does not protect speech that promotes religious discrimination. In the case of *I.A. v. Turkey*, the applicant published a novel which insulted the Islamic prophet.[42] An Istanbul court sentenced him to two years' imprisonment, which was later converted to a fine, for insulting God, the prophet and the holy book. The ECtHR stated that "the measure taken in respect of the statements in issue was intended to provide protection against offensive attacks on matters regarded as sacred by Muslims. In that respect it finds that the measure may reasonably be held to have met a 'pressing social need'."[43]

Many issues relating to hate speech are associated with works of art. The ECtHR considered in the case of *Alinak v. Turkey* the content of a novel which discriminated against the various ethnic groups in Turkey and promoted inter-ethnic hatred and intolerance.[44] A Turkish court therefore prohibited sale of the book and ordered seizure of unsold copies.[45] The ECtHR noted that some parts of the novel "might be construed as inciting readers to hatred, revolt and the use of violence. In deciding whether they in fact

36 *Ibid.*, para. 62.
37 *Ibid.*, para. 63.
38 *Ibid.*, para. 64.
39 *Leroy v. France,* no. 36109/03, judgment of 2 October 2008.
40 *Vejdeland and Others v. Sweden,* no. 1813/07, judgment of 9 February 2012.
41 *Le Pen v. France*, no. 18788/09, decision of 20 April 2010.
42 *I. A. v. Turkey,* no. 42571/98, judgment of 13 September 2005. See also *Hizb Ut-Tahir and Others v. Germany*, no. 31098/08, judgment of 19 June 2012.
43 *Ibid.*, para. 30.
44 *Alinak v. Turkey*, no. 40287/98, judgment of 29 March 2005, para. 11.
45 *Ibid.*, paras. 12–13.

did so, it must nevertheless be borne in mind that the medium used by the applicant was a novel, a form of artistic expression that appeals to a relatively narrow public compared to, for example, the mass media..."[46] The Court held that the "the order to seize the applicant's book was disproportionate to the aims pursued and accordingly not 'necessary in a democratic society'" and that the Turkish authorities had violated Article 10 of the ECHR.[47] In the case of *Soulas and Others v. France* the ECtHR examined the merits of a judgment of the Paris Court of Justice, which ordered the publisher and author of the book *The Colonization of Europe* to pay fines as the book promoted intolerance, hatred and violence against Muslim communities in France.[48] Thereafter, the ECtHR confirmed the decision of the French courts, since prohibition of incitement to hatred is necessary in a democratic society and therefore did not find a violation of Article 10 of the ECHR.[49] In the case of *Orban and Others v. France*, the Court examined whether the criminal convictions of the author and editors of a book on operations by French forces in Algeria between 1955 and 1957 violated their freedom of expression.[50] Since the book did not encourage violence and contributed to public debate in a democratic society,[51] the Court did not find that the conviction of applicants was necessary in a democratic society.[52]

Prohibition of Hate Speech and Democracy

Freedom of expression enjoys broad protection. The ECtHR in its jurisprudence has so far distinguished between two categories of prohibition of hate speech. The first category comprises the worst forms of hate speech, where the ECtHR finds abuse of rights under Article 17 of the ECHR and thereafter does not examine the merits of the complaint. The second category includes cases in which the ECtHR addresses hate speech on the basis of the principle of proportionality under Article 10(2) of the ECHR. What is more, freedom of expression is very much dependent on the notion of democracy so that courts must address dilemmas of extreme speech hand in hand with protection of pluralism in a given society. This approach is particularly important with regard to the second category of cases arising from prohibition of hate speech. Democracy is a form of political system where people exercise power indirectly through their representatives. Elections play a central role in a pluralistic democratic process. A pluralistic democracy breathes hand in hand with a plurality of political parties representing the contrasting opinions among the population. Periodic democratic and pluralistic elections must be accompanied by the separation of public powers, pluralistic public debate, and faith in

46 *Ibid.*, para. 41.

47 *Ibid.*, para. 47. See also *Karatas v. Turkey* [GC], no. 23168/94, judgment of 8 July 1999, para. 52; *Gerger v. Turkey* [GC], no. 24919/94, judgment of 8 July 1999, para. 50; *Kizilyaprak v. Turkey*, no. 27528/95, judgment of 20 October 2003, para. 37.

48 *Soulas and Others v. France*, no. 15948/03, judgment of 10 June 2008, paras. 9,11.

49 *Ibid.*, para. 47.

50 *Orban and Others v. France*, no. 20985/05, judgment of 15 January 2009, paras. 5–9.

51 *Ibid.*, para. 52.

52 *Ibid.*, para. 54.

the media and the freedoms of expression, association, and assembly. Moreover, a democratic society requires much more than mere compliance with formal normative protections and democratic safeguards. Those democratic safeguards need to be employed in practice on a daily basis. Although the right to freedom of expression is not absolute and must be reconciled with other rights, it has often taken precedence over other values. Value judgments, promoting hatred and intolerance, or alleged factual statements not based on fact are not protected by freedom of expression. The next paragraphs therefore discuss and analyse the interrelation between prohibition of hate speech and a functioning democracy. The first category of hate speech in the jurisprudence of the ECHR prohibits only its most extreme forms. In cases where the applicant denies or downplays crimes of genocide, crimes against humanity, war crimes and the Holocaust, the ECtHR immediately rejects the complaint and does not examine its merits. Substantive democracy derives from the fundamental values of rule of law, pluralism, human rights protection, mutual respect and integrity.[53] Substantive democracy requires that the ECtHR examines every contested expression on the basis of the principle of proportionality. The path to substantive democracy cannot be trodden by insisting on opposite narratives and avoiding taking responsibility for one's own mistakes. Consolidation of democracy and reconciliation is therefore possible only on the basis of a pluralistic debate. As long as those conditions are not met, people will continue to live in an immature and subconsciously crippled society. The question is whether an absolute prohibition of hate speech is necessary in a democratic society, or would it be better for the ECtHR to examine all complaints on the basis of the principle of proportionality? In this way, it is submitted that prohibition of the worst forms of hate speech is more than clear through the case law of the ECtHR. Freedom of expression does not protect hate speech based on glorification of genocide, crimes against humanity and the Holocaust, or on discriminatory and xenophobic statements against racial, religious or ethnic group(s). This prohibition is also the lowest common denominator among the national legal orders of the member states of the Council of Europe. Nonetheless, the ECtHR's approach is convincing, particularly in a diverse and plural European context.

The second category includes cases of hate speech protected by the right to freedom of expression, which the ECtHR can limit on the basis of one of the exceptions provided in Article 10(2) of the ECHR. In doing so, the ECtHR applies the principle of proportionality. In assessing interference with freedom of expression the ECtHR must first determine whether the state interfered with the applicants' right to freedom of expression or whether it is covered by appropriate safeguards, or interference was prescribed by law and pursued a legitimate aim and whether such interference was necessary in a democratic society.

This category of hate speech leads to dilemmas of *what, who, whom, where and how*. To this end, the Court needs to examine what has been expressed, who expressed it and against whom, the context in which the words were spoken and how they were expressed. Cram notes that the "level of threat posed by the anti-democratic group at the time of the

[53] Matej Avbelj, "(Ne)demokratičnost ustavnosodnih odločb," *Pravnik* 58, no. 9 (2003): 747–766.

ban is critical to any analysis of the legality of the restraint."[54] For instance, if words have been expressed or written in a tense interracial, ethnic or inter-religious atmosphere, then the ECHR will not afford it protection. It will rather refer to any of the values of Article 10(2) of the ECHR. However, the ECtHR and national courts should give equal importance to all five questions as a partial approach often leads to a result lacking an argumentative basis. In other words, a holistic approach must be employed to properly examine the dilemma between freedom of expression and democracy.

For instance, in the case of *Sürek v. Turkey* (no. 1), the ECtHR considered interference by the Turkish authorities in the applicant's right to freedom of expression.[55] Sürek was the majority owner of the weekly *Haberde Yorumda Gerçek*.[56] The weekly published on 23 August 1992 two letters by readers, who strongly condemned the operation and the brutality of the Turkish army against the Kurds.[57] The Istanbul National Security Court sentenced the applicants on 12 April 1993. The ECtHR stated that the two contributions used terms such as "fascist Turkish army" and "murderous gang," "massacres," "brutality" and "slaughter." The ECtHR held that the letters urged bloody revenge, which encouraged and strengthened already established biases. The ECtHR stated that "the letters were published in the context of the security situation in south-east Turkey, where since approximately 1985 serious disturbances have raged between the security forces and the members of the PKK involving a very heavy loss of life and the imposition of emergency rule in much of the region."[58] Letters were therefore employed in order to promote further violence. The ECtHR held that "it must also be observed that the letter ... identified persons by name, stirred up hatred for them and exposed them to the possible risk of physical violence."[59] Therefore, the ECtHR found that the criminal conviction of the applicants was necessary in a democratic society. However, not all the judges agreed. Judges Palm and Bonello emphasized the importance of a holistic approach. In this way, Judge Palm noted in his partially dissenting opinion that "the majority has attached too much weight to the admittedly harsh and vitriolic language used in the impugned letters and insufficient attention to the general context in which the words were used and their likely impact. Undoubtedly the words in question shock and disturb the reader with their general accusatory tone and their underlying violence. But in a democracy, as our Court has emphasised, even such "fighting" words may be protected by Article 10."[60] Judge Palm concluded that there was "no real or genuine risk of the speech at issue inciting to hatred or to violence and that the applicant was sanctioned because of the political message of the letters rather

54 Ian Cram, "Constitutional responses to extremist political associations – ETA, Batasuna and democratic norms," *Legal studies* 28, no. 1 (2008): 88.

55 *Sürek v. Turkey (no. 1)* [GC], no. 26682/95, judgment of 8 July 1999. See similar cases: *Özgür Gündem v. Turkey*, no. 23144/93, judgment of 16 March 2000; *Önal v. Turkey*, no. 41445/04, 41453/04, judgment of 2 October 2012; *Sürek v. Turkey (no. 4)* [GC], no. 24762/94, judgment of 8 July 1999.

56 *Ibid.*, para. 9.

57 *Ibid.*, paras. 10–11.

58 *Ibid.*, para. 62.

59 *Ibid.*

60 *Ibid.*, partially dissenting opinion of judge Palm.

than their inflammatory tone."[61] Judge Bonello emphasized in his concurring opinion that:

> in order to support a finding of clear and present danger which justifies restricting freedom of expression, it must be shown either that immediate serious violence was expected or was advocated, or that the past conduct of the applicant furnished reason to believe that his advocacy of violence would produce immediate and grievous action. It is not manifest to me that any of the words with which the applicant was charged, however pregnant with mortality they may appear to some, had the potential of imminently threatening dire effects on the national order ...[62]

Nonetheless, harsh political statements and contributions will not be *a priori* excluded from the scope of protection of freedom of expression. The Court noted in *Batasuna and Herri Batasuna v. Spain* that "there is no democracy without pluralism. Indeed, one of the main characteristics of democracy lies in the opportunity it offers to debate through dialogue, without recourse to violence, issues raised by various currents of political opinion, even when they bother or disturb. Democracy thrives because of the freedom of expression."[63] Flauss correctly observes that the Court in such cases "simply confers more extensive discretionary powers to national authorities in order to implement limitations on the exercise of freedom of speech."[64] Therefore, the use of either approach is different from case to case and depends on the historical, cultural and legal circumstances. The balancing exercise between legitimate concerns under Article 10(2) and protection of freedom of expression has been and will remain delicate. However, the Court's judgments will be much more persuasive if they follow a holistic approach when addressing cases on prohibition of hate speech, particularly where the values of democratic political process are involved. On the other hand, if participants in public debate use speech which promotes violence, hatred and intolerance, they overstep the protection of freedom of expression, which only protects peaceful expression. When violence breaks out against participants in public debate, the public authorities must safeguard public order, national security or other values. Freedom of expression does not protect statements which incite discrimination, hatred and violence. The ECtHR noted that in *Erkaban v. Turkey* that "tolerance and respect for the dignity of all people ... constitute the foundations of a democratic and pluralistic society. It follows that in principle it may be considered necessary in certain democratic societies to sanction or even prevent all forms of expression which spread, incite, promote or justify hatred based on intolerance ..."[65] The ECtHR and national courts must be mindful of both protection of freedom of expression and of a pluralistic democratic process, and must act within those limits. Such are the demands of a democratic, pluralistic and free society.

61 *Ibid.*
62 *Ibid.*, partially dissenting opinion of judge Bonello.
63 *Herri Batasuna and Batasuna v. Spain*, no. 25803/04, 25817/04, judgment of 30 June 2009, para. 76.
64 Jean-François Flauss, "The European Court of Human Rights and Freedom of Expression," *Indiana Law Journal* 84, no. 3 (2009): 841.
65 *Erbakan v. Turkey*, no. 59405/00, judgment of 6 July 2006, para. 56.

Conclusions

Although in its case law the ECtHR has emphasized that the right to freedom of expression also protects those statements which "offend shock or disturb the state or any sector of the population," this is, however, not an absolute right. Freedom of expression does not in any case protect promotion and/or incitement of national, racial, religious or and other discrimination, hatred, intolerance and violence. Such expression falls outside the protected field. Prohibition of hate speech has been taken for granted as it is often pushed to the periphery by society itself. Effective implementation of prohibition of hate speech can contribute to a more tolerant dialogue in European societies. However, mere normative protection is not sufficient. Individuals also bear a key responsibility in creating a tolerant, open-minded and pluralistic public sphere in the respective European societies.

Prohibition of hate speech is one of most radical measures to be employed by democratic states. States must therefore be mindful of protection of fundamental human rights and must act within those limits. Prohibition of hate speech is a restriction on freedom of expression and may be necessary at times to protect society's fundamental freedoms and rights. However, if speech does not promote violence, hatred, intolerance and discrimination and society does not face an unacceptable and real threat to national security and the pluralistic democratic process, then the individual's right should be given priority.

Discussion on political pluralism and hate speech is often underpinned by deeply-rooted emotions that suppress argumentative dialogue and reasoning and have led to the long-term polarization of European societies. There are no simple answers to the fundamental questions raised by extreme speech. This chapter has attempted to argue that the ECtHR and national courts should employ a holistic approach to examining potential hate speech. Courts should strike a better balance by assessing the *real* level of threat to the democratic order represented by alleged hate speech and by protecting fundamental human rights and freedoms.

Bibliography

Avbelj, Matej. "(Ne)demokratičnost ustavnosodnih odločb." *Pravnik* 58, no. 9 (2003): 747–66.

Cannie, Hannes, and Dirk Voorhoof. "The Abuse Clause and Freedom of Expression under the European Human Rights Convention: an Added Value for Democracy and Human Rights Protection?" *Netherlands Quarterly for Human Rights* 27, no. 1 (2011): 54–83.

Cram, Ian. "Constitutional responses to extremist political associations – ETA, Batasuna and democratic norms." *Legal studies* 28, no. 1 (2008) 68–95.

Černič, Jernej Letnar. "Freedom of press in the European context: Klein v. Slovakia." *Edinburgh Law Review* 11, no. 3 (2007): 444–46.

Flauss, Jean-François. "The European Court of Human Rights and Freedom of Expression." *Indiana Law Journal* 84, no. 3 (2009): 810–84.

Keane, David. "Attacking hate speech under article 17 of the European Convention on Human Rights." *Netherlands Quarterly of Human Rights* 25, no. 4 (2007): 641–64.

Weinstein, James. "An Overview of American Free Speech Doctrine and its Application to Extreme Speech," In *Extreme Speech and Democracy*, edited by Ivan Hare and James Weinstein, 81–91. Oxford: Oxford University Press, 2009.

Weinstein, James. "Extreme Speech, Public order, and Democracy: Lessons from The Masses." In *Extreme Speech and Democracy*, edited by Ivan Hare and James Weinstein, 23–61. Oxford: Oxford University Press, 2009.

Aleksandra
Gliszczynska-Grabias*

COPING WITH THE PAST IN A MULTICULTURAL EUROPE: THE EUROPEAN COURT OF HUMAN RIGHTS ON MEMORY AND LAW

Introduction

The dramatic history of the last century still plays a predominant role in today's Europe, determining its current political, social and legal realm. It is also present and sometimes even predominant in places such as the Strasbourg courtroom of the European Court of Human Rights (ECtHR).[1] Many times over the past 50 years Strasbourg judges have had to decide on matters related to the memory and identity of European societies and to search for answers to the following questions: which of the historical claims deserve legal protection offered by the so-called "memory laws"? When does an otherwise justified action against abuse of historical truth turn into a state-sponsored decreeing of an official version of history? How far can judges inquire into the historical background of societies in order to decide if a human right of an individual had been violated? Those questions become even more urgent if we take into account the ever greater social, national and ethnic diversification of today's Europe as well as the myriad existing cultures, traditions, religions and beliefs. The legal space currently created in Europe through memory laws may be misunderstood or even not accepted by those groups in European societies whose historical identity and memory do not encompass events which are crucial from the European perspective. Tensions which arise against this background are among the most important challenges in the field of current social relations within multicultural communities.

* PhD, senior researcher at the Poznán Human Rights Centre, Institute of Legal Studies of the Polish Academy of Sciences.

1 One of the most significant cases concerning history and responsibility for historical human rights violations is the complaint against Russia filed by the relatives of the Polish military prisoners executed in Katyn in 1940. The Strasbourg Court found Russia in violation of Article 3 of the European Convention on Human Rights (ECHR) on the prohibition of torture, stating that the Russian government did not provide the applicants with sufficient information regarding the fate of their relatives. However, the judges did not pass a decision on the violation of Article 2 on the right to life. Controversially, in the Grand Chamber verdict, the ECtHR held not only that it has no competence to examine the complaint under Article 2 of the Convention, but also overruled its previous finding concerning violation of Article 3 and deciding that such violation did not take place. *Janowiec and Others v. Russia* [GC], no. 55508/07, 29520/09, judgment of October 21, 2013.

This chapter will examine a variety of answers so far provided by the ECtHR to the above questions. In particular the almost uniform case-law in matters related to the Holocaust and the National Socialist regime will be analysed.[2] One may ask whether, by doing so, the Strasbourg Court is contributing to the creation of a particular hierarchy of dramatic events in European history. And if so, what kind of arguments has it expressed in order to support its position? This is another question which is to be reflected upon in this chapter. Three cases (complaints lodged against Germany, France and Hungary) are of particular relevance for the analysis and will be considered in detail, also from the perspective of the narrative so far dominating in the Court's jurisprudence on free speech.[3]

The chapter will also address the persistence of other, non-European historical narratives in the current case law of the ECtHR, and dilemmas raised by the existence of the dominant model in a Europe which is multi-cultural and diverse,

Struggling with the Past

It is usually extremely difficult to distinguish between acceptable exercise of freedom of speech and unacceptable abuse of this right.[4] Each limitation in this regard deprives an individual of the ability to freely express their opinion, emotions and beliefs. Moreover, as Wiktor Osiatyński has noted, freedom of speech protects an individual not only from the repressive attempts of a state but also from capture of public debate by powerful and influential non-state actors.[5]

Thus, if legal provisions limit freedom of expression in a way which obstructs historical debate on key events in the history of a given country and society, those in power can be accused of imposing an orthodox version of history, which in many cases turns out to be distant from the historical memory of particular ethnic, national or religious groups within societies. Thus such legal provisions may be considered as a factor of exclusion from rather than inclusion in the community. Such limitations may also justifiably be regarded as closing down the debate for contradictory narratives. In some historical contexts they even risk serving those who hide the truth and deny the state's liability for past events.[6] Therefore, in the case of memory laws, the reasonableness,

2 This applies in particular to cases concerning limiting the freedom of speech of Holocaust deniers. See Emanuela Fronza, "The Punishment of Negationism: The Difficult Dialogue Between Law and Memory," *Vermont Law Review* 30 (2006): 609–26.

3 On various aspects of free speech case-law of the ECtHR see Josep Casadevall et al., *Freedom of Expression: Essays in Honour of Nicolas Bratza, President of the European Court of Human Rights* (Strasbourg: Wolf Legal Publishers, 2012).

4 It is particularly difficult in the case of hate speech bans, as the concepts of hate, hostility or prejudice lack legal definition. For comprehensive analysis of many aspects of the dilemma of punishing for hate speech see Ivan Hare and James Weinstein, *Extreme Speech and Democracy* (Oxford: Oxford University Press, 2009).

5 Wiktor Osiatyński, *Human Rights and Their Limits* (Cambridge: Cambridge University Press, 2009), 195.

6 Among eminent scholars opposing criminal law sanctions in the case of memory laws are: Pierre Emmanuel Vidal-Naquet, Deborah Lipstadt, and Timothy Garton Ash.

necessity and proportionality of limitations imposed on the participants in historical discussions must be proved under strict scrutiny.

Memory laws can be defined on the basis of various criteria, with reference to historical events being their key component. They take the form of legal recognition of a certain historical fact such as a crime of genocide or crime against humanity (e.g. in 2013 the British parliamentary recognition of the Kurdish genocide in Iraq); they may also prescribe by law the commemoration of historical events. Another example of memory law is legal prohibition of interpreting historical events in a particular manner, subject to a sanction.[7] Importantly, sanctions primarily apply if the very occurrence of crimes of genocide is denied or if such crimes are interpreted in a certain way described by the legislator, which most often involves their endorsement, severe downgrading or belittling and trivialising. However, memory laws may also prohibit public display and dissemination of certain historical symbols (such as the swastika or the hammer and sickle), or registration of organisations that base their agenda on the totalitarian and criminal heritage of the Third Reich or Fascist Italy.

One particular example of memory law is the Spanish 2007 Law of Historic Memory, which includes prohibition of political events at the Valley of the Fallen – Franco's burial place – and orders the removal of Francoist symbols from public buildings and spaces, with the exception allowed for artistic or architectural reasons, or for religious spaces.[8] The statute was enacted as a way of addressing the matter of coping with the recent Francoist and nationalist past, as demanded mainly by the Left, despite resistance by those who warned against such enactments and who did not discern major problems regarding the Franco legacy in Spanish society today. In the context of the multicultural character of Spanish society, which at the same time grapples with the process of including immigrants in a common social space, it may be worth considering the problem of the impact of such memory laws on the aforementioned process. It seems that in this case it is possible to find arguments which both support and refute the creation of such laws. The argument for memory laws similar to that concerning the past of the Franco regime emphasises the need for all citizens to know state history, which will facilitate creation of a more comprehensive identity. A counter-argument would rather be based on the conviction that such laws are created for a select part of society, to which immigrants, refugees and all "others" will never belong, and to which they will have to submit. They are placed beyond the pale of the common memory, so to speak.

7 For example in Poland it is legally forbidden to contradict publicly and contrary to the facts, Nazi crimes, communist crimes and other crimes constituting crimes against peace, crimes against humanity or war crimes, perpetrated against persons of Polish nationality and Polish citizens of other ethnicity or nationalities in the period between 1 September 1939 and 31 July 1990. Violation attracts a fine or a penalty of deprivation of liberty of up to three years and the judgment is to be made publicly known. Polish Official Journal no.155, item 1016, 18 December 1998. http://isap.sejm.gov.pl/.

8 Ley 52/2007, de 26 de diciembre, por la que se reconocen y amplían derechos y se establecen medidas en favor de quienes padecieron persecución o violencia durante la guerra civil y la dictadura. www.derechos.org/nizkor/espana/doc/lmheng.html. For an analysis of the legal dimension of the transitional justice period in Spain, see Joseph M. Tamarit Sumalla, *Historical Memory and Criminal Justice in Spain. A Case of Late Transitional Justice* (Cambridge – Antwerp – Portland: Intersentia, 2013).

Another memory law, fortunately no longer in force, was a provision included in the Polish penal code in 2006, establishing a crime of "defamation of the Polish Nation." The offence defined in this provision consisted in accusing the Polish Nation of participation in Nazi and Communist crimes. The regulation was a response by then-incumbent political forces, partly far-right, to facts revealed by the historian Jan Tomasz Gross in his books, concerning crimes and wrongs committed by Poles against Jews during and directly after the Second World War.[9] In a judgment of 19 September 2008, the Constitutional Tribunal ruled that the provision in question did not conform to the Constitution of Poland, holding that the unconstitutionality was caused by defects which had occurred in the course of legislative works. Yet the Tribunal failed to address the fact that the provision, which penalised claims about Polish participation in crimes of Nazism and Communism, in effect used the authority of the Polish state to endorse a lie. This proves clearly that instead of preserving the truth, memory laws may, if the legislator so decides, contribute to obscuring it. Even though in Poland the national and ethnic social structure is clearly much simpler than the current one in Spain, it is also worth considering how alien the law on defamation of Polish society must have been for all those members of Polish society who did not have a historical and cultural background that would allow them to understand the reasons for passing such absurd laws.

For their proponents, the purpose of laws regulating historical facts and events and their interpretation is to safeguard the truth about the past and protect the memory of victims of history's darkest moments. However, opponents of memory laws protest against decreeing historical dogmas through legal sanctions. The ECtHR had to resolve which party to the above dispute is right not only in a particular case, but also referring to the elements of the legal rationale for establishing memory laws. The Strasbourg judges therefore ruled on general issues sometimes related to the very essence of a given nation's identity and history. So far, they have been dealing with this difficult challenge in a variety of ways, performing their task which is both easy and cumbersome at the same time. As far as memory laws are concerned, the "easy part" is that the judges most often are not personally involved in historical conditions and events which constitute the content of the cases they hear. Yet this personal detachment is the very factor that causes the difficulties they experience in resolving memory law cases: placed outside the centre of a given historical narrative, judges may face problems with fully comprehending the lawmakers' intent as well as the effects brought about by particular enactments of memory laws.[10]

9 On these shameful and hurtful events see Jan Grabowski, *Hunt for the Jews: Betrayal and Murder in German-Occupied Poland* (Bloomington: Indiana University Press, 2013).

10 The concept of margin of appreciation seems particularly relevant and important in cases concerning the specifics – historical, social or political – of a given state. However, some consider granting the margin by the ECtHR to a wide extent allows judges to avoid expressing legal opinions on controversial issues. For critical analysis of the concept see Arai Yutaka, *The Margin of Appreciation Doctrine and the Principle of Proportionality in the Jurisprudence of the ECHR* (Cambridge: Intersentia, 2002).

The ECtHR on Holocaust Denial, Marshal Pétain and the Communist Red Star

A major part of ECtHR case-law concerning memory laws refers to the issue of penalising public expressions of Holocaust denial and prohibitions on approving crimes committed by the Nazi regime. In an overwhelming majority of cases, the Court explicitly took the side of the state-parties, declaring applications lodged by Holocaust deniers inadmissible.

In a complaint submitted by the Munich-Upper Bavaria regional branch of the National Democratic Party of Germany (NDP) the applicant challenged a series of obligations imposed on the NDP by the Munich municipal authorities in connection with a conference held by the applicant.[11] The conference was entitled "Germany's future in the shadow of political extortion?" and was to host a lecture by the well-known negationist David Irving.[12] The organisers of the conference were obliged to ensure that the event would not feature statements denying the Holocaust and advise the conference participants on penal sanctions for inciting hatred, or insulting or defiling the memory of the dead. The organisers were also requested to terminate the conference immediately after any such statements were made.

The application submitted to Strasbourg asserted that statements denying the persecution of Jews by the Nazis and existence of gas chambers were protected by the European Convention for Human Rights. The gas chambers in Auschwitz were described as not authentic, according to scientific research. The applicant further argued that the conference was solely to discuss anti-German "extortion propaganda." In its decision, the Strasbourg court considered the application inadmissible, holding that interference by the German authorities had been proportional and necessary in a democratic society to protect the rights and reputation of Jews. Citing Article 17 of the Convention, the Commission – at that time part of the Strasbourg system – held that statements calling into question the persecution of Jews under the National-Socialist regime in the context of a discussion of "anti-German extortion propaganda" are contrary to the axiological basis of the Convention.[13]

11 *Nationaldemokratische Partei Deutschlands, Bezirksverband München-Oberbayern v. Germany*, no. 25992/94, decision of November 29, 1995.

12 David Irving is a notorious Holocaust denier and one of the leaders of the negationist movement in Europe. In 1996 Irving filed a libel suit against Deborah Lipstadt and her British publisher Penguin Books for publishing a British edition of Lipstadt's book, Denying the Holocaust, in which Lipstadt called Irving a Holocaust denier, falsifier, and bigot. Irving lost the case. The court trial which resulted from Irving's suit was one of the most controversial and disturbing legal battles in the field of memory, history and law. See Deborah Lipstadt, *History on Trial: My Day in Court with David Irving* (New York: Ecco, 2005).

13 The most explicit and firm statement of the Strasbourg Court on the incompatibility of Holocaust denial with the very foundations of the European Convention was expressed in a case against France (*Garaudy v. France*, no. 65831/01, decision of 24 June 2003). The ECtHR summed up its argument in the following quotation:

> Denying crimes against humanity is therefore one of the most serious forms of racial defamation of Jews and of incitement to hatred of them. The denial or rewriting of this type of historical fact undermines the values on which the fight against racism and anti-Semitism are based and constitutes a serious threat to public order. Such acts are incompatible with democracy and human rights because they infringe the rights of others.

A number of other applications brought by negationists to the ECtHR were similarly dismissed as manifestly ill-founded. This approach was justified in the Court's jurisprudence by the fact that the assertions made by applicants were examples of discrimination based on race and religion,[14] a continuation of the traditional discrimination against the Jewish people and incitement to hatred against Jews[15] as well as defamation and deprivation of reputation resulting from reproaching them with lying and extortion and thus portraying them as particularly abominable.[16]

In a high-profile case against France the above line of judicial reasoning in respect of Holocaust denial was generally upheld, or even amplified by a determination that article 17, which prohibits destruction of any of the rights and freedoms set forth in the Convention, may constitute the exclusive basis for dismissing negationists' applications as manifestly ill-founded, hence being a certain kind of prohibitive clause restricting their ability to seek protection of freedom of expression in Strasbourg.[17] Although the case generally concerned criminal liability for defending the reputation of Marshal Philippe Pétain, conduct considered in France as equal to endorsing war crimes, controversy was raised by another aspect of the ECtHR's judgment in *Lehideux*, namely the assessment of sanctions imposed by French national courts against persons defending the good name of Marshal Pétain, who had been found guilty of endorsing war crimes.

The applicants in this case were French nationals. The former was the President of the Association for the Defence of the Memory of Marshal Pétain, and Minister for Industrial Production in the Vichy Government. The latter was a defence lawyer for Marshal Pétain during his post-war trial.[18] In July 1984 the daily newspaper "Le Monde" published a one-page advertisement starting with the subsequently repeated passage "People of France, you have short memories if you have forgotten that…," followed by a series of assertions presenting the figure of Marshal Pétain in a positive, or even laudatory, way. Organisations of former members of the French Resistance filed a criminal complaint, accusing the advertisers and the editor of "Le Monde" of public endorsement of war crimes and collaboration with the enemy. The accusations were later affirmed by domestic courts.

In its judgment, finding a violation of article 10 of the Convention, the Strasbourg Court faced a difficult challenge in assessing what constituted an abuse of freedom of expression in the French historical context. The Court emphasised that no endorsement of pro-Nazi policy could enjoy the protection afforded by article 10 but noted that in the instant case the applicants explicitly stated their disapproval of "Nazi atrocities and persecutions" and of "German omnipotence and barbarism" though they failed to mention that Marshal Pétain had knowingly contributed to their occurrence, particularly through his responsibility for the persecution and deportation of French Jews.[19] The

14 *Remer v. Germany*, no. 25096/94, decision of 6 September 1995.
15 *Walendy v. Germany*, no. 21128/93, decision of 11 January 1995.
16 *X. v. Germany*, no. 9235/81, decision of 16 July 1982.
17 *Lehideux and Isorni v. France* [GC], no. 55/1997/839/1045, judgment of 23 September 1998.
18 On 15 July 1945 Marshal Pétain was convicted and sentenced to death by a one-vote majority of the Tribunal of State.
19 On the crimes of the Vichy regime see in particular Robert Aron, *The Vichy Regime, 1940–44* (Boston: Beacon Press, 1969).

ECtHR found that the applicant's silence on the Marshal's responsibility, though "morally reprehensible," needed to be assessed together with a number of other circumstances in the case, above all the fact that nearly 40 years had passed since the events mentioned in the advertisement took place. The ECtHR also referred to the state's duty to make efforts to hold an open public debate on even the most controversial subjects concerning its own history. The Strasbourg Court noted that the case would have been resolved differently if the applicants had negated the Holocaust thus contradicting clearly established historical facts.[20] In that case, however, the history of the Vichy regime and the personal role played by Marshal Pétain were still a part of an ongoing debate.

Still, the judgment was not unanimous – in their dissenting opinions several judges emphasised that limitation of the applicants' right to freedom of speech was necessary in a democratic society.[21] The dissenting judges took note of the form of the published material – a press advertisement – and argued that the advertisement, entirely one-sided and of a "promotional" character, had brought no "added value" to historical debate. Above all, the dissenters pointed to the Court's improper assessment of the margin of appreciation afforded to the state. The argument was based on a contention that the circumstances of the case clearly indicated that it concerned historical events in France whose specific features could be best considered by French courts.[22] An important critical statement was also expressed by Judge Casadevall, who opposed the majority argument that the passage of 40 years after the events discussed in the advertisement

20 The ECtHR stated that in the case of clearly established historical facts, such as the Holocaust, their negation or revision would be removed from the protection of Article 10 by Article 17 of the ECHR.

21 See in particular the dissenting opinion of judges Foighel, Loizou and Freeland, which is worth quoting at length: "As regards the content of the advertisement, the applicants have, in order to distance Philippe Pétain from personal responsibility for the darker side of what was done in France during the Vichy era and as part of the vindication of his actions during the period, pointed to the references in the text to 'Nazi atrocities and persecutions' and its claim that he afforded protection to the French people from 'German omnipotence and barbarism'. Yet, as the Paris Court of Appeal observed in its judgment of 26 January 1990, the text said nothing at all about the notorious racist, and in particular anti-Jewish, activities undertaken by the Pétain regime itself, beginning with the Act relating to aliens of Jewish race which was signed by him on 3 October 1940. … The distortion inherent in this contrasting silence about one of the most unsavoury features of the Pétain regime is capable of being understood as amounting to implicit support for what was done. Even if such a distortion is, however, insufficient, because too indirect or remote, to constitute an "activity or … act aimed at the destruction of any of the rights and freedoms set forth" in the Convention, within the meaning of its Article 17, so as to disable the applicants from relying on Article 10, the principle which underlies Article 17 is a factor which can properly be taken into account in the assessment of the exercise of the margin of appreciation and the existence of necessity. That principle is one of firm discouragement of the promotion of values hostile to those embodied in the Convention. Having regard to the conclusions reached in the judgment of the Paris Court of Appeal of 26 January 1990 as to the effect to be given to the wording of the advertisement, and having regard to the concern which the French authorities, with their particular familiarity with the historical background and current context, could legitimately have to demonstrate that racism and, in particular, anti-Semitism, are not to be condoned, we consider that the margin of appreciation should not be treated as having been exceeded and that the test of necessity in a democratic society has been satisfied in this case."

22 The argument concerning granting France a wider margin of appreciation was included in the dissenting opinions of judges Morenilla and Casadevall.

should be considered an "alleviating" factor. Moreover, Judge Casadevall agreed with the opinion expressed in the dissenting opinion to the Commission's report regarding the very favourable and lenient approach to far-right ideas in the 1990s in Europe.

It seems that the dissenting judges in *Lehideux* were right in their conclusions that in this case the state should have been awarded a wider margin of appreciation in assessing what constituted endorsement of the Nazi regime and collaboration with the enemy. At the moment the advertisement was published, historical knowledge of the crimes of the Vichy regime and French collaboration with the Nazis had already been well-established as undoubtedly conducive to such atrocities as deportations of French Jews to death camps. Further, although the Strasbourg Court rightly stated in its argument that the Convention should be interpreted and applied in individual cases in the light of "present-day" conditions and circumstances, it seems unreasonable to apply this rule to cases involving negation of the Holocaust or other forms of falsifying historical truth.[23] This is so because the more time passes after a negated or falsified event, the greater the risk of encountering the adverse effects of such behaviour, because with the passage of time there are fewer direct witnesses and therefore a greater risk that the falsehood will be accepted at face value.[24]

Yet the Strasburg standards applicable to memory laws relating to the Nazi regime have not been mechanically transferred by the ECtHR into memory laws concerning the Stalinist and Communist regime. In this peculiar way the Court voiced its opinion in the debate on the equal treatment of the crimes committed by Hitler and those perpetrated by Stalin, which has been becoming increasingly emotional over recent decades.[25] In particular the Baltic States, themselves former Soviet republics, have been making attempts, also in the legal sphere, to vindicate such an equalisation of both regimes.[26]

In July 2008 the ECtHR delivered a landmark decision in a case against Hungary which hinged on the question about the admissibility of restricting a public display of Communist symbols.[27] The applicant in this case, Vice-President of the Hungarian Workers' Party, complained about infringement of his right to freedom of expression. In 2004, he was found guilty of a violation of the law prohibiting a public display of totalitarian symbols which he had allegedly committed by placing a red star symbol on his jacket and wearing it during a legal demonstration. The Hungarian authorities argued

23 *Tyrer v. United Kingdom*, no. 5856/72, judgment of 25 April 1978.

24 As regards Holocaust denial, such threat has been especially visible over the period of the last few years which mark the departure of the last generations of death camp prisoners, direct witnesses to the Holocaust. In January 2012 the Forsa Research Institute revealed the results of a survey, which proved that 21% of Germans aged between 18 and 30 asked about Auschwitz Nazi extermination camp had never heard of it. Data reported by Education News: www.educationnews.org/international-uk/20-of-german-students-do-not-know-about-auschwitz/.

25 For a multitude of examples proving the ECtHR's differential treatment of two totalitarian regimes: Communism and Nazism, see James A. Sweeney, *The European Court of Human Rights in the Post-Cold War Era. Universality in Transition* (London: Routledge, 2013).

26 In 2008 prominent European politicians, former political prisoners and historians signed the Prague Declaration on European Conscience and Communism, which called for "Europe-wide condemnation of, and education about, the crimes of communism." The text of the declaration is available at www.webcitation.org/64otCtAyz.

27 *Vajnai v. Hungary*, no. 33629/06, judgment of 8 July 2008.

for the necessity of counteracting dangers related to the totalitarian Communist regime. However, the ECtHR held that the applicant's right had been infringed and the authorities' interference was not necessary in a democratic society owing to the absence of a real danger of reinstatement of the former regime. The Court observed that the red star symbol might be associated with mass violations of human rights occurring in the age of Communist rule in Hungary. Notwithstanding, it ruled that the sign itself might also symbolise the entire international workers' movement and legally recognised political parties.In a very important element of its judgment, the ECtHR refers to the danger involved in translating social feelings and opinions into legal regulations:

> The Court is of course aware that the systematic terror applied to consolidate Communist rule in several countries, including Hungary, remains a serious scar in the mind and heart of Europe. It accepts that the display of a symbol which was ubiquitous during the reign of those regimes may create uneasiness amongst past victims and their relatives, who may rightly find such displays disrespectful. It nevertheless considers that such sentiments, however understandable, cannot alone set the limits of freedom of expression. Given the well-known assurances which the Republic of Hungary provided legally, morally and materially to the victims of Communism, such emotions cannot be regarded as rational fears.

The judgment should be considered an outcome of balancing the actual magnitude of threats against particular limitations of rights and freedoms with respect to memory laws.[28] There exist no public opinion polls that would reveal a likelihood of the return of Communist rule in a form involving crimes and mass violations of human rights. At the same time, a similar decision probably would not be made in respect of a public display of the swastika symbol on a jacket of a member of the National Democratic Party of Germany speaking in public in Berlin since there is a conceivable danger that far-right, neo-Nazi political movements may actually gain certain political significance.[29] The ECtHR also noted that the red star symbol did not represent an unequivocal political meaning. Arguably, in the case of the swastika, the meaning and symbolism it conveyed from the moment the Nazis took power in Germany would rightly prevent the Strasbourg Court from reaching a conclusion similar to that expressed in the Hungarian case.

(De)legitimised Heritage and Memory of the Other

There is yet another dimension to European ways of coping with the past, as often reflected in legal acts and judgments. This is the dimension of the memory and legacy of various minorities which also seek recognition of their historical narratives which often clash with the dominant or majoritarian narrative in their country or throughout

[28] This approach taken by the ECtHR was confirmed in *Fratanoló v. Hungary*, no. 29459/10, judgment of 11 November 2011.

[29] The drastic example of the Hungarian far-right Jobbik party clearly demonstrates that traditional anti-Semitic and racial attitudes and slogans, similar to those observed in the Nazi era, are still alive. See reports on Hungary by the European Commission against Racism and Intolerance: www.coe.int/t/dghl/monitoring/ecri/Country-by-country/Hungary/Hungary_CBC_en.asp.

Europe. One must emphasize: there is rarely a single "memory" in a given society; there are numerous memories, some more on the surface and enjoying majoritarian support, others more hidden and often neglected or even persecuted.

Among many examples of such "memory clashes" one may consider the case of the recent French law which mandated a positive account of the role of French colonialism in school curricula and textbooks.[30] Naturally, descendants of peoples from French colonial territory who now live in France protested vigorously. Another problematic case is that of the historical memory of Germans who, increasingly, have sought recognition of German sufferings at the hands of the Red Army and the Allies at the end of the Second World War. The Centre against Expulsions which opened in Berlin with the support of the German authorities triggered strong protests, mainly by many Poles.[31] There is some analogy with attempts by sexual orientation minorities, especially by homosexuals, to commemorate crimes against members of these minorities committed by the Nazis.[32] For a long period after the end of the Second World War their victimhood remained unacknowledged. In this way, part of European historical memory centred around the 2nd World War remained diminished.

As an effect of such exclusion from the common circle of historical narratives, often reinforced by legal rules, there is a reinforced separation between "Us" and "Them," an increase of xenophobia, and radicalization of the position of those who perceive recognition of the commonality of legacy and memory as a threat to the legitimacy of the established order.

This is directly related to the question of limits to freedom of speech in a multinational, multicultural and multi-religious society. The "Others" who are excluded from the common circle of legacy and memory, and who are usually also denied legal protection for their sensibilities, are usually most vulnerable when it comes to manifestations of hate speech. In his recent book, Jeremy Waldron made this point very well.[33] The history of enslavement, persecution and humiliation suffered by African Americans throughout history became part of the official story about the US past only with the achievements of the movement led by Martin Luther King Jr.[34] As a result, those internal "Others" became the main targets of racist assaults. But Waldron's observations can also be extrapolated to the European scene. While in many European countries Muslim minorities have been present for many generations, feelings of Islamophobia have intensified. It seems that this worrying phenomenon is related to the fact that Muslim history, culture and religious practices have not been included, on equal grounds, as part of the generally recognized European heritage.

30 *Loi Rapatriés* of 15 February 2005.

31 In the 2002 resolution, the German Parliament called for establishing 'A centre against displacement with a European alignment,' In none of its paragraphs does the resolution mention the word 'Nazism' or indicate the reasons for the displacements. The text of the declaration is available at www.z-g-v.de/english/aktuelles/?id=61 (accessed December 16, 2013).

32 See Richard Plant, *The Pink Triangle: The Nazi War Against Homosexuals* (New York: Holt Paperbacks, 1988).

33 See Jeremy Waldron, *The Harm in Hate Speech* (Cambridge: Harvard University Press, 2012).

34 For a bitter description of the Afro-Americans, see James Baldwin, *The Fire Next Time* (New York: The Dial Press, 1963).

The problem of applying the same legal reasoning towards the "other," non-European historical memory has been well displayed in an ECtHR case against Switzerland concerning sanctions imposed for rejection of the legal characterisation as "genocide" of the 1915 massacre of Kurds by the Turks.[35] Finding violation of the applicant's rights under article 10 of the Convention, the ECtHR, by a majority, clearly distinguished between the "Armenian genocide" and the Holocaust, granting only to the latter the status of undisputed fact of clear legal and historical qualification. The judgment is troublesome and will undoubtedly be a subject of stormy comments, part of which will point to the inadmissibility of creation by the ECtHR of a "hierarchy of genocides." Indeed it seems that in order to provide convincing arguments for different treatment of Holocaust denial cases, the Court will need to go beyond mere reference to internationally approved legal definitions and elaborate in more detail on historical narratives which emerge from other than European backgrounds.

Concluding Remarks

Considering the arguments for and against memory laws one is confronted with a dilemma, which is captured in two powerful quotations. The first is a call by Ellie Wiesel, a survivor from the Holocaust and a Nobel Peace Prize winner, who asks for securing the truth about the past when he says "Remembering is a noble and necessary act. The call of memory, the call to memory, reaches us from the very dawn of history,"[36] The second is the call by the signatories of the "Appel de Blois":

> History must not be a slave to contemporary politics nor can it be written on the command of competing memories. In a free state, no political authority has the right to define historical truth and to restrain the freedom of the historian with the threat of penal sanctions... We ask government authorities to recognize that, while they are responsible for the maintenance of the collective memory, they must not establish, by law and for the past, an official truth whose legal application can carry serious consequences for the profession of history and for intellectual liberty in general.[37]

Meeting halfway between these demands is not an easy task, but a necessary one, as law cannot stay indifferent to situations when under the cover of free academic debate some try to spread hatred, and at the same time are obliged to protect the rights and freedoms of the individual.

Still, an important comment must be made here. The law as a measure that penalises promotion of certain views and ideas should interfere only when a speaker acts out of racist, xenophobic or other hateful motives, when intending to incite hatred or violence

35 *Perinçek v. Switzerland*, no. 27510/08, judgment of 17 December 2013.

36 Elie Wiesel. "Hope, Despair and Memory." (Nobel Lecture, presented in Oslo, Norway, 11 December 1986).

37 The full text of the Appeal is available at: www.lph-asso.fr/index.php?option=com_content&view=article&id=47&Itemid=14&lang=en.

against individuals or groups differentiated because of their race, ethnicity, nationality, religion, or when the aim is to restore one of the genocidal totalitarian regimes. These are the only instances in which the law should be given the green light to interfere, not so much to safeguard and preserve the historical memory of societies – since this may not be enforced by a decree or a binding court ruling – but to protect individuals and groups whose rights and freedoms are violated. Freedom of expression, assembly or association must not disguise incitement to hatred, discrimination or violence against anyone.

The Strasbourg Court has on many occasions had to meet the challenge of deciding cases involving memory laws, with some of its findings being considered at least controversial. It is also worth noting that no jurisprudence on memory laws to-date, (neither that of the national legislature nor that of the Strasbourg Court), grapples with the difficult central problem, which is the question of how the historical narrative, shaped by the law, may become accepted by all members of the multicultural societies of many European states. It may be that initiating such a debate is too challenging a task, but I believe that soon it will be impossible to ignore the question if certain memory laws are not to pose yet another barrier to creation of social (and historical) space for all members of society. At the same time, legislative changes observed in some Council of Europe member states particularly in the area of penalizing genocide denial will inevitably lead to proliferation of individual complaints lodged with the ECtHR.

Bibliography

Arai, Yutaka. *The Margin of Appreciation Doctrine and the Principle of Proportionality in the Jurisprudence of the ECHR*. Cambridge: Intersentia, 2002.

Aron, Robert. *The Vichy Regime, 1940–44*. Boston: Beacon Press, 1969.

Baldwin, James. *The Fire Next Time*. New York: The Dial Press, 1963.

Casadevall, Josep, Egbert Myjer, Michael O'Boyle and Anna Austin. *Freedom of Expression: Essays in Honour of Nicolas Bratza, President of the European Court of Human Rights*. Strasbourg: Wolf Legal Publishers, 2012.

Fronza, Emanuela. "The Punishment of Negationism: The Difficult Dialogue Between Law and Memory." *Vermont Law Review* 30 (2006): 609–26.

Grabowski, Jan. *Hunt for the Jews: Betrayal and Murder in German-Occupied Poland*. Bloomington: Indiana University Press, 2013.

Hare, Ivan, and James Weinstein. *Extreme Speech and Democracy*. Oxford: Oxford University Press, 2009.

Lipstadt, Deborah. *History on Trial: My Day in Court with David Irving*. New York: Ecco, 2005.McNamara, Lawrence. "History, Memory and Judgment: Holocaust Denial, The History Wars and Law's Problems with the Past." *Sydney Law Review* 26 (2004): 353–94.

Osiatyński, Wiktor. *Human Rights and Their Limits*. Cambridge: Cambridge University Press, 2009.

Plant, Richard. *The Pink Triangle: The Nazi War Against Homosexuals*. New York: Holt Paperbacks, 1988.

Sweeney, James A. *The European Court of Human Rights in the Post-Cold War Era. Universality in Transition*. London: Routledge, 2013.

Tamarit Sumalla, Joseph M. *Historical Memory and Criminal Justice in Spain. A Case of Late Transitional Justice*. Cambridge – Antwerp – Portland: Intersentia, 2013.

Waldron, Jeremy. *The Harm in Hate Speech*. Cambridge: Harvard University Press, 2012.

Wiesel, Elie. "Hope, Despair and Memory." *Nobel Lecture*, presented in Oslo, Norway, 11 December 1986.

Mónica
López Lerma*

WHAT JUDICIAL MEMORY FOR THE AMNESTY LAW OF 1977?

On 18 July 1936, Franco's military uprising put an end to the democratic government of the Spanish Second Republic (1931–1936), leading the country to a bloody Civil War (1936–1939) and subsequent repressive dictatorship (1939–1975). After his victory in 1939, Franco justified the Civil War as necessary to "liberate" Spain from the public chaos of a Republic led by "evil and degenerate Marxists," and devoted his efforts to eradicating the values and institutions of the Second Republic (i.e., secularization, democracy, federalism).[1] To do so, he centred the regime's discourse on restoration of traditional catholic values (*National-Catholicism*); exaltation of the myth of the Spanish Empire in Latin America (*Hispanity*); assertion of Spain as one and indissoluble territorial integrity (*Fatherland*); and rejection of communism (what he called the "New Crusade").[2] Franco himself defined his military uprising as a necessary "national crusade" to protect *la patria* from "the bastardized, Frenchified, Europeanizing" doctrines of modern liberalism.[3] Franco distanced Spain from the European democracies and promoted a homogenizing vision of the nation. Thus, any mention of pluralism, or cultural and national diversity was considered a dangerous conspiracy of "reds" and "masons."

After the War, a series of laws was enacted to eliminate all opposition.[4] For instance, the Law of Political Responsibilities (9 February 1939) was passed against those who "after 1 October 1934 and before 18 July 1936 contributed to create or aggravate the subversion of any kind of which Spain was made a victim, and of those others, who from the second of said dates have opposed the National Movement with concrete acts or serious passivity" (Article 1).[5] Through the concept of "serious passivity" the law "ensured

* Faculty of Law, University of Helsinki.

1 Paul Preston, *The Triumph of Democracy in Spain* (London and New York: Methuen, 1986), 4.

2 Carlos Closa, "The Domestic Basis of Spanish European Policy and the 2002 Presidency," trans. Stephen J. Wilkins, *Notre Europe, European Studies* 16 (2001), www.notre-europe.eu.

3 Ibid., 4. See also Pablo Jáuregui, "National Pride and the Meaning of 'Europe': a Comparative Study of Britain and Spain," in *Whose Europe? The Turns Towards Democracy*, ed. Dennis Smith and Sue Wright (Oxford: Balckwell, 1999), 274.

4 See Marc Carrillo, "El marco legal en la represión en la dictadura franquista durante el periodo 1939–1959," in *El derecho a la memoria*, ed. Felipe Gómez Isa (Bilbao: Alberdania, 2006), 501–527.

5 See Paul Preston, *The Spanish Holocaust, Inquisition and Extermination in Twentieth-Century Spain* (London: Harper Press, 2012), 503. See also Julius Ruiz, *Franco's Justice: Repression in Madrid after the Spanish Civil War* (New York: Oxford University Press, 2005), 131–164.

that no Republican would go unpunished and justified 'legal' persecution of any individual who had not actively fought in the insurgent ranks."[6] The Law for the Repression of Masonry and Communism (1 March 1940) and the Law of Public Order (30 July 1959) were passed to "legalize" the persecution, torture, and execution of those who had been vanquished and anyone suspected of threatening the new order.[7] Women were no exception. In the name of the Francoist concept of "redemption," the wives and mothers of Republican soldiers or sympathizers were imprisoned, raped, and executed because of the behaviour of a son or a husband.[8] Furthermore, to purify Spain from Republican evils, more than 30,000 children were removed from their imprisoned mothers and sent to state institutions or given to adoption to families that could raise them according to the values and moral teachings of the new regime.[9] Thus, on 14 December 1941 a law was passed to allow the state to legally change the names of these "stolen" children, making the victims' past legally untraceable.[10] The justification for this enforced adoption policy was provided by Antonio Vallejo Nágera, Director of Military Psychiatric Services and of the Cabinet of Psychological Investigations during the dictatorship. Vallejo Nágera claimed to have demonstrated through psychological experiments the infrahuman, dangerous, and evil condition of the Republican enemies.[11] In 1954, Franco reformed the *Ley de Vagos y Maleantes* (Vagrancy Act) of 1933 in order to include homosexuals (together with gypsies, drug addicts, and vagrants) and declare homosexuality illegal. The law's stated goal was to protect and correct, rather than to punish, "those subjects who had fallen to the lowest levels of morality."[12] Once arrested by the police, homosexuals could be sent to prison or correction camps for up to three years. In prison, they were often raped by other inmates and tortured by officials in order to get more information about other homosexuals or just to humiliate them.[13] To

6 Preston. *The Spanish Holocaust*, 503.

7 Ruiz, *Franco's Justice*, 192–223.

8 Brincat Report (Informe Brincat), Parliamentary Assembly of Council of Europe, *Need for International Condemnation of the Franco Regime*, Doc. 10737, 4 November 2005, www.assembly.coe.int/Main.asp?link=/Documents/WorkingDocs/Doc05/EDOC10737.htm. During Franco's dictatorship laws such as marital permission ("permiso marital") were passed, with the support of the Catholic Church, to maintain a conservative and patriarchal society. Women were not allowed to sign contracts, pursue a career, apply for a job or take a trip without the permission of their fathers or husbands. P. B. Radcliff, "Imagining female citizenship in the 'New Spain': Gendering the democratic transition, 1975–1978," *Gender and History* 13, no. 3 (2011): 505.

9 See Brincat Report. See also Ricard Vinyes, *Los niños perdidos del franquismo* (Barcelona: Plaza & Janes, 2002).

10 Preston, *The Spanish Holocaust*, 515. In 2010, the National Association of those Affected by Irregular Adoptions (*Asociación Nacional de Afectados por las Adopciones Irregulares*, ANADIR) was founded to initiate the investigations necessary to locate and identify those who were victims of illegal adoptions during Franco's dictatorship and the early years of democracy. See http://anadir.es/asociacion/.

11 Ibid., 514. See also José María Ruiz Vargas, "Trauma y memoria de la Guerra Civil y la dictadura franquista," *Hispana Nova. Revista de Historia Contemporánea* 6 (2006): 325–328.

12 Ley de Vagos y Maleantes, BOE n 198, 17 July 1954. In 1970, the *Ley de Peligrosidad y Rehabilitación Social* (Dangerousness and Social Rehabilitation Law) replaced the Vagrancy Act to declare homosexuals socially dangerous subjects.

13 Nikolaos Tsinonis, "Memoria y Homosexualidad: Sufrimiento, Olvido y Dignidad," in *El derecho a la memoria*, ed. Felipe Gómez Isa, (Bilbao: Alberdania, 2006), 483–484. See also Jordi Terrasa Mateu, "La

conceal the regime's crimes, thousands of "prisoners were taken far from their home towns, executed and buried in unmarked graves."[14] It is estimated that, by the end of the dictatorship, hundreds of thousands of people had been imprisoned, tortured, executed, subjected to medical experiments, sent to concentration camps, and forced into labour, exile, or "disappeared" under the auspices of the law.[15]

The transition to democracy after Franco's death in 1975 might have provided Spain the opportunity to provide recognition and justice for the countless victims of the regime.[16] Instead, the prominent political forces of the transition agreed that securing a successful and peaceful transition to democracy (1975–1978) required leaving the past behind – what has been referred to as the "pact of forgetfulness" or "pact of silence." Unlike in countries such as Argentina, Chile or South Africa, in Spain no trials were conducted to judge those responsible for crimes committed during Franco's dictatorship, and no truth commissions were created to investigate them. In the name of national reconciliation, a parliamentary majority passed the Amnesty Law of 1977 covering all "political crimes" committed before 1976 and precluding their prosecution. The Amnesty Law, which gave legal form to the pact of oblivion,[17] became the cornerstone of the new democratic national identity, and the Spanish transition was celebrated as an exemplary model of national reconciliation and consensus.[18]

This chapter examines the first *judicial* attempt since the transition to open a criminal investigation into the crimes of Francoism – a decision by Investigating Judge of the *Audiencia Nacional* Baltasar Garzón[19] – and the ensuing judicial proceedings before the Supreme Court that effectively put an end to this attempt.[20] On 16 October 2008, Judge Garzón, who had come to international prominence when he indicted Chile's former dictator Augusto Pinochet, took the unprecedented decision of authorizing a

Legislación Represiva," in *Una Discriminación Universal. La Homosexualidad bajo el Franquismo y la Transición*, ed. Javier Ugarte-Pérez (Barcelona-Madrid: Editorial Egales, 2008).

14 Preston, *The Spanish Holocaust*, xvii.

15 Preston, *The Spanish Holocaust.*

16 The UN General Assembly's "Basic Principles and Guidelines on the Right to a Remedy and Reparation for Victims of Gross Violations of International Human Rights Law and Serious Violations of International Humanitarian Law" defines victims as "persons who individually or collectively suffered harm, including physical or mental injury, emotional suffering, economic loss or substantial impairment of their fundamental rights, through acts or omissions that constitute gross violations of international human rights law, or serious violations of international humanitarian law. Where appropriate, and in accordance with domestic law, the term 'victim' also includes the immediate family or dependants of the direct victim and persons who have suffered harm in intervening to assist victims in distress or to prevent victimization." UN General Assembly Resolution 60/147, 16 December 2005 (A/Res/60/147), para. 8.

17 As Diane Orentlicher has pointed out, the word "amnesty," like "amnesia," comes from the Greek word "amnēstia," connoting "forgetfulness" or "oblivion" of a crime and constitutes a declaration that the government intends to *erase* rather than forgive any record of a previously condemned crime. Diane F. Orentlicher, "Settling Accounts: the Duty to Prosecute Human Rights Violations of a Prior Regime," *Yale Law Journal* 100, no. 8 (1991): 2543.

18 Bénédicte André-Bazzana, *Mitos y mentiras de la Transición* (Barcelona: El Viejo Topo, 2006), 14.

19 Juzgado Central de Instrucción No. 5 de la 'Audiencia Nacional' (National High Court of Spain).

20 For an overview of these judicial proceedings see Josep M. Tamarit Sumalla, *Historical Memory and Criminal Justice in Spain. A Case of Late Transitional Justice* (Cambridge: Intersentia, 2013).

criminal investigation into crimes committed during Franco's regime, categorizing them as crimes against humanity and hence not shielded by the Amnesty Law of 1977. Garzón's decision caused a chain of judicial reactions. Less than a week later, the Public Prosecutor's Office filed an appeal before the Criminal Chamber of the *Audiencia Nacional* to dismiss Garzón's investigation for lack of jurisdiction and alleging that the Amnesty Law prevented prosecution of those crimes. Two months later, the Chamber decided in favour of the Public Prosecutor. The main setback came on 3 February 2010, when, following a complaint filed by three far right wing organizations, the Supreme Court decided to prosecute Garzón for the crime of *prevaricación* (knowingly dictating an unjust decision).[21] According to the complaint, Garzón had knowingly violated the principle of legality by applying international human rights law to circumvent the Amnesty Law. Although Garzón was eventually acquitted on 12 January 2012, the decision of the Supreme Court closed off the possibility of investigating those crimes on the grounds that the Amnesty Law had already settled the issue, which is highly problematic from the perspective of the victims of those crimes.

The main goal of this chapter is to inquire into the Amnesty Law of 1977 as part of the unquestioning myth of Spanish democracy – one that prevents Spain from fully coming to terms with one of the most violent times in its modern history. The chapter is divided into four sections. Section I reviews the Amnesty Law of 1977 and the parliamentary debate concerning its enactment, examining the memories and "forgettings" imprinted in the law. Section II turns to the Law of Historical Memory of 2007, the first legislative attempt to respond to victims' demands for truth and justice since the transition and the limitations of which led the victims to seek the assistance of the judiciary. Section III analyses Judge Garzón's decision to investigate the crimes of Francoism in spite of the Amnesty Law of 1977. Finally, Section IV analyses the criminal proceedings opened against Judge Garzón for this very reason and the decision of the Supreme Court finally to acquit him. The analysis shows how under the guise of defending the legitimacy of the Spanish transition, Spanish Courts have shielded any revision of the Amnesty Law of 1977 in light of present-day circumstances. In failing to bring to light the memory of the victims that the Amnesty Law inevitably suppressed in 1977, the Courts have once again reinstated silence and impunity over truth and justice.

The Amnesty Law of 1977: the Pact of Legal Oblivion

On 14 October 1977, following the first general elections since the Second Republic, the newly elected democratic Parliament unanimously approved the Amnesty Law 46/1977 (of the 317 votes counted, 296 were affirmative, 2 negative, 18 abstentions from the right wing party *Alianza Popular*, and 1 null).[22] One of the law's main novelties was to extend

21 Article 446.3 of the Spanish Penal Code provides that: 'The judge or magistrate who, knowingly, dictates an unjust sentence or resolution' commits the crime of *prevaricación*.

22 Ley 46/1977, de 15 de octubre, de Amnistía Jefatura de Estado (BOE n. 248 de 17/10/1977). The Amnesty Law was passed in order to eliminate some of the limitations of its predecessor, the Royal Decree-Law of 1976, which amnestied "all crimes and misdemeanours of political intentionality and opinion,

the amnesty to "[a]ll acts of political intentionality, whatever the outcome, classified as crimes and misdemeanours committed before December, 15, 1976" (Article 1). In so doing, the law granted amnesty to those political prisoners (mostly members of the Basque organization ETA) who had actively (and violently) opposed Francoism since the 60s and 70s.[23] But most importantly for our present concerns, the law also exonerated all "authorities, officers and agents of public order who, prior to December of 1976, committed crimes and misdemeanours against the exercise of people's rights" (Article 2). As Paloma Aguilar explains, "in exchange for the liberation of political prisoners who had committed violent crimes, ... the impunity of the Francoist regime was established as its perpetrators could no longer be taken to court."[24]

Even though the Amnesty Law does not include a preamble explaining its goals and reasons, some of these can be inferred from the parliamentary debate concerning its enactment.[25] The debate opened with the abstention of the *Alianza Popular*, the political party led by former Francoist Minister Manuel Fraga. The party claimed that, while they were in favour of amnesty for those who were serving sentences for acts that in the new regime "constitute the legitimate exercise of democratic freedoms or rights," they could not support an amnesty for "real terrorists."[26] They argued that "rather than contributing to a national reconciliation... [amnesty would] result in a ferment of social insecurity, the lack of institutionalization of the rule of law, and a deep erosion of authority."[27] Publicly, the *Alianza Popular* questioned the legitimacy of the law by arguing that the amnesty covered acts of bloodshed (referring to ETA terrorist attacks).[28] However, the same argument could have been applied to crimes committed by Franco and his followers during the long years of repression, which they failed to "remember." For historian Carme Molinero, the real goal behind their abstention was "to avoid putting into question the legitimacy of Francoist legality," because amnesty entails "retrospective repeal of the criminal law."[29]

All the rest of the political parties voted in favour of the law. The recently legalized Communist party demanded an "[a]mnesty for all political crimes, without exception,"[30] arguing that only such an amnesty... would allow national reconciliation" and "open the way for peace and freedom."[31] The *Grupo Parlamentario Mixto* appealed for

except those that had harmed or endangered peoples' life and integrity." Royal Decree-Law (*Real Decreto-Ley*) 10/1976 (BOE no. 186, 4 August 1976).

23 Paloma Aguilar, "Transitional Justice in the Spanish Case, Argentinian and Chilean Case," *Study Workshop 10-Alternative Approaches to Dealing with the Past* (June 2007), 5.

24 Ibid., 5. Paradoxically, as Aguilar observes, the law did not stop ETA's killings, nor did it prevent the coup d'état of 1981. Ibid., 6.

25 Diario de sesiones del Congreso de los Diputados. Sesión Plenaria n. 11, celebrada el viernes, 14 de Octubre de 1977, n. 24, 953–983. All translations in this chapter are mine, unless specified otherwise.

26 Ibid., 957.

27 Ibid.

28 Ibid., 957.

29 Carme Molinero, "La Ley de Amnistía de 1977: la reivindicación antifranquista y su lectura treinta años después," in *30 años de la Ley de Amnistía (1977–2007)*, ed. M. Jesús Espuny Tomás and Olga Paz Torres (Madrid: Dykinson, 2009), 47.

30 Diario de sesiones, 961.

31 Ibid., 960.

the need to "assume [the] past, but forget its mistakes."[32] For the Catalan party *Socialistes de Catalunya* and *Grupo Socialista del Congreso* (the second largest political party) this total amnesty meant closing "definitely a historical period" of Spain, as "amnesty eliminates what has been considered as political crimes by the former regime,"[33] and "the beginning of a new era of trust … in the future."[34] In their view, amnesty would mean to "bury the Civil War, division among Spaniards, and the responsibilities of whom, in defence of freedom, opposed those who tried to destroy the power of reason by force of violence and the exercise of authoritarian power."[35] During its turn, the Basque Minority group stated that amnesty "is just oblivion, … an amnesty for everybody to everybody, a forgetting from everybody to everybody;"[36] claiming that since "acts of bloodshed [had] been committed by both parties," it was necessary to "forget … everything."[37] Finally, for the *Union de Centro Democrático* (the party of government), amnesty represented "the ethical-political presupposition of democracy," because amnesty "does not look back, rather, it seeks fervently to overcome and transcend the divisions that separated and confronted [Spaniards] in the past."[38] In a nutshell, all parties covering the entire political spectrum considered that a total amnesty was the only way to put the crimes of the past aside: for only through forgetting (= amnesty) could people's demands for democracy and national reconciliation (= peaceful coexistence among Spaniards) be accomplished.

Analysis of the parliamentary debates leaves clear that the prospect of amnesty was mainly aimed at those who had been imprisoned for their opposition to Franco. Thus, no political party openly discussed or even mentioned Article 2 of the law; nor did they demand prosecution and punishment of those responsible for crimes committed under the dictatorship.[39] Moreover, no one discussed the impact that such blanket impunity would have on those who had been victimized by the regime. Although some of the political parties that voted in favour expressed their dissatisfaction with the limitations of the law and urged the government to correct them in the near future, they justified their vote in terms of "imposition" and "inevitability."[40] In their view, the exceptionality of the historical circumstances required putting the future of democracy above the injustices of the past.[41] All political parties concentrated on celebrating the virtues of

32 Ibid., 963.
33 Ibid., 964.
34 Ibid., 964–965.
35 Ibid., 966.
36 Ibid., 968.
37 Ibid., 969.
38 Ibid., 973.
39 Javier Chinchón Alvarez, "El viaje a ninguna parte: Memoria, leyes, historia y olvido sobre la guerra civil y el pasado autoritario en España (Un examen desde el derecho internacional)," *Revista IIDH*, 45 (2007): 134.
40 Diario de Sesiones, 963. During their interventions, several tributes were made to those would not benefit from the law: common criminals, social prisoners, and women who had been imprisoned for adultery.
41 According to Aguilar, it is "[t]he traumatic memory of the fratricidal conflict" and fear of its repetition, that best explains "why Spaniards persistently gave priority to values relating to peace, order and stability" over justice. Paloma Aguilar, "Collective Memory of the Spanish Civil War: The Case of the

forgetting and reconciliation, while "suppress[ing] or de-emphasiz[ing] those memories felt to be likely to endanger stability and consensus."[42] Therefore, even if the memory of the (painful) past was present throughout the political debates, and the law was the direct result of this memory as some scholars have argued,[43] the Amnesty Law effectively erased, both in its wording and implementation, the trace of Franco's crimes, consigning them and its victims to legal oblivion.[44] It is precisely this "suppressed memory" which became the object of both the Law of Historical Memory of 2007 and of Garzón's judicial investigation.

Remembering the Victims: the Law of Historical Memory

Peter Digester suggests that "[w]hat may look like [a voluntary act of] forgetting may be symptomatic of a deeper injustice in which the voice of the victim is effectively silenced."[45] Thus, the fact that the Amnesty law consigned Franco's crimes to legal oblivion did not mean that the victims of these wrongs had similarly forgotten the past. The hypothesis of a "dormant memory" may help to understand why, at the beginning of the 21st century, grassroots organizations such as the *Asociación para la Recuperación de la Memoria Histórica* (Association for the Recovery of Historical Memory, ARMH) mobilized to demand recognition for Franco's victims.[46] The ARMH claimed that around 30,000 bodies remained buried in unmarked mass graves and asked the government for support in order to locate, exhume, and identify them.[47] The ARMH also demanded the establishment of a truth commission to investigate the circumstances surrounding the fate of "the disappeared" (*los desaparecidos*). Lacking the support of domestic legislation, the ARMH based their demands on existing instruments of Human Rights and International Law.

These demands were rejected by the then Prime Minister Jose María Aznar (*Partido Popular*, formerly *Alianza Popular*, 1996–2004), with the argument that they would

Political Amnesty in the Spanish Transition to Democracy," *Estudio/Working Paper* 1996/85 (December 1996), 2.

42 Madeleine Davis, "Is Spain Recovering its Memory? Breaking the 'Pacto del Olvido'," *Human Rights Quarterly* 27 (2005): 867.

43 Historian Santos Juliá argues that, "neither in its gestation, or discussion, nor in its enactment was the amnesty law the result of amnesia." In his view, it was rather the "triumph of memory" that "aimed at closing the past and opening a future that has never been absent." Santos Juliá, "Amnistía como triunfo de la memoria," *El País*, 24 November 2008, and "Amnistía nunca fue amnesia," *España Siglo XX, Blog de Tendencias 21 sobre la historia reciente de España*, 22 February 2010, www.tendencias21.net/espana/archives/2010/2/ (my own translation).

44 See W. James Booth, "The Unforgotten: Memories of Justice," *American Political Science Review* 95, no. 4 (2004): 784.

45 Peter Digester, "Forgiveness and Political Reconciliation" (Paper for the Political Studies Conference-UK 50th Annual Conference, London, 10–13 April 2000), 15, footnote 17.

46 The response in the international community to Truth Commissions, such as in South Africa and Latin America, and charging Pinochet for crimes against humanity in Spain in 1998, influenced the creation of different civic associations. Among others: Forum for Memory; Association for the Creation of Archives of the Civil War; the Children of War; the Spanish Resistance and Exile (AGE).

47 Recent estimates, however, raise this number to more than 150,000 victims. Preston, *The Spanish Holocaust*, xviii.

shatter the reconciliation achieved in the transition and endanger democracy. In response to the government's lack of support, ARMH referred their case to the United Nations Working Group on Enforced or Involuntary Disappearances.[48] In 2002, Spain officially entered the UN list of countries with unresolved cases of enforced disappearances, placing the PP government in the spotlight of the international community.[49] The same year, the government agreed to support a non-binding resolution condemning Franco's military uprising and proclaiming moral recognition of the victims of the civil war and dictatorship as proposed by the opposition parties. The motion was unanimously approved by the Constitutional Commission of Congress on 20 November 2002 (the 27th anniversary of Franco's death).

With the coming to power of the Socialist government of José Luis Rodríguez Zapatero in 2004, the demands of the ARMH and similar associations were addressed for the first time. The Socialist government established a Commission for the Study of the Situation of the Victims of the Civil War and Francoism.[50] Following the Commission's recommendations, two so-called "Memory Laws" were passed by Congress: First, Law 24/2006 of 7 July, declaring 2006 as the Year of Historical Memory,[51] and commemorating the 75th anniversary of the Second Republic and the 70th anniversary of the beginning of the Civil War. Second, Law 52/2007 of 26 December, in favour of those who had suffered persecution or violence during the Civil War and subsequent dictatorship.[52] This law incorporates the Declaration of the Constitutional Commission of Congress of 20 November 2002, which states that: "No one is entitled to use violence, as it has occurred in our past, for the purpose of imposing political ideology or totalitarian regimes that are contrary to our liberty and our dignity, and that deserve condemnation and rejection by democratic society." The law also incorporates the Resolution of the Parliamentary Assembly of the Council of Europe of 17 March 2006, condemning the "severe violations of human rights" that occurred in Spain from 1939 to 1975. Furthermore, the law establishes a series of economic, legal, and symbolic measures: economic compensation for different categories of victims (Articles 5–10); assistance to private citizens for locating and identifying bodies that remain in unmarked graves (Articles 11–14); a ban on Francoist symbols and monuments from buildings and public spaces (Articles 15–16); creation of the Centre for Documentation of Historical Memory; and maintenance and development of the General Archives of the Civil War and the private right to access them (Articles 20–22). For our purposes here, it is important to mention that the law

48 Davis, "Is Spain Recovering its Memory?," 872–874.

49 Ibid., 873.

50 *Comisión Interministerial para el Estudio de las Víctimas de la Guerra Civil y del Franquismo*, established by Real Decreto 1891/2004, 10 September 2004, Boletín Oficial de Estado n 227 (20 September 2004). For the final report see: *Informe General de la Comisión Interministerial para el Estudio de las Víctimas de la Guerra Civil y del Franquismo*, 28 July 2006, 1–93.

51 Ley 24/ 2006 de 7 de julio sobre declaración del año 2006 como Año de la Memoria Histórica. 25573, Sábado 8 Julio 2006. BOE. n. 162.

52 Ley 52/2007, de 26 de diciembre, *por la que se reconocen y amplían derechos y se establecen medidas en favor de quienes padecieron persecución o violencia durante la guerra civil y la dictadura*. 53410, 27 December 2007. BOE n. 310.

also incorporated a provision stating that the law "is fully compatible with the exercise of rights and access to ordinary and extraordinary judicial proceedings established in the laws and international treaties and agreements ratified by Spain" (Second Additional Provision).

Despite these positive measures, the law had certain limitations.[53] As Giulia Tamayo points out, even though the law includes the Resolution of the Parliamentary Assembly of the Council of Europe of 17 March 2006, it does not follow its main recommendation: "to set up a national commission to inquire into violations of human rights committed under the Franco dictatorship" with a clear mandate to establish the factual truth.[54] The Law obligated the authorities only to "provide assistance" to individuals and families for the identification of corpses in mass graves. However, the task of location and exhumation of bodies was left to the initiative of private citizens, making it very hard in practice to recover the remains and establish the truth surrounding their deaths.[55] Finally, although the law establishes its compatibility with judicial actions, it does not take a position on the Amnesty Law, which was going to be the object of litigation.[56]

Garzón against Francoism: Breaking the Judicial Silence

The real turning point arrived in 2008. In response to an official request by thirteen associations representing victims of Francoism, Investigating Judge Baltasar Garzón opened a criminal investigation into 114,266 (in contrast to the previous official estimation of 30,000) cases of enforced disappearance perpetrated by Franco and his supporters during the Civil War and the early years of the dictatorship (1936–1951).[57] In his decision, Garzón accused Franco and thirty-four of his high commanding officers of designing a "preconceived and systematic plan" to end the "legitimate government of the Second Republic" and to exterminate political opponents through mass killings, tortures, exile, and enforced disappearances (illegal detentions).[58] He found that under the Penal Code of 1995 (Article 607*bis*), and in line with the jurisprudence of the

53 For an analysis of the law as a site of commemoration of the Spanish Transition see Mónica López Lerma, "The Ghosts of Justice and the Law of Historical Memory," *Conserveries mémorielles* 9 (April 2011).

54 Giulia Tamayo, "Los derechos de las víctimas de la Guerra Civil española y el franquismo en el contexto de la experiencia mundial y las obligaciones internacionales sobre la verdad, justicia y reparación," *Entelequia. Revista Interdisciplinar* 7 (2008): 271.

55 Ibid.

56 Ursula Urdillo, "Impunity for Enforced Disappearances in Contemporary Spain. The Spanish Search for Truth," *Interdisciplinary Journal of Human Rights* 6. no. 1 (2011–2012): 53.

57 Garzón maintains that such an investigation is impartial because while Francoist authorities had "used all their resources to locate, identify and repair the victims from the winning side, they did not give the same respect to the victims from the 'losing' side, who were persecuted, jailed, disappeared and tortured during both the Civil War and the dictatorship." Baltasar Garzón, Auto del 16 Octubre 2008. Diligencias Previas Proc. Abreviado 399/2006 V, Juzgado Central de Instrucción No. 5, Audiencia Nacional, 5.

58 Ibid., 8, 17.

Supreme Court,[59] such crimes could now be characterized as "crimes against humanity" without violating the principle of non-retroactivity,[60] and to which the statute of limitations did not apply.[61] On these grounds, he declared his court competent to investigate what he qualified as "permanent crimes of illegal detention without revealing the detainee's whereabouts, within the context of crimes against humanity of enforced disappearance."[62]

The most significant aspect of Garzón's reasoning was his decision to qualify alleged crimes of illegal detention or enforced disappearance as crimes against humanity and, therefore, as not covered by the Amnesty Law of 1977.[63] He argued that the Amnesty Law could not extinguish Spain's duty under international law to investigate, prosecute, and punish this type of crime and recalled that impunity is a violation of both the *jus cogens* norms of International Human Rights Law,[64] and the victims' rights to truth, reparation, and justice.[65] To support his decision he relied on the case law of International Tribunals, such as the European Court of Human Rights, the Special Court for Sierra Leone, or the Inter-American Court of Human Rights, which had upheld the inadmissibility of amnesties in cases of serious violations of human rights, and reaffirmed the State's duty to prosecute these crimes. In his decision, Garzón also referred to the UN International Covenant on Civil and Political Rights of 1966, which Spain ratified in 1977, requiring states to investigate cases of disappearance and execution and to provide effective judicial remedies to the victims. He also cited the UN Convention on the Protection of all Persons from Enforced Disappearances of 26 December 2006, which Spain ratified in 2007, prohibiting blanket amnesties (article 18). Accordingly, Garzón affirmed that "any amnesty law that seeks *to erase a crime against humanity* which cannot be classified as a political crime or offence, should be declared null and void."[66]

Garzón finally argued that the permanent character of the crimes of illegal detention or enforced disappearance (already typified in the Penal Code of 1932) also excludes the applicability of the Amnesty law because these are crimes that are ongoing until the fate or whereabouts of the victim are known or an effective criminal investigation is opened.[67] In addition, Garzón claimed that the Law of Historical Memory of 2007 "does

59 Caso Scilingo, Sentencia del Tribunal Supremo, Sala de lo Penal, 1 de Octubre 2007 (No. 798/2007).

60 For this type of crime, he concluded that the criminal principle of non-retroactivity cannot apply since the prohibition of retroactivity would be in conflict with the norms of International Customary Law (*jus cogens*). Garzón, "Auto," 32.

61 Article 134(1) of the Penal Code establishes that "Statutes of limitations shall not apply to crimes against humanity and genocide and crimes against protected persons and objects in war time, excepting for those punished in Article 614."

62 Garzón, "Auto," 20.

63 Ibid., 44.

64 See International Amnesty Report: "España: poner fin al silencio y a la injusticia. La deuda pendiente con las víctimas de la Guerra Civil Española y del régimen franquista," 18 July 2005, www.derechos.org/nizkor/espana/doc/aifranq.html.

65 See UN General Assembly's "Basic Principles and Guidelines."

66 Garzón, "Auto," 47, emphasis added.

67 Ibid., 16.

not exhaust the requirement of accountability and is fully compatible… *with the exercise of rights and access to ordinary and extraordinary proceedings established in the laws and international treaties and agreements ratified by Spain*."[68] Garzón concluded that his decision was not only in strict compliance with the law, but more importantly, and regardless of the success or failure of his investigation, *already* a form of institutional rehabilitation. In his view, *the silence deployed to date* had brought an unjustified impunity in addition to a *de facto* extinction of criminal liability.[69] Therefore, failure to open a criminal investigation into the case would be "a negative instrumentalisation of justice."[70] Garzón thus ordered proof of the death of General Franco and his thirty-four high commanders and requested the exhumation and identification of victims still buried in 19 unmarked mass graves, including the grave believed to hold the remains of the poet and playwright Federico García Lorca.

The Struggle over Judicial Memory

Garzón's judicial initiative caused fierce opposition. A week later, Javier Zaragoza, the Chief Public Prosecutor of the *Audiencia Nacional*, filed an appeal to dismiss Garzón's investigation, which "breaks the most elementary rules of criminal procedure and leads to a general inquisition."[71] Zaragoza argued that, under the Spanish Penal Code of 1932, those offences were not punishable as crimes against humanity but as ordinary crimes, which prescribe within a 20-year period of limitation.[72] By default, these crimes were covered by the Amnesty Law of 1977.[73] To justify his position, Zaragoza launched a passionate defence of the Amnesty Law of 1977. He began by recalling the differences between the Spanish Amnesty Law and the laws of "Full Stop" and "Due Obedience" passed in countries such Argentina and Chile. He argued that while the Argentinian and Chilean Laws "can be openly described as 'impunity laws'" – because they were enacted (and sustained under threat of a military coup) with the purpose of precluding prosecution, the Spanish Law was "a demand by democratic political forces, widely supported by Spanish society, and approved by the [first democratically elected] Spanish Congress."[74] For this reason, he affirmed, "it would be legally absurd to question the legitimacy of the origin of the [Spanish] law, or worse, to attribute to it the stigma of 'law of impunity'."[75] Finally, Zaragoza maintained that the victims' rights to truth, reparation, and justice could be satisfied through the mechanisms established by the Law of Historical Memory of 2007. At any rate, he concluded that the investigation did not fall under the jurisdiction of the *Audiencia Nacional* (the Court of Judge Garzón) but under

68 Ibid., 57, emphasis in the original.
69 Ibid., 56, emphasis added.
70 Ibid.
71 Javier-Alberto Zaragoza Aguado, "Recurso de apelación ante la Sala de lo Penal de la Audiencia Nacional," 20 October 2008, 12.
72 Ibid., 14.
73 Ibid., 32.
74 Ibid., 34.
75 Ibid.

the various territorial courts where the crimes had been committed. On 18 November, after verifying the death of the perpetrators of the alleged crimes, Garzón declined jurisdiction in favour of Spain's provincial courts, hoping that the investigation would continue. Contrary to his wishes, Garzón soon found himself in the midst of a criminal investigation opened against him.

On 3 February 2010, Investigating Judge of the Supreme Court Luciano Varela admitted a complaint filed by three far right organizations (*Manos Limpias, Libertad y Identidad*, and *Falange Española y de las JONS*) accusing Judge Garzón of the crime of *prevaricación* for authorizing a criminal investigation into Francoist crimes.[76] Varela found the complaints admissible, on the grounds that Garzón "acted with the intent to elude the legislator's decision about the regime of locating and exhuming the victims of the horrible crimes of Francoism… knowing that these crimes had been subjected to amnesty by the democratic Parliament of Spain, whose will he consciously decided to ignore or circumvent."[77] The key to Varela's decision lay in his interpretation of the Amnesty Law of 1977.

Varela argued that Garzón's interpretation was "legally unacceptable."[78] First, the Amnesty Law did not apply to crimes of a "political nature" as Garzón suggested, but rather to crimes "committed with political intent," which are precisely the type of crimes Garzón "unreasonably" qualified as crimes against humanity – that is, those "*committed out of a systematic plan to exterminate a political adversary.*"[79] Second, in Varela's view, the permanent character of the alleged crimes of illegal detention or enforced disappearance does not exclude application of the Amnesty law. Finally, he maintained that neither the International Covenant on Civil and Political Rights nor the European Convention of Human Rights were applicable, for they "were incorporated into the Spanish legal system… *after the occurrence of the acts* to which the amnesty law refers."[80] Accordingly, Varela rejected Garzón's decision to declare the Amnesty law null and void and accused him of "plac[ing] himself as an ethical referee of the political decision taken by democratic forces in 1977, under the pretext of axiological standards taken from instruments of International Law."[81]

Varela also reproached Garzón for neglecting the democratic origin of the Amnesty Law, echoing Judge Zaragoza's previous criticism, that "only out of an *inexcusable ignorance of the law* can one equate the Amnesty Law [approved by a democratic Parliament] with unilateral amnesties or *auto-amnesties* to which generally international

76 Luciano Varela Castro, Causa Especial 3/20048/2009, Sala Segunda del Tribunal Supremo, Sobreseimiento Querella, 3 February 2010.

77 Ibid., 53.

78 Ibid., 39.

79 Ibid.,41, emphasis in the original.

80 Ibid. To support this argument, Varela also mentioned Article 6 of the Additional Protocol II to the Geneva Conventions, which "applies to the prosecution and punishment of criminal offences *related to* the armed conflict. What are exactly the facts of the proceedings initiated by [Garzón]"; and Article 18 of the International Convention for the protection of all persons against enforced disappearances approved on 20 December 2006 by the General Assembly of the UN, which, in contrast to Garzón's interpretation, "does not veto possible amnesties for such crimes.' Ibid., 41–43.

81 Ibid., 40.

instruments and decisions from international bodies refer."[82] He averred that if the alleged crimes had never been subject to a criminal investigation in Spain this was not because of some sort of judicial "conspiracy of silence" or judicial "insensitivity" to the victims as Garzón seemed to imply, but rather because of the validity and legitimacy of the Amnesty Law of 1977, which exempts criminal liability for such crimes. As he put it:

> *It is unreasonable* to think that we are facing some sort of conspiracy of silence of which protagonists would be all those who preceded him in the judicial ladder and in the Office of the Public Prosecutor, not to mention citizens' organizations, which, before and after the Constitution, have shown a commendable sensitivity to the massacre and tragedy that the Civil War and the subsequent dictatorship inflicted on the most basic human rights.[83]

According to Varela, Garzón constructed an "artificial argument" to circumvent the application of the Amnesty Law.[84] In his view, the real goal behind Garzón's criminal investigation was "to control the conduct of exhumations," which the Law of Historical Memory of 2007 explicitly conferred on the lower courts, and "in order to facilitate this goal he repeatedly manifested his willingness to tamper with *the will* of democratic society and the state authorities manifested in the Amnesty Law."[85] On these grounds, Varela concluded that there was "enough probable cause" to prosecute Garzón for *prevaricación*.[86] While Varela insisted that the Amnesty Law precluded the application of International Law, he failed to mention that Article 1.c excluded acts that "involved serious violence against the life or the integrity of persons" and, hence, could be interpreted as allowing an investigation into the crimes in question.[87]

On 27 February 2012, the majority of the Supreme Court acquitted Judge Garzón of the crime of *prevaricación*, but it stated nevertheless that he had committed "an erroneous application of the law."[88] Basically agreeing with Varela's reasoning, the Court maintained that Garzón's decision was erroneous because the alleged facts could not qualify as crimes against humanity, for they were not typified as such either in the national Penal Code or under international law at the time they were committed.[89] Even if the Amnesty Law were considered, as Garzón declared, a violation of International Law and the victims' right to truth, reparation and justice, that categorization could not

82 Ibid., emphasis added.

83 Ibid., 50.

84 Ibid., 52.

85 Ibid., 51.

86 Ibid., 49.

87 Mónica Zapico Barbeito, "La investigación de los crímenes del franquismo: entre el procesamiento por prevaricación abierto contra el Juez Baltasar Garzón y la querella presentada en Argentina en virtud del ejercicio de la jurisdicción," *AFDUDC* 14 (2010): 910.

88 Sentencia del Tribunal Supremo. Sala de lo Penal. n. 20048/2009. Juicio Oral. 27 February 2012, 10.

89 13 The Court also stated that "it is not possible, however strongly it may be argued in some doctrinal areas, that the requirements of the principle of legality be satisfied by the provisions of customary international criminal law, if the act is defined as an offence in domestic law." Ibid., 12.

be applied retroactively.[90] Likewise, the Court affirmed that the jurisprudence of the Inter-American Court of Human Rights was non-binding on Spain.[91]

The most revealing aspect of the decision, however, is that the Court launched yet another passionate defence of the Amnesty Law and the Spanish transition. Like Zaragoza and Varela, the Court began by recalling the democratic origin of the law, noting that the law "was passed with the full consensus of all political forces during the constituent period resulting from the democratic elections of 1977" and that "in no case was a law approved by the victors, those in power, to cover up their own crimes."[92] The law, the Court claimed, "constituted an essential, irreplaceable, and necessary pillar to overcome Francoism."[93] The Court also emphasized the reconciliatory character of the Amnesty law, stating that the law "had an evident sense of reconciliation since … the 'transition' required that all political forces ceded something in their different positions… The fundamental idea of the 'transition'…was to achieve a peaceful reconciliation among Spaniards, and both the Amnesty Law and the Spanish Constitution were essential milestones in that historical process."[94] Most significantly, the Court concluded that "because the 'transition' was the will of the Spanish people, which is embodied in a law [of Amnesty], no judge or court can in any way call into question the legitimacy of such a process. It is a valid law, the potential repeal of which would attach exclusively to the Parliament."[95]

Conclusion

The legislative history of the Amnesty Law of 1977 demonstrates its democratic origins. And yet, it ought to be borne in mind that, as Chinchón Alvarez has argued, the international legality of a given measure in response to grave crimes depends ultimately not on "whether it has been adopted by a democratic parliament or not," but on "whether the content of that measure is contradictory to international legal obligations."[96] According to Carlos Closa, the Courts have "shielded the Amnesty Law behind a tight and strict interpretation of the principle of legality which kept at bay potential empowerment against the law coming from international law."[97] In doing so, "Spanish Courts successfully avoided any revision of the *specific* provisions of the Amnesty Law in the *specific* case at hand,"[98] with the argument that it would undermine

90 See Naomi Roht-Arriaza, "The Spanish Civil War, Amnesty, and the Trials of Judge Garzón," *ASIL* 16, no. 24 (25 July 2012).

91 Sentencia del Tribunal Supremo, 17.

92 Ibid., 19.

93 Ibid.

94 Ibid.

95 Ibid., 20.

96 Javier Chinchón Alvarez, "The challenges posed to the recent investigation of crimes committed during the Spanish Civil War and Francoism," in *The Role of Courts in Transitional Justice. Voices from Latin America and Spain*, ed. J. Almqvist and C. Espósito (Oxford-New York: Routledge, 2012), 155–156.

97 Carlos Closa, "Truth, Truth Shall You Pursue: Spanish Courts and Transitional Criminal Justice," unpublished manuscript, cited with the permission of the author, 18.

98 Ibid., emphasis added.

the legitimacy of the transition. In the Courts' view, the Amnesty Law should be remembered as an essential milestone in the consolidation of Spanish democracy after Francoism and any critical assessment could be regarded "as a criticism of democracy itself."[99] However, to open an investigation into the crimes of Francoism is not to question the legitimacy of the transition, let alone to threaten national reconciliation, but rather to comply with Spain's international obligations towards the victims in the present.

In this respect, thousands of bodies remain buried in unmarked graves and their exhumation and identification require official investigation. While the Law of Historical Memory of 2007 left this task in private hands of friends and families of the victims, the elimination of the state budget to support this exhumation sends a worrisome message.[100] In a preliminary report issued on 3 February 2014 UN Special Rapporteur Pablo de Greiff bemoaned the "immense distance" between the position of state institutions and the victims.[101] He found especially surprising that state institutions have not done more for the victims, considering the absence of risks to the stability of the democratic order, and recalled that "genuine reconciliation" requires giving full effect to the victims' rights to truth, justice, and reparation.[102] The UN expert recommended setting up mechanisms to "officialise the truth" and seek information of underexplored themes such as forced labour, stolen children, concentration camps, and impact on women.[103] Finally, he also expressed his concern regarding the Public Prosecutors' decision to deny Argentina's request to extradite a former police officer for alleged torture committed during the last years of Franco's dictatorship, on the grounds that that they were bound by the Amnesty Law of 1977. Having already closed the door to justice in the Spanish judicial system, this decision would close victims' access to justice in other countries. Seeing Spain's record of ignoring all UN recommendations thus far, there is increasingly less and less hope that the Spanish authorities will ever decide to investigate the serious human rights violations committed under Franco's dictatorship.

99 Salvador Cardús, "Politics and the Invention of Memory. For a Sociology of the Transition to Democracy in Spain," in *Disremembering the Dictatorship: The Politics of Memory in the Spanish Transition to Democracy*, ed. Joan Ramón Resina (Amsterdam: Ediciones Rodopi, 2000), 18.

100 Samantha Salsench i Linares, "Francoism Facing Justice. Enforced Disappearances before Spanish Courts," *Journal of International Criminal Justice* 11 (2013): 482.

101 See UN preliminary report: "Observaciones preliminares del Relator Especial para la promoción de la verdad, la justicia, la reparación y las garantías de no repetición, Pablo de Greiff, al concluir su visita oficial a España," 3 February 2014. www.ohchr.org/EN/NewsEvents/Pages/DisplayNews.aspx?NewsID=14216&LangID=E. The UN expert will present his final report on his visit to the Human Rights Council in September 2014.

102 Ibid. See also "Spain should trust its democracy and work for victims' rights" – UN expert on transitional justice. www.ohchr.org/EN/NewsEvents/Pages/DisplayNews.aspx?NewsID=14220&LangID=E.

103 Ibid.

Bibliography

Aguilar, Paloma. "Collective Memory of the Spanish Civil War: The Case of the Political Amnesty in the Spanish Transition to Democracy." *Estudio/Working Paper* 1996/85 (December 1996).

— "Transitional Justice in the Spanish Case, Argentinian and Chilean Case." *Study Workshop 10-Alternative Approaches to Dealing with the Past* (June 2007): 1–25.

"Amnistía nunca fue amnesia." *España Siglo XX, Blog de Tendencias 21 sobre la historia reciente de España*, February 22, 2010. www.tendencias21.net/espana/archives/2010/2/.

André-Bazzana, Bénédicte. *Mitos y mentiras de la Transición*. Barcelona: El Viejo Topo, 2006.

Brincat Report (Informe Brincat), Parliamentary Assembly of Council of Europe, Need for International Condemnation of the Franco Regime, Doc. 10737, 4 November 2005. www.assembly.coe.int/Main.asp?link=/Documents/WorkingDocs/Doc05/EDOC10737.htm

Booth, W. James. "The Unforgotten: Memories of Justice." *American Political Science Review* 95, no. 4 (2004): 777–91.

Cardús, Salvador. "Politics and the Invention of Memory. For a Sociology of the Transition to Democracy in Spain." In *Disremembering the Dictatorship: The Politics of Memory in the Spanish Transition to Democracy*, edited by Joan Ramón Resina. Amsterdam: Ediciones Rodopi, 2000.

Carrillo, Marc. "El marco legal en la represión en la dictadura franquista durante el periodo 1939–1959." In *El derecho a la memoria*, edited by Felipe Gómez Isa, 501–27. Bilbao: Alberdania, 2006.

Chinchón Alvarez, Javier. "El viaje a ninguna parte: Memoria, leyes, historia y olvido sobre la guerra civil y el pasado autoritario en España (Un examen desde el derecho internacional)." *Revista IIDH* 45 (2007): 119–233.

— "The challenges posed to the recent investigation of crimes committed during the Spanish Civil War and Francoism." In *The Role of Courts in Transitional Justice. Voices from Latin America and Spain*, edited by J. Almqvist and C. Espósito, 132–58. Oxford and New York: Routledge, 2012.

Closa, Carlos. "The Domestic Basis of Spanish European Policy and the 2002 Presidency." Translated by Stephen J. Wilkins. *Notre Europe, European Studies* 16 (2001), www.notre-europe.eu.

— "Truth, Truth Shall You Pursue: Spanish Courts and Transitional Criminal Justice." Unpublished.

Davis, Madeleine. "Is Spain Recovering its Memory? Breaking the 'Pacto del Olvido'." *Human Rights Quarterly* 27 (2005): 858–80.

Digester, Peter. "Forgiveness and Political Reconciliation." Paper for the Political Studies Conference - UK 50th Annual Conference, London, April 10–13, 20007.

"España: poner fin al silencio y a la injusticia. La deuda pendiente con las víctimas de la Guerra Civil Española y del régimen franquista." International Amnesty Report, 18 July 2005. www.derechos.org/nizkor/espana/doc/aifranq.html.

Garzón, Baltasar. Auto del 16 Octubre 2008. Diligencias Previas Proc. Abreviado 399/2006 V, Juzgado Central de Instrucción No. 5, Audiencia Nacional, 5.
Informe General de la Comisión Interministerial para el Estudio de las Víctimas de la Guerra Civil y del Franquismo, July 28, 2006, 1–93.
Jáuregui, Pablo. "National Pride and the Meaning of 'Europe': a Comparative Study of Britain and Spain." In *Whose Europe? The Turns Towards Democracy*, edited by Dennis Smith and Sue Wright, 275–87. Oxford: Balckwell, 1999.
Juliá, Santos. "Amnistía como triunfo de la memoria." *El País*, November 24, 2008.
López Lerma, Mónica. "The Ghosts of Justice and the Law of Historical Memory." *Conserveries mémorielles* 9 (2011).
Molinero, Carme. "La Ley de Amnistía de 1977: la reivindicación antifranquista y su lectura treinta años después." In *30 años de la Ley de Amnistía (1977-2007)*, edited by M. Jesús Espuny Tomás and Olga Paz Torres, 41–55. Madrid: Dykinson, 2009.
"Observaciones preliminares del Relator Especial para la promoción de la verdad, la justicia, la reparación y las garantías de no repetición, Pablo de Greiff, al concluir su visita oficial a España." UN preliminary report, February 3, 2014. www.ohchr.org/EN/NewsEvents/Pages/DisplayNews.aspx?NewsID=14216&LangID=E.
Orentlicher, Diane F. "Settling Accounts: the Duty to Prosecute Human Rights Violations of a Prior Regime." *Yale Law Journal* 100, no. 8 (1991): 2537–615.
Preston, Paul. *The Spanish Holocaust, Inquisition and Extermination in Twentieth-Century Spain*. London: Harper Press, 2012.
— *The Triumph of Democracy in Spain*. London and New York: Methuen, 1986.
Radcliff, P. B. "Imagining female citizenship in the 'New Spain': Gendering the democratic transition, 1975–1978." *Gender and History* 13, no. 3 (2011): 498–523.
Roht-Arriaza, Naomi. "The Spanish Civil War, Amnesty, and the Trials of Judge Garzón." *ASIL*, 16, no. 24 (2012).
Ruiz, Julius. *Franco's Justice: Repression in Madrid after the Spanish Civil War*. New York: Oxford University Press, 2005.
Ruiz Vargas, José María. "Trauma y memoria de la Guerra Civil y la dictadura franquista." *Hispana Nova. Revista de Historia Contemporánea* 6 (2006): 299–336.
Salsench i Linares, Samantha. "Francoism Facing Justice. Enforced Disappearances before Spanish Courts." *Journal of International Criminal Justice* 11 (2013): 463–83.
"Spain should trust its democracy and work for victims' rights" – UN expert on transitional justice. www.ohchr.org/EN/NewsEvents/Pages/DisplayNews.aspx?NewsID=14220&LangID=E
Tamarit Sumalla, Josep M. *Historical Memory and Criminal Justice in Spain. A Case of Late Transitional Justice*. Cambridge: Intersentia, 2013.
Tamayo, Giulia. "Los derechos de las víctimas de la Guerra Civil española y el franquismo en el contexto de la experiencia mundial y las obligaciones internacionales sobre la verdad, justicia y reparación." *Entelequia. Revista Interdisciplinar* 7 (2008): 255–71.
Terrasa Mateu, Jordi. "La Legislación Represiva." In *Una Discriminación Universal. La Homosexualidad bajo el Franquismo y la Transición*, edited by Javier Ugarte-Pérez. Barcelona-Madrid: Editorial Egales, 2008.

Tsinonis, Nikolaos. "Memoria y Homosexualidad: Sufrimiento, Olvido y Dignidad." In *El derecho a la memoria*, edited by Felipe Gómez Isa, 483–84. Bilbao: Alberdania, 2006.

Vinyes, Ricard. *Los niños perdidos del franquismo*. Barcelona: Plaza & Janes, 2002.

Urdillo, Ursula. "Impunity for Enforced Disappearances in Contemporary Spain. The Spanish Search for Truth." *Interdisciplinary Journal of Human Rights* 6, no. 1 (2011–2012): 41–60.

Zaragoza Aguado, Javier-Alberto. "Recurso de apelación ante la Sala de lo Penal de la Audiencia Nacional." October 20, 2008.

Zapico Barbeito, Mónica. "La investigación de los crímenes del franquismo: entre el procesamiento por prevaricación abierto contra el Juez Baltasar Garzón y la querella presentada en Argentina en virtud del ejercicio de la jurisdicción." *AFDUDC* 14 (2010): 891–927.

IUS COMMUNE EUROPAEUM

A peer-reviewed book series in which the common foundations of the legal systems of the Member States of the European Union are the central focus.

The *Ius Commune Europaeum* series includes horizontal comparative legal studies as well as studies on the effect of treaties within the national legal systems. All the classic fields of law are covered. The books are published in various European languages under the auspices of METRO, the Institute for Transnational Legal Research at Maastricht University.

Recently published:
Volume 123: *The Treaty on European Union 1993-2013. Reflections from Maastricht*, M. De Visser and A.P. van der Mei (eds.)
Volume 124: *Inside Policy Custody. Training Framework on the Provisions of Suspects' Rights*, T. Spronken, J. Blackstock, E. Lloyd-Cape, J. Hodgson, A. Ogorodova and M. Vanderhallen
Volume 125: *Coordinating Ombudsmen and the Judiciary. A Comparative View on the Relations between Ombudsmen and the Judiciary in the Netherlands, England and the European Union*, M. Remac
Volume 126: *Legal Evolution and Hybridisation. The Law of Shares Transfer in England*, M. Solinas
Volume 127: *The Role of EU State Aid Law in Promoting a Pro-Innovation Policy. A Review from the Perspective of University-Industry R&D Cooperation*, M. Cisneros
Volume 128: *Tradition, Codification and Unification. Comparative - Historical Essays on Developments in Civil Law*, J.M. Milo, J.H.A. Lokin and J.M. Smits
Volume 129: *Nobody's Perfect. Comparative Essays on Appeals and Other Means of Recourse Against Judicial Decisions in Civil matters*, A. Uzelac and C.H. van Rhee (eds.)
Volume 130: *Legal Aid in the Low Countries*, B. Hubeau and A. Terlouw (eds.)
Volume 131: *State Aid and Public Procurement in the European Union*, S. Schoenmaekers, W. Devroe and N. Philipsen (eds.)
Volume 132: *Property Law Perspectives III*, A. Apers, S. Bouly et al. (eds.)
Volume 133: *Multi-Party Redress Mechanisms in Europe: Squeaking Mice?*, V. Harsági and C.H. van Rhee (eds.)

www.ingramcontent.com/pod-product-compliance
Ingram Content Group UK Ltd.
Pitfield, Milton Keynes, MK11 3LW, UK
UKHW051927100926
8556IPUK00022B/1417

9 781780 683065